Effective Classroom Management

Models and Strategies for Today's Classrooms

Carlette Jackson Hardin

Austin Peay State University

PEARSON

Merrill
Prentice Hall

Upper Saddle River, New Jersey
Columbus, Ohio

Library of Congress Cataloging in Publication Data

Hardin, Carlette Jackson.
    Effective classroom management : models and strategies for today's classrooms / Carlette
Jackson Hardin.
        p. cm.
    Includes bibliographical references and index.
    ISBN 0-13-096809-w9
    1. Classroom management. I. Title.

    LB3013.H343 2004
    371.102'4—dc22   2003060934

Vice President and Executive Publisher: Jeffery W. Johnston
Executive Editor: Debra A. Stollenwerk
Editorial Assistant: Mary Morrill
Production Editor: Kris Robinson-Roach
Production Coordination: nSight
Photo Coordination: Cynthia Cassidy
Design Coordinator: Diane C. Lorenzo
Cover Designer: Terry Rohrbach
Cover image: Getty One
Production Manager: Susan Hannahs
Director of Marketing: Ann Castel Davis
Marketing Manager: Darcy Betts Prybella
Marketing Coordinator: Tyra Poole

This book was set by Laserwords. It was printed and bound by R. R. Donnelley & Sons Company. The cover
was printed by Coral Graphic Services, Inc.

Photo Credits: Scott Cunningham/Merrill, 55, 72, 100, 123, 138, 161, 242; Jean Greenwald/Merrill, 117; Larry
Hamill/Merrill, 62, 187; Anthony Magnacca/Merrill, 3, 17, 24, 37, 44, 107, 130, 146, 167, 173, 202, 206, 246; Gail
Meese/Merrill, 235; Barbara Schwartz/Merrill, 196; Rhoda Sidney/PH College, 91; Anne Vega/Merrill, 221; Tom
Watson/Merrill, 82; Todd Yarrington/Merrill, 1, 178

Pearson Education Ltd.
Pearson Education Singapore Pte. Ltd.
Pearson Education Canada, Ltd.
Pearson Education—Japan

Pearson Education Australia Pty. Limited
Pearson Education North Asia Ltd.
Pearson Educación de Mexico, S.A. de C.V.
Pearson Education Malaysia Pte. Ltd.

10 9 8 7 6 5 4 3 2
ISBN 0-13-096809-9

Dedication

For my sister and friend, Martha Jackson Barnes, who lovingly shared the wisdom gleaned from 30 years of teaching.

Preface

A friend, who knew I was writing this text, recently shared a textbook used by her aunt when she was training to be a teacher in the 1930s. The text, *Classroom Organization and Control* by Jesse Sears, was published in 1928 and left little doubt about the role of the teacher, with chapters devoted to order, discipline, and punishments. The text was a reminder of how much classroom management has changed in the last 70 years. The text from the 1930s is a far cry from many current classroom-management texts that focus less on teacher-centered control and punishment and more on building communities and creating safe learning environments.

The purpose of *Effective Classroom Management: Models and Strategies for Today's Classrooms* is to provide a synthesis of these changing views of classroom management. The text presents 12 models of classroom management that fall into three distinct categories: Classroom Management as Discipline, Classroom Management as a System, and Classroom Management as Instruction. This book is a scholarly review of the research base on classroom management. However, it is written and formatted in a way that is easy for students to read, understand, and apply.

INTENDED AUDIENCE

Effective Classroom Management: Models and Strategies for Today's Classrooms is especially appropriate as the sole text for an undergraduate or graduate course on classroom management. In addition, it may be used for staff-development programs for inservice teachers. This text provides a foundation for selecting a model to follow or for the development of an individual classroom-management plan. The content is applicable for teachers and preservice teachers at all levels—elementary, middle, and high school.

ORGANIZATION

Chapter 1 provides the theoretical framework of the text, in which a rationale is given for considering classroom management as discipline, as a system, or as instruction. The chapter presents a brief review of the major research in the field, and ends with a discussion of how individual management plans are developed.

Part 1 Classroom Management as Discipline presents four models of classroom management. Chapter 2 presents basic behavioral concepts, including a review of B. F. Skinner's theory of operant conditioning. Lee and Marlene Canter's model, Assertive

Discipline, is presented in Chapter 3. Chapter 4 provides a different approach to using behavioral theory in Fredric Jones's model, Positive Classroom Discipline. Chapter 5 presents the work of two theorists, Rudolf Dreikurs and Linda Albert.

Part II Classroom Management as a System highlights four models that are systematic in approach. The changing theories of William Glasser are the focus of Chapter 6. Chapter 7 presents Richard Curwin and Allen Mendler's model, Discipline with Dignity. Chapter 8 focuses on building communities and discusses the theories of Haim Ginott and Alfie Kohn. The research of Carolyn Evertson is the foundation of her model, Classroom Organization and Management Program (COMP), which is presented in Chapter 9.

Part III Classroom Management as Instruction provides four models that have the teaching of prosocial skills as their central focus. The first model, presented in Chapter 10, is Barbara Coloroso's Inner Discipline. Chapter 11 reviews Ellen McGinnis and Arnold Goldstein's model, Skillstreaming. Several approaches to teaching conflict resolution and peer mediation are presented in Chapter 12. Finally, Forrest Gathercoal's model, Judicious Discipline, is the focus of Chapter 13.

Part IV Developing a Personal System provides information to assist the teacher in designing a personal system of classroom management. Chapter 14 provides information for creating a safe learning environment for all students and explores issues related to multicultural and socioeconomic factors, physical and mental disabilities, and at-risk behaviors. Chapter 15 helps the individual teacher combine all elements of classroom management into a comprehensive program.

SPECIAL FEATURES

The following features make *Effective Classroom Management: Models and Strategies for Today's Classrooms* both instructor and reader friendly:

- Information and chapter activities are directly tied to Interstate New Teacher Assessment and Support Consortium (INTASC) standards. The table on the inside front cover provides the INTASC standards and the chapters in which these standards are addressed.
- Tips from the Field appear throughout the text. These tips offer sage advice from practicing teachers.
- Each chapter contains case studies and scenarios that illustrate the concepts presented. Although most of the case studies and scenarios are based on actual events that occurred in typical classrooms, the names of teachers and students are fictitious.
- Chapter Activities are designed to help readers reflect on the model presented, develop portfolio material, and develop a personal philosophy of classroom management.
- A glossary of the Key Terms presented in each chapter appears at the end of the text.

ACKNOWLEDGMENTS

Many people provided support and guidance as I prepared this book. A very special thanks goes to my husband, William, whose patience and encouragement enabled me to complete the project. The faculty of the School of Education at Austin Peay State University provided daily encouragement and support. I'm especially grateful to Dr. Sutton Flynt, who challenged me to stay focused and to trust my vision for this text. My sister, Martha Jackson Barnes, lovingly read each word of this text. I must also thank Dr. Ann Harris and Dr. Heraldo Richards, who read specific chapters and provided feedback. Leigh Bonds was a wonderful reviewer and suggested ways to make the text student-friendly. I must thank all the teachers who graciously provided Tips from the Field, and I encourage readers of the text to submit tips for the next edition. I also want to thank the following reviewers for their thoughtful comments: Sue R. Abegglen, Culver-Stockton College; Carrie Dale, Michigan State University; Sandra L. DiGiaimo, University of Scranton; Joyce Lynn Garrett, Boise State University; Dennis Heim, California Sate University—Los Angeles; Shirley W. Jacob, Southeastern Louisiana University; Daniel J. Lucas, Alabama State University; Suzanne MacDonald, The University of Akron; Bruce M. Mitchell, Eastern Washington State University; and Judy Sander, Texas A&M University—Texarkana.

Finally, eternal gratitude goes to Debbie Stollenwerk at Merrill/Prentice Hall for her faith in me.

Carlette Jackson Hardin

Educator Learning Center: An Invaluable Online Resource

Merrill Education and the Association for Supervision and Curriculum Development (ASCD) invite you to take advantage of a new online resource, one that provides access to the top research and proven strategies associated with ASCD and Merrill—the Educator Learning Center. At **www.EducatorLearningCenter.com** you will find resources that will enhance your students' understanding of course topics and of current educational issues, in addition to being invaluable for further research.

How the Educator Learning Center will help your students become better teachers

With the combined resources of Merrill Education and ASCD, you and your students will find a wealth of tools and materials to better prepare them for the classroom.

Research

- More than 600 articles from the ASCD journal *Educational Leadership* discuss everyday issues faced by practicing teachers.
- A direct link on the site to Research Navigator™ gives students access to many of the leading education journals, as well as extensive content detailing the research process.
- Excerpts from Merrill Education texts give your students insights on important topics of instructional methods, diverse populations, assessment, classroom management, technology, and refining classroom practice.

Classroom Practice

- Hundreds of lesson plans and teaching strategies are categorized by content area and age range.
- Case studies and classroom video footage provide virtual field experience for student reflection.
- Computer simulations and other electronic tools keep your students abreast of today's classrooms and current technologies.

Look into the value of Educator Learning Center yourself

Preview the value of this educational environment by visiting **www.EducatorLearningCenter.com** and clicking on "Demo." For a free 4-month subscription to the Educator Learning Center in conjunction with this text, simply contact your Merrill/Prentice Hall sales representative.

Brief Contents

Contents

CHAPTER
8

Building Community   123

CHAPTER
9

*Classroom Organization
and Management Program (COMP)   138*

Part III   *Classroom Management as Instruction*   *159*

CHAPTER 10   *Inner Discipline*   *161*

CHAPTER 11   *Skillstreaming*   *173*

CHAPTER 12 *Conflict Resolution and Peer Mediation   187*

CHAPTER 13 *Judicious Discipline   202*

Part IV *Developing a Personal System   219*

CHAPTER **14** *Creating Safe and Welcoming Classrooms for All Students   221*

Chapter 1

Changing Views
of Classroom Management

Objectives

Chapter 1 prepares preservice teachers to meet INTASC standards #2 (Student Development), #5 (Motivation and Management), and #9 (Reflective Practitioner) by helping them to:

- evaluate different classroom-management approaches.
- select or create the classroom-management model that best fits their needs.
- analyze classroom environments and interactions.
- use research on effective classroom management to select strategies and methods for managing the classroom.
- understand the theoretical background of different approaches to classroom management.
- reflect on personal skills and philosophy about teaching and classroom management.

Scenario

For the past week, Marcus Holmes has been going to sleep during Ms. Salerno's math class. Today, one of his classmates reaches over and pokes Marcus while he sleeps. Startled, Marcus jumps from his seat and curses the other student. Before Ms. Salerno can react, Marcus runs from the room.

INTRODUCTION

Ms. Salerno has only seconds to react to the situation that just occurred: she must deal with a student who has left the classroom, a classroom in uproar, and several violations of the school's and her classroom rules. What she will do in the next few minutes and in the days to follow will be determined by many factors. Marcus's age and grade level will play a major role in her handling of the situation. If a fellow teacher or teacher's aide is available, she may elect to leave the classroom to find Marcus. If she doesn't have such assistance, she must weigh the consequences of searching for Marcus with the cost of leaving the other students unsupervised. How well Ms. Salerno can predict where Marcus may have gone will impact her decision regarding whether to search for Marcus or stay with her students. She will need to consider whether Marcus has a disability that may have contributed to his behavior. She must be cognizant of school policies regarding such situations. She must decide if Marcus will be punished for his cursing or for his leaving the classroom. Eventually, she must decide what should happen to the student who poked Marcus and set the events in motion. This incident, which occurred in less than a minute, will require Ms. Salerno to make a multitude of decisions.

If Ms. Salerno were teaching in the first part of the twentieth century instead of in the first part of the twenty-first century, the answer to this classroom management situation would be simple: Marcus and the student who poked him would be headed to the woodshed for a spanking. In 1949, Dorothy Walter Baruch in *New Ways in Discipline* suggested that the days of corporal punishment and taking students to the woodshed were over. Many parents, teachers, and legislators lament the end of such trips to the woodshed and suggest that teachers no longer have options when handling classroom-management issues. However,

The technology for managing classrooms changes as educators gain more knowledge about how students learn and develop.

nothing could be further from the truth, because teachers now have more options in managing students' behavior than in any other period in history.

Each year hundreds of books and articles are written that provide advice on the best way to handle situations like the one facing Ms. Salerno. Theoretically, the vast amount of research available about the nature of students and effective classroom-management practices makes teachers more thoughtful and less reactive in their handling of classroom situations. Unfortunately, the research fails to provide all of the answers teachers need to effectively manage their classrooms. Teachers like Ms. Salerno have learned that there is no *one* answer to discipline or effective classroom management, and ultimately teachers are left to do what they think is best for their students.

CHANGING VIEWS OF CLASSROOM MANAGEMENT

Teachers have entered a new age of classroom management. Faced with new challenges during the first part of the twenty-first century, teachers, teacher educators, and school administrators have searched for alternate ways to manage classrooms. However, finding answers to classroom-management situations is difficult, because there is disagreement about what constitutes effective classroom-management approaches.

Some administrators and teachers think of classroom management and discipline as being synonymous terms. Vasa (1984) describes classroom management as behaviors related to maintenance of on-task student behaviors and the reduction of off-task or disruptive behaviors. Those who share his view define effective classroom management as the process of controlling students' behaviors.

Those with a more student-centered approach view classroom management as a way of preparing students for life. They focus not on controlling students' behaviors today but on preparing students for the world they will live in tomorrow. Teachers and administrators who approach classroom management from this perspective define effective classroom management as the process of creating a positive social and emotional climate in the classroom (Morris, 1996).

How teachers and administrators define effective classroom management depends on their focus and goals. These conflicting views are the basis for classroom models that vary in approach and philosophy.

Classroom Management as Discipline

In the 1970s and 1980s, the emphasis of classroom management was on making the classroom safe, establishing the rules of behavior, and maintaining discipline. For teachers, discipline was viewed as both a noun and a verb (Hoover & Kindsvatter, 1997). As a noun, *discipline* was defined as the rules established to maintain classroom order. As a verb, *discipline* was defined as what teachers do to help students behave acceptably in school. Both definitions tie discipline to misbehavior, because if there is no misbehavior, no discipline is required (Edwards, 1999). As Doyle (1990) notes, preventing misbehavior has been the dominant theme in classroom management, because the need for management and discipline is most evident when students are misbehaving.

Those who viewed classroom management as discipline turned to psychological theories in counseling, mental health, and behavior modification for answers to classroom-management problems. Most of these theories were developed outside classroom settings and dealt with individual students rather than with groups of students (Brophy, 1983). However, studies in behavior management were the first to show experimentally that teacher behavior could shape and maintain student misbehavior (Freiberg, 1999). Since the 1960s, behavior management has been the most common approach to classroom management. Schools throughout the United States quickly adopted these early models, because they were simple to use and allowed teachers to meet the need to stop inappropriate behavior immediately. For these same reasons, they continue to be used today.

This text contains four models that have discipline as their major focus. Although different in approach, they share the following principles:

- the teacher is responsible for maintaining classroom control
- discipline comes before instruction
- consequences must exist for inappropriate behavior

The four models presented are Skinner's *Behavioral Management*, Canter's *Assertive Discipline*, Jones's *Positive Classroom Discipline*, and Dreikurs's *Logical Consequences*. The chapter on Logical Consequences is expanded to include Linda Albert's *Cooperative Discipline* model, because her model is based on the work of Dreikurs.

For praise to be effective, it must be:

- Age appropriate—don't talk down to high school students
- Private—don't embarrass a student in front of peers
- Earned—students know when praise is fake!

Kathy Buckner
High School History Teacher
Fort Campbell High School
Fort Campbell, KY

Classroom Management as a System

In the late 1970s, teachers began to reject earlier models that focused on discipline. Many found that earlier models did not adequately serve teachers who sought to create calm and safe learning environments for all their students (McEwan, 2000). For these teachers, classroom management and instruction are interdependent rather than separate functions. Therefore, effective classroom management is not seen as a few isolated techniques or learned gimmicks but rather as a system of management skills (Brophy, 1983; Evertson & Harris, 1992). Kohn (1995) notes that many educators reject discipline models, because they have found punishment and threats to be counterproductive, in that they produced temporary compliance at best. Others stress that it is better to have a plan to *prevent* misbehavior than to have a response plan when misbehavior occurs. Doyle (1990) stresses that the new focus on prevention has transformed both research and theory in classroom management.

For these reasons, many teachers have come to believe that the best approach to classroom management is one that is systematic, beginning with preparation before the school year begins and continuing throughout the year. Such an approach includes planning and conducting activities in an orderly fashion, keeping students actively engaged in lessons and seatwork activities, and minimizing disruptions and discipline problems (Brophy & Evertson, 1976).

Management programs that use a systematic approach provide solid instruction and create a purposeful learning climate (Hoover & Kindsvatter, 1997). Kohn (1995) suggests that many discipline problems are the result of the teacher asking students to do uninteresting, inappropriate, or unreasonable tasks. When teachers change their instructional strategies, behaviors improve. Carolyn Evertson (as cited in Marchant & Newman, 1996) stresses that classroom management based on control and discipline is not compatible with building the kinds of learning communities in which students have a stake in their own learning and their own school community. Rather, systematic approaches create a positive social and emotional climate stemming from good interpersonal relationships between students and teacher, as well as among students.

This text includes four models that emphasize a systematic approach to classroom management. They include Glasser's *Reality Therapy and Choice Theory*, Curwin and Mendler's *Discipline with Dignity*, Kohn's *Beyond Discipline: From Compliance to Community*, and Evertson's *Classroom Organization and Management Program (COMP)*. These models view classroom management and instruction as interwoven, with the focus being on *preventing* problems rather than *responding* to problems. Each emphasizes that effective management begins before the first child arrives for the first day of school. Recognizing that each child is unique, the creators of these models reject one-size-fits-all approaches to maintaining classroom control. Instead, these approaches are based on the belief that when students' basic needs are met, misbehavior can be avoided.

Classroom Management as Instruction

There are those who argue that classroom-management models focusing on rewards, rules, consequences, and procedures overlook the needs of individual students. The necessity to meet individual needs has become more critical as classrooms have become more diverse and as students' needs have become more intense. Wolfgang and Kelsay (1992) contend that childhood has changed, and traditional discipline methods do not work for children who grow up in nontraditional circumstances. Therefore, as Weinstein (1999) notes, "a major change is occurring in our thinking about classroom management—this change can be characterized as a shift from a paradigm that emphasized the creating and application of rules to regulate student behavior to one that also attends to students' need for nurturing relationships and opportunities for self-regulation" (p. 151). Many schools are accepting this philosophy and are replacing rule-bound discipline programs with instruction that helps the student make ethical judgments and decisions.

These new classroom-management models focus on teaching prosocial skills to students. Peterson (1997) stresses that the teaching of some form of conflict mediation, negotiation procedures, and conflict-resolution skills should be included in the curriculum of every classroom. In addition, some teachers use conflict resolution as part of their classroom-management practices. Many schools have adopted schoolwide programs in which participation, support, and resources extend beyond a single classroom. Girard (1995) found that there were approximately fifty school-based conflict-resolution programs in 1984. By 1995, the number of such programs had risen to 5,000 and continues to increase. Because the goal is for students to learn self-discipline, these methods take longer to develop and implement but invite more risk-taking on the part of the teacher. However, Curwin and Mendler (1988) feel that these models may be more effective, because they encourage improved teaching as well as improved learning.

Many of these models advance a violence-prevention approach. As Gold and Chamberlin (1996) note, all children who are eventually identified as juvenile delinquents can be reliably identified by age eight. Therefore, effective violence-prevention programming begins in the early grades, in which the habits of peacemaking are first being learned, and continues throughout middle and high school, with the hope that if violence is learned, it can be unlearned. Remboldt (1998) states that "the key to preventing violence lies in shaping children's beliefs, attitudes, and behaviors before violence becomes an automatic manifestation of their anger" (p. 33).

TABLE 1.1 *Three Views of Classroom Management*

	Concepts:	Chapters:
Classroom Management as Discipline	The teacher is responsible for maintaining classroom control. Discipline comes before instruction. Consequences must exist for inappropriate behavior.	2: Behavioral Management 3: Assertive Discipline 4: Positive Classroom Discipline 5: Cooperative Discipline
Classroom Management as a System	Classroom management is systematic. Management and instruction are interwoven. There is a focus on the building of learning communities. Planning is essential.	6: Reality Therapy and Choice Theory 7: Discipline with Dignity 8: Building Communities 9: Classroom Organization and Management Program (COMP)
Classroom Management as Instruction	There is a focus on teaching prosocial skills. The goal is to establish habits of peacemaking. Schoolwide programs teach the skills of conflict resolution and peer mediation. Teachers help students make ethical judgments and decisions.	10: Inner Discipline 11: Skillstreaming 12: Conflict Resolution and Peer Mediation 13: Judicious Discipline

This text presents four models that have the teaching of prosocial skills as their central focus. The models presented include Coloroso's *Inner Discipline*, Goldstein and McGinnis's *Skillstreaming*, Bodine and Crawford's *Conflict Resolution and Peer Mediation*, and Gathercoal's *Judicious Discipline*. The purpose of these programs is to teach appropriate behavior and social skills, with the focus being on helping students develop positive interactions throughout their lifetime rather than on behavior at a particular moment. Table 1.1 presents the three views of classroom management covered in this book, outlines their basic concepts, and lists the chapters that discuss them.

RESEARCH ON EFFECTIVE CLASSROOM MANAGEMENT

Ms. Salerno's reaction to the situation described at the beginning of this chapter should also be influenced by the classroom-management research conducted during the last fifty years. Researching in the 1950s, Fritz Redl and William Wattenberg were the first to suggest that group behaviors differ from individual behaviors and that the influence of group dynamics must be considered in creating an effective classroom-management plan. Before Redl and Wattenberg, much of the focus of classroom management had been on the individual "problem" student, not on the interactions of a class of thirty or more students that might include several "problem" students. Redl and Wattenberg (1959) also noted that each classroom had what they described as "key students" who influence the other students in the classroom. They emphasized that it is important for classroom teachers to understand the influence of class leaders, class clowns, and instigators in creating or destroying a positive classroom environment. Therefore, teachers were encouraged to anticipate certain behaviors, to be aware of group interactions, and to handle problems from a group perspective.

Most experts in the field of classroom management agree that the work of Jacob Kounin in the 1970s was pivotal and continues to influence the development of classroom-management approaches. Kounin investigated the effects of classroom procedures and activities on students' on-task behaviors. Like Redl and Wattenberg, Kounin designed his research to gain knowledge about group-management techniques, emphasizing that classrooms are made up of more than one student, and to support the idea that it is the management of group behavior that identifies a successful classroom manager. He identified successful classroom managers as those teachers who "produced a high rate of work involvement and a low rate of deviancy in the academic setting" (Kounin, 1970, p. 63). Therefore, his work focused on both classroom management and lesson management. Through his research, Kounin identified the following management techniques that remain valid in describing management strategies:

Desists: the teacher's actions and words used to stop misbehavior. Kounin found that the clarity, firmness, intensity, and focus of the desist greatly influenced the behavior of the student disciplined and the other students in the classroom.

Ripple Effect: the teacher's method of handling misbehavior by one student, which influences the behavior of other students in the classroom. Kounin found that the ripple effect for high school students was related to the students' degree of motivation to learn the material and to their positive feelings toward the teacher.

Withitness: the teacher's ability to know everything that is happening in the classroom and an awareness of the verbal and nonverbal interactions of students with the teacher and their classmates. The withitness quality was measured by the following criteria:

- The ability to stop misbehavior before it spreads.
- The ability to stop misbehavior before it increases in seriousness.
- The ability to correct a child who is misbehaving rather than correcting the wrong child.
- The ability to stop serious misbehavior rather than focusing on a less-serious misbehavior (Vasa, 1984).

Overlapping: the teacher's ability to manage two issues simultaneously. This involves managing multiple groups or assignments. In more modern language this would be known as multi-tasking.

Transition Smoothness: the teacher's management of various activities throughout the day. Because the teacher must initiate, sustain, and terminate many activities throughout the day, transitions are constant. The ability to make such transitions in a smooth and orderly fashion influences the teacher's management effectiveness.

As Brophy (1999) notes, the results of Kounin's research stressed the point that effective classroom managers were not effective merely because they could handle disruptions

Tips from the Field

I use a small plastic bucket to address the issue of tattling. I decorate the bucket with a sad face, a nose, eyes and some big ears. After I discuss tattling with the class, I tell my students that if they want to tattle, they must write their concern on a piece of paper and place it in Mr. Bucket. This has been a great help in stopping the tattling because kids don't get my attention. Later, I read what is placed in Mr. Bucket and then decide if anything needs to be addressed.

Kirk Ver Halen
Gifted and Talented Teacher
Elisha M. Pease Elementary School
Dallas, TX

when they occurred; they were effective because they prevented disruptions from occurring in the first place by establishing the classroom as an effective learning environment, preparing and teaching good lessons, and monitoring students as they worked. Kounin's research changed the way teachers thought about classroom management by moving the focus on disciplining students to creating and maintaining classroom environments that support learning.

For over twenty-five years, Carolyn Evertson has researched effective classroom-management practices. Her work continues to be valid today. Her program for effective classroom management, *Classroom Organization and Management Program (COMP)*, is discussed in Chapter 9. Working with a number of fellow researchers (Edmund Emmer, Linda Anderson, Barbara Clements, Jere Brophy, Alene Harris), Evertson sought to verify the results of Kounin's study and to determine the impact of effective classroom management on student achievement.

In the late 1970s, Evertson was part of a research project at the Research and Developmental Center for Teacher Education located at the University of Texas at Austin. In a study of third-grade classrooms that recorded behaviors of teachers and students from the first day of school and throughout the school year, Emmer, Evertson, and Anderson (1980) found that better classroom managers:

- *Analyzed the classroom tasks.* Better managers were able to analyze in precise detail the procedures and expectations required for students to function well in a classroom.
- *Taught going-to-school skills.* Better managers provided instructions in the classroom rules and procedures as part of the curriculum and gave students practice in classroom procedures. They viewed the classroom through the child's eyes. Better managers could analyze the student's needs for information about how to participate in class activities.

- *Monitored student behavior*. Better managers kept their students in view and dealt with problems quickly.
- *Took the student's perspective*. Effective managers were able to predict and deal with students' confusions, distractions, and concerns.

Evertson studied the behaviors of effective junior high classrooms as well. Researching with Emmer (Evertson & Emmer, 1982), Evertson found that better managers:

- *Explained rules and procedures*. Better managers had explicit rules, procedures, and expectations that are communicated to students.
- *Monitored student behavior*. Better managers were consistent. They were aware of and dealt with disruptive behavior and potential threats to the management systems.
- *Held students accountable*. Better managers developed detailed systems for keeping track of student academic work.
- *Communicated effectively*. Better managers presented information clearly, reduced complex tasks to their essential steps, and had a good understanding of student skill levels.
- *Organized instruction*. More effective managers preserved their instructional time and had more students engaged in academic work.

Jere Brophy, too, has researched the topic of classroom management for over twenty-five years. His research indicates that the crucial classroom-management skills involve planning, organizing, and maintaining a learning environment in which students are engaged in productive activities. Brophy (1988) stressed that the main concern of teachers should be on the quality of instruction rather than on the ability to exert control over students. Therefore, according to Brophy, to be effective managers, teachers must have prepositional knowledge (knowledge of effective classroom-management principles), procedural knowledge (knowledge of how to implement these principles), and conditional knowledge (knowledge of when and where to implement these principles).

Brophy and Evertson (1976) found that teachers whose students consistently gained in achievement had organized classrooms that ran smoothly, with a minimum of disruptions. Their research during the last twenty-five years provides evidence supporting specific ways to systematically organize the classroom and provide instruction that supports both the academic and social goals of the classroom.

SUMMARY OF RESEARCH FINDINGS

In the past fifty years, researchers have spent thousands of hours observing the behaviors of teachers who successfully and unsuccessfully managed their classrooms. These fifty years of research have produced the following findings:

- Group behaviors differ from individual behavior.
- Effective classroom management starts with careful planning for the school year and each school day. The order created during the first few days of school reliably predicts the degree of student engagement and disruption for the rest of the year.

- Effective classroom management prevents disruptions from occurring rather than merely reacting to situations.
- Effective teachers weave instructional and disciplinary strategies together.
- Better managers provide instruction in classroom rules and procedures as part of the curriculum.
- Academic achievement and effective classroom management are tied together.

DEVELOPING A PERSONAL SYSTEM OF CLASSROOM MANAGEMENT

McEwan (2000) notes that the issues associated with classroom management are as complex as the time in which we live and as diverse as the students we teach. Different children, and even the same children at different levels of development, require different treatment for optimal results. Therefore, there are no easy answers to discipline problems, nor is there one most effective classroom-management plan. Figure 1.1 describes factors that should be considered in formulating a personal classroom-management plan.

Ultimately, the best classroom-management plan is the one developed by an individual teacher, designed to meet the needs of his or her students. The last two chapters of this text provide information to assist in the design of a personal system. Chapter 14 provides information for creating a safe learning environment for all students, and explores issues related to multicultural and socioeconomic factors, physical and mental disabilities, and at-risk behaviors. Chapter 15 helps the individual teacher put together all elements of classroom management into a comprehensive program.

There is not one perfect discipline approach. Teachers must discover what works best for themselves, their students, and their specific situations. The goal of this text is to provide theories and research from which individual teachers can select, blend, and create the best classroom-management plan to meet their needs.

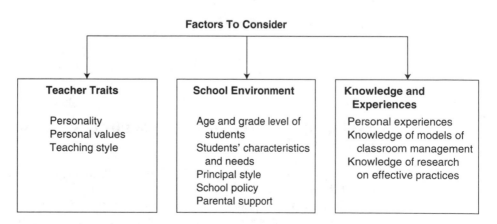

FIGURE 1–1 Developing a Personal Classroom-Management Plan

KEY TERMINOLOGY

Definitions for these terms appear in the glossary:

Desists   Transition smoothness
Overlapping   Withitness
Ripple effect

CHAPTER ACTIVITIES

Reflecting on the Material

1. Consider the situation with Marcus described at the beginning of this chapter.

   a. What additional information would you want to consider in deciding how to handle this situation?
   b. What strategies could Ms. Salerno have used to prevent the situation from occurring?
   c. In what ways could Ms. Salerno's instructional strategies have created or prevented the situation?
   d. Does the motivation of the student who poked Marcus play in your decision making?
   d. How would you have handled the situation?

2. Kounin's research identified "withitness" as a skill of effective classroom managers. Describe a teacher you have observed who has "withitness." How did the teacher's "withitness" prevent discipline problems or help the teacher in correcting inappropriate behavior?

Developing Your Portfolio

1. The research on classroom management speaks to the importance of classroom rules. List the rules you are considering for your classroom. What is your rationale for selecting these rules?

Developing Your Personal Philosophy of Classroom Management

1. This chapter provides several definitions of classroom management. Which definition most closely reflects your personal definition of classroom management? Why?
2. This chapter describes classroom management as discipline, a system, and instruction. Which of these models most closely fits your philosophy of classroom management? Why?

CHAPTER REFERENCES

Baruch, D. W. (1949). *New ways in discipline.* New York: Whittlesey House.

Brophy, J. E. (1983). Classroom organization and management. *Elementary School Journal, 83*, 275–285.

Brophy, J. E. (1988). Educating teachers about managing classrooms and students. *Teacher and Teacher Education, 4*, 1–18.

Brophy, J. (1999). Beyond behaviorism. In H. Jerome Freiberg (Ed.), *Beyond behaviorism: Changing the classroom management paradigm.* Boston: Allyn & Bacon.

Brophy, J. E., & Evertson, C. M. (1976). *Learning from teaching: A developmental perspective.* Boston: Allyn & Bacon.

Curwin, R. L., & Mendler, A. N. (1988). Packaged discipline programs: Let the buyer beware. *Educational Leadership, 46*, 68–73.

Doyle, W. (1990). Classroom management techniques. In O.C. Moles (Ed.), *Student Discipline Strategies: Research and Practice.* Albany: State University of New York Press.

Edwards, C. H. (1999). *Building classroom discipline* (3rd ed.). New York: Longman.

Emmer, E., Evertson, C., & Anderson, L. (1980). Effective management at the beginning of the school year. *Elementary School Journal. 80*, 219–231.

Evertson, C., & Emmer, E. (1982). Effective management at the beginning of the school year in junior high classes. *Journal of Educational Psychology, 74*, 485–498.

Evertson, C. M., & Harris, A. H. (1992). What we know about managing classrooms. *Educational Leadership, 49*, 74–78.

Freiberg, H. J. (1999). Beyond behaviorism. In H. Jerome Freiberg (Ed.), *Beyond behaviorism: Changing the classroom management paradigm.* Boston: Allyn & Bacon.

Girard, K. (1995). Preparing teachers for conflict resolution in the schools. *ERIC Digest 94.*

Gold, V. E., & Chamberlin, L. J. (1996). School/student violence: A primer. *American Secondary Education, 24*, 27–32.

Hoover, R. L, & Kindsvatter, R. (1997). *Democratic discipline: foundation and practice.* Upper Saddle River, NJ: Merrill/Prentice Hall.

Kohn, A. (1995). Discipline is the problem—not the solution. *Learning, 24*, 34.

Kounin, J. S. (1970). Discipline and group management in classrooms. New York: Holt, Rinehart, & Winston.

Marchant, G. J., & Newman, I. (1996). Mentoring education: An interview with Carolyn M. Evertson. *Mid-Western Educational Researcher, 9*, 26–28.

McEwan, B. (2000). *The art of classroom management.* Upper Saddle River, NJ: Merrill/Prentice Hall.

Morris, R. C. (1996). Contrasting disciplinary models in education. *Thresholds in Education, 22*, 7–13.

Peterson, G. J. (1997). Looking at the big picture: School administrators and violence reduction. *Journal of School Leadership, 7*, 456–479.

Redl, F., & Wattenberg, W. W. (1959). Mental hygiene in teaching. New York: Harcourt.

Remboldt, C. (1998). Making violence unacceptable. *Educational leadership, 56*, 32–38.

Vasa, S. (1984). Classroom management: A selected review of the literature. In Robert Egbert and Mary Kluender (Eds.), *Using Research to Improve Teacher Education.* The Nebraska Consortium. Teacher Education Monograph No. 1. (ERIC Document Reproduction Services No. 246 026).

Weinstein, C. S. (1999). Reflections on best practices and promising programs: Beyond assertive classroom discipline. In H. Jerome Freiberg (Ed.), *Beyond behaviorism: Changing the classroom management paradigm.* Boston: Allyn & Bacon.

Wolfgang, C. H., & Kelsay, K. L. (1992). Problem students in class: Disobedient—or just "devalued"? *Education Digest, 57,* 58–60.

Part
I

Classroom Management as Discipline

Four models of classroom management are presented in Part I: Classroom Management as Discipline. Chapter 2 presents basic behavioral concepts with a review of B.F. Skinner's theory of operant conditioning. Lee and Marlene Canter's model, Assertive Discipline, is presented in Chapter 3. Chapter 4 provides a different approach to using behavioral theory in Fredric Jones's model, Positive Classroom Discipline. Chapter 5 presents the work of two theorists, Rudolf Dreikurs and Linda Albert. Although different in approach, the models presented in these four chapters share the following principles:

- The teacher is in control and responsible for all decisions concerning classroom management.
- Discipline is separate from instruction and comes before instruction.
- Consequences must exist for inappropriate behavior and are the same for all students.
- Rules are developed by the teacher and are clearly defined.
- Strategies are reactive, not proactive.
- Students choose to misbehave and must face the consequences of their decisions.
- Rewards are extrinsic rather than intrinsic.
- Strategies are based on behavioral theory.

Chapter 2

Behavioral Approaches to Classroom Management

Objectives

Chapter 2 prepares preservice teachers to meet INTASC standards #2 (Student Development), #5 (Motivation and Management), and #9 (Reflective Practitioner) by helping them to:

- use knowledge about human behavior drawn from the research of Pavlov, Thorndike, Watson, and Skinner to develop strategies for classroom management.
- understand the basic principles behind a behavioral approach to classroom management.
- evaluate research concerning the impact of reinforcement and punishment on learning and behavior.
- evaluate the role of extrinsic rewards on students' behaviors.
- learn techniques for applying behavioral techniques in the classroom.
- determine whether they will incorporate behavioral strategies into their classrooms.

Scenario

Student teacher Tennill Johnson is nervous about her ability to control the classroom. With the permission of her cooperating teacher, she develops a plan to reward her students for good behavior. Addressing the class, she unveils a twenty-four-inch-square jigsaw puzzle. The puzzle features balloons and confetti and the word "Party" appears several times on the picture. Getting the children's attention, she removes all the pieces of the puzzle and places them in a basket. She explains that each day the class can earn puzzle pieces when they display excellent behavior. At the end of each day, they will discuss the behavior of the class during the day and Ms. Johnson will determine whether they have earned a piece of the puzzle. Placing a piece of the puzzle back on the board, she demonstrates how the pieces will be placed on the board. "When the puzzle is complete," she explains, "you will get what the puzzle says—a party. I will provide the food and drinks, and we will watch a video you select."

Hands go up around the room. "Can we earn more than one piece in a day?"

"Yes," Ms. Johnson explains, "if I am pleased with how you act during a certain activity, I might put an extra piece on for that day."

"Can we lose pieces if we are bad?"

"No, I will never remove pieces. They are your rewards. I won't take them back."

Carmen raises her hand, "What about David? He is bad all the time. He will make us lose our puzzle pieces."

Ms. Johnson took a deep breath, "First, I would never assume David will be bad, and neither should you, Carmen." She looked at David, "I am confident David will help the class earn the party." Then, looking back at Carmen, she continued, "This is a class reward, so no individual student will prevent you from getting a puzzle piece. Now, if there are no more questions, it is time to work on our spelling."

When the class returned from lunch, Ms. Johnson explained that she was very pleased with their behavior in the lunchroom. Taking a puzzle piece, she filled in the first piece of the puzzle. At the end of the day, she spent a few minutes talking about the overall behavior of the class for that day. Pleased with their behavior, she put another piece on the puzzle. The second day, the students weren't as attentive, and Ms. Johnson had to correct several students throughout the day. At the end of the day, she explained that no puzzle pieces had been earned that day and that she hoped the following day would be a better one.

Four days before the end of her teaching assignment, the puzzle was complete, and the students were rewarded with the promised party. Ms. Johnson was also rewarded when her cooperating teacher gave her an excellent evaluation for her student-teaching experience.

INTRODUCTION

Whether the result of training, good teaching skills, or logic, the approach Ms. Johnson used is one of the oldest classroom-management techniques in existence. The practice of providing consequences for both good and bad behaviors has been used in classrooms since the first cave teacher taught the first cave student to make fire. It is only during the past fifty years, however, that the process of systematically applying rewards (reinforcements) and punishment has been part of classroom-management training. This model of classroom management is known by many terms, including behaviorism, behavioral techniques, behavior modification, and social-learning theory (Wielkiewicz, 1986). For the purpose of this chapter, the term **behavioral techniques** will refer to the practices used to modify classroom behaviors, and the term **behavior modification** will be used for the programs developed for individual students.

This behavioral approach to classroom management has its roots in the work of Pavlov (1849–1936), Watson (1878–1958), Thorndike (1874–1949), and Skinner (1904–1990). Focusing on how organisms learn, the behavioral model is concerned with the scientific modification of observable behaviors. Pavlov, considered the father of classical conditioning, began the behaviorist movement with his discovery that when a conditioned stimulus is applied with an unconditional response, the result is a conditioned response. He is best remembered for his conditioning of dogs to salivate (unconditioned response) at the sound of a bell (conditioned stimulus). Thus the concept that learning and behavior can be controlled and manipulated was developed. Watson, who called himself a behaviorist, found that learning was the process of conditioning responses through the substitution of one stimulus for another. Learning, according to Watson, could explain most behaviors. Thorndike was one of the first researchers to apply operant conditions. He developed the concept known as the **Law of Effect,** which states that a rewarded behavior will be repeated, and an unrewarded behavior will cease. Skinner developed operant conditioning as a theory and concentrated on the observation and manipulation of behaviors. Operant conditioning describes the relationship between behavior and environmental events and focuses on the use of reinforcement to obtain desired behaviors (Zirpoli & Melloy, 1997). Classroom management was never the goal of these researchers; however, their research changed the concept of classroom management, because their studies demonstrated experimentally how a teacher's behavior could shape and maintain students' behaviors.

In 1954, Skinner stressed that "special techniques have been designed to arrange what are called 'contingencies of reinforcement'—the relation which prevails between behavior on the one hand and the consequences of that behavior on the other—with the result that a much more effective control of behavior has been achieved" (p. 86). Through reinforcements, Skinner suggested, the behavior of an individual—student, spouse, employee—could be shaped almost at will. Although some behaviors required successive stages to change behaviors, other behaviors could be changed in a single reinforcement.

Therefore, according to behaviorists, all behaviors (good and bad, appropriate and inappropriate) are learned and maintained by reinforcement. Behavior is conditioned by its consequences: strengthened if followed immediately by reinforcement, weakened if not reinforced. Drawing upon the findings of operant conditioning is the belief that the causes of behavioral problems are not in individual personality variables or emotional well-being but in the interactions among the child, his or her peers, the parents, and the teacher (Skiba, 1983). Consider the following situations:

> Every day seventh-grader Jacob manages to disrupt the class to the point that he is eventually sent to the office or to in-school suspension. Twice he has been suspended from school. Jacob's teacher, his principal, and his parents are confused about what to do with Jacob and fail to understand the reasons that none of the punishments imposed on Jacob have been effective. Unfortunately, they have not consulted with Jacob's bus driver. He could explain that each day Jacob gets in trouble, Jacob is greeted with high-fives from the other kids on the bus who have bets that Jacob can get more suspensions in one year than any other student in the history of his school.

> Because Timothy is always off task, Ms. Sloan often walks by his desk and stands beside Timothy until he returns to work. Timothy, who is raised by his father, likes having Ms. Sloan beside him, because he thinks she smells good and reminds him of his mom. So, as soon as Ms. Sloan walks away, Timothy puts his pencil down and stares into space. In a few seconds, Ms. Sloan is beside him again.

> Kindergartener Latisha clung to her mother's skirt and cried when she tried to leave the room. Trying to console Latisha, her mother agreed to stay a few minutes longer. Unfortunately, the crying became louder and stronger as weeks went by, and now Latisha's mother is spending most of her day in the kindergarten classroom. She agrees with Latisha's teacher that she needs to leave but can't bring herself to leave her crying child.

> Whenever Ms. Carter asks a question, Carla raises her hand. If Ms. Carter doesn't call on her immediately, Carla waves her hand wildly. Eventually, Ms. Carter always calls on Carla.

> Mr. Reynolds controls his tenth-grade basic-science class by yelling and screaming. The students have learned that when he is especially angry he will begin to stutter and spit. Mr. Reynolds's loss of control is the source of much lunchroom laughter, and eventually most of his classes are pushing him to the point that he is constantly red faced, stuttering, and spitting.

In all the situations described, behavior was modified because of reinforcement. Unfortunately, the modified behavior was not always the behavior desired. In some cases, the adults had *their* behavior modified. To be used effectively in the classroom, there are several basic assumptions about behavioral theory that must be understood:

- Behaviors are learned. Individuals tend to exhibit behaviors that are reinforced and avoid behaviors that have not been previously reinforced or have been punished.
- Behaviors are stimulus specific—that is, individuals behave differently in different environments. This is because each environment contains its own sets of cues (antecedents) and consequences (reinforcers or punishments) for the behavior exhibited. Behaviors have environmental, situational, and social roots. Therefore, teachers should never question when parents say, "He never acts that way at home," because it may be the school environment that creates the behavior.
- Behaviors can be taught, changed, or modified. Because behaviors are learned, teachers and parents can teach new behaviors and modify current behavior.
- Behavioral change should focus on the here and now. Behaviorists are not concerned with past events; instead, they concentrate on current events within a student's environment, in order to identify the influences on current behaviors (Walker & Shea, 1999; Zirpoli & Melloy, 1997).

ELEMENTS OF BEHAVIOR MANAGEMENT

The relationship between behaviors and consequences represent the heart of behavior-management strategies. **Consequences** are events or changes in the environment following a behavior. According to Jones and Jones (2001), there are three basic consequences of behavior:

1. Behavior followed immediately by a reward (reinforcement) will occur more frequently.
2. Behavior followed closely by a punishing consequence will occur less often.
3. Behavior will be extinguished (stopped) when it is no longer reinforced.

Reinforcement is a powerful tool used to teach new behaviors and change current behaviors, and is the foundation of Skinner's operant conditioning (Zirpoli & Melloy, 1997). Reinforcement leads to an increase in behavior. Extinction is the cessation of a particular behavior resulting from a lack of reinforcement (Whitman & Whitman, 1971). Reinforcement and extinction are opposite phenomena but should not be confused with punishment. Whereas extinction consists of withholding a reinforcer after a behavior is displayed, punishment involves the application of negative consequences for inappropriate behavior. Thus, when confronted with inappropriate behavior, a teacher has three choices:

- Rewarding appropriate behavior in order to increase the chances the desired behavior will occur again.
- Ignoring the inappropriate behavior in hopes of extinction.
- Punishing the child for inappropriate behavior.

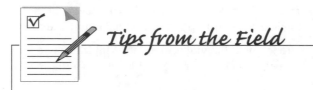

Tips from the Field

Call all parents at the beginning of the school year to welcome them and their child to your class. Find something positive to say. Invite them to visit your classroom. Making a positive first contact will help gain support when you need their help in resolving discipline problems.

Alma Dark
Grade 5 Teacher
Caldwell Middle School
Schriever, LA

Consequences of Behavior

Reinforcement involves the use of consequences to *strengthen* the behavior. **Reinforcement** following a behavior operates on the likelihood that the desired behavior will be repeated under the same or similar circumstances. Reinforcement can be both positive and negative, and both positive and negative reinforcement increase behavior. **Positive reinforcement** is the presentation of a reinforcer wanted by the student after the desired behavior has been exhibited. Typically, the student will repeat this behavior in order to get another reward. Positive reinforcement can come in many forms. Examples are:

Jennifer's high school English teacher wrote a note at the bottom of the first assignment that read, "I really enjoyed your writing. I can't wait to read your next paper." Jennifer was so pleased, she spent hours making sure her next paper was perfect.

Julio's principal stops him on his way back from lunch and tells him that she is proud of the way he helped a classmate who had dropped her lunch tray. She gives Julio a good citizenship slip that qualifies him for a drawing for a prize at the end of the six weeks.

Brian's teacher places a peppermint on his desk because he is working hard on his math problems.

Ms. Foster announces that the class will get fifteen extra minutes on the playground because they acted so well during assembly.

Mr. Bader's principal names him Teacher of the Month because of his work with the debate club. Along with the title comes free lunch in the cafeteria for a month.

Unfortunately, positive reinforcement does not always have the desired effect. Walker and Shea (1999) stress that reinforcement is most effective in maintaining or increasing a behavior when:

- Reinforcement is given only if the student exhibits the desired behavior. If students are rewarded when they haven't earned the reward, there is little chance of getting the desired behavior in the future.
- Reinforcement is individualized for a particular child. Some reinforcements are more effective with some children than others. By asking the child and testing different reinforcers, teachers can generate a reinforcement menu. Brian, in the example given earlier, would not find the peppermint rewarding if he hated peppermint candy.
- The desired behavior is reinforced immediately after it is exhibited. As the interval between the behavior and reinforcement increases, the relative effectiveness of the reinforcer decreases. Initially, an effective reinforcement program reinforces immediately after the desired behavior. Later, the time between the behavior and reinforcement can be increased.
- Verbal praise is combined with the reinforcement. It is important to remind the child of the connection between the desired behavior and the reinforcement.
- The target behavior is reinforced each time it is exhibited. When the target behavior becomes routine for the student, it can be reinforced intermittently. However, if all reinforcement ceases, the behavior may end as well.
- The reinforcement is given by someone the child loves, likes, or respects.

Negative reinforcement also strengthens the behavior. However, unlike positive reinforcement, it involves the removal of an aversive stimulus following a desired behavior. There are two key words or phrases in this definition. The first is *removal*; rather than presenting something to the student, as in positive reinforcement, something aversive is removed. The second key phrase is *desired behavior*. In negative reinforcement, the aversive stimulus continues until the desired behavior is achieved. Because there is relief when the aversive stimulus is removed, the student is rewarded, and the likelihood increases that the desired behavior will occur again. There are fewer examples of negative reinforcement in the classroom, because most teachers prefer to avoid introducing aversive stimuli into the classroom. Examples of negative reinforcement would include:

> When Ms. Evans's class becomes too loud, she blows a whistle until the noise level drops. The students find the sound of the whistle aversive and stop talking so Ms. Evans will stop blowing the whistle.

> Simone and Dana like to whisper to each other during class. When Mr. Morris notices that they are whispering, he stands behind the girls until they stop whispering and return to their work.

> Because the class is too loud as they line up for lunch, Ms. Harris tells the class that they will not go to lunch until their work is put away and they are quietly in line. The students remain in the classroom until all work is put away and every student is standing quietly in line.

Because negative reinforcement requires the use of aversive stimuli, teachers must be careful in its application. If in the earlier example, Ms. Harris had kept the students in the classroom throughout the lunch period and the children had had no lunch that day, she

Desired behaviors, such as raising one's hand, will be repeated if reinforced.

would have found that using effective negative reinforcement practices resulted in her having to deal with angry parents and administrators.

It is important to remember that negative reinforcement is not punishment. The main difference between the two is that reinforcement *strengthens* behavior, whereas punishment *suppresses* behavior (Morris, 1996). For example, if Ms. Smith tells Michael he has to miss recess because he failed to complete his work, Ms. Smith has punished Michael. Ms. Smith has no guarantee that Michael will now finish his work. In fact, Michael may reason that because he already missed recess, there is no need for him to finish his work. On the other hand, if Ms. Smith tells Michael that he must miss recess (something Michael finds aversive) *until* he has finished his work (the desired behavior), Michael will realize he must finish the assigned work before he can have recess. It may take Michael five minutes to finish, and he can then join his classmates on the playground, or it may mean that Michael misses several days of recess until he completes the assigned work.

Punishment is the application of an unpleasant stimulus or the withdrawal of a pleasant reward in an attempt to weaken a response. It differs from negative reinforcement in that the student may *never* display the desired behavior. Punishment comes in many forms and typically falls into two categories. The first type is **presentation punishment**, which involves the presentation of an aversive stimulus in order to decrease inappropriate behavior. Examples include:

> The lunchroom monitor tells Ms. Henderson that her class left the tables messy when they left the cafeteria. Ms. Henderson took the class to the cafeteria where they had to clean all the tables.

> Grandpa tells Phillip that when he was a boy, he was whipped for sassing the teacher.

> Ms. Nelson's principal felt Ms. Nelson mishandled a situation with a parent and placed a letter of reprimand in her file.

The second type of punishment is removal punishment. In **removal punishment**, a pleasant stimulus or the eligibility to receive a positive reinforcement is taken away. Examples would be:

> Two of Adams High School's best football players are caught cutting class so they can go to lunch at the local McDonald's. The coach and principal agree that, as punishment for skipping class, they should not be allowed to play in the next game.

> Ms. Richards allows her students thirty minutes of computer time each week. During that time they can play computer games or search the Internet. Daniel loses his time, because he shot a rubber band at a fellow student.

> Each day, Ms. Smith's students wear two clothes-pin bumble bees (the school mascot) clipped to their clothes. One reads, "I'm a busy bee." The other reads, "I will always bee a good citizen." Students who are still wearing the pins at the end of the day get to pick a prize from the treasure box. When students misbehave, they must remove a pin and place it in a box. Students who lose both pins lose the opportunity to receive a prize.

Detention, in-school suspension, and time-out are examples of removal punishments, because they prevent students from receiving positive stimuli from their classmates (Eggen & Kauchak, 2001). As Alberto and Troutman (2002) explain, time-out is a shortened term for time-out from positive reinforcement. During time-out, students are denied the opportunity to earn reinforcement, such as participation in an activity. There are three types of time-out:

1. **nonseclusionary:** the student remains in the classroom but must be completely silent or is required to put his or her head on the desk;
2. **exclusionary:** a disruptive child is removed from the immediate instructional area to another part of the room;
3. **seclusionary:** the disruptive child is removed from the classroom (Smith & Misra, 1992).

Skinner (1968) cautioned against the use of punishment; he stressed that the main lesson learned from punishment is how to avoid or escape punishment in the future. As

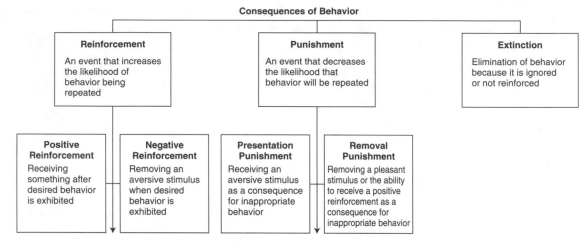

FIGURE 2-1   Elements of Behavior Management

Skinner explained, children do not learn to tie their shoestrings by being punished when they cannot. In addition, Biehler and Snowman (1990) stress that the results of punishment are neither predictable or dependable for the following reasons:

- Mild punishment does not eliminate undesirable behaviors permanently. To be effective, punishment must be much more harsh than desired when working with children.
- Punished behaviors may continue when the punishers are not present.
- The punishment itself may be reinforcing. Sometimes the attention given to the student is rewarding, and the behavior will increase rather than decrease.
- The punishment may produce undesirable emotional side effects such as fear, trauma, or hatred of school.
- Punishers model a type of behavior that they would find unacceptable if exhibited by the student who is punished. If the teacher's goal is to produce children who are not aggressive and who can settle differences in a peaceful manner, the teacher must not demonstrate behavior that is counter to this goal.

When reinforcement is no longer forthcoming, a response becomes less and less frequent. This process of ending undesired behaviors by withholding reinforcement is known as **extinction**. Teachers can use extinction to stop undesired behavior by ignoring behavior. For example, had the teacher in the example given early in this chapter ignored Carla's waving hand and refused to call on Carla unless she was holding up her hand in an appropriate manner, Carla's hand waving would have stopped. Unfortunately, desired behaviors can also be extinguished if they are never rewarded. If Carla's classmate Joe is never called on, even though he is holding up his hand and waiting quietly to be called on, he will soon stop behaving appropriately and begin the hand waving that seems to work for Carla.

Extinction is also useful when the behavior is one that the teacher wishes to discourage but does not consider punishable. For example, if Chris often uses baby talk when he is tired, ignoring the behavior would be a more appropriate way of handling the situation than punishing Chris for his baby talk.

Extinction does not occur quickly and will take longer when there has been a long history of reinforcement. Although there is no simple relation between the number of reinforced and nonreinforced responses necessary for extinction, disruptive behavior can be extinguished if it is ignored. Unfortunately, the teacher is not the only person in the classroom, and misbehavior may still be maintained by peer attention or other elements outside the control of the teacher (Whitman & Whitman, 1971). If Chris's parents think his baby talk is sweet and reinforce the behavior at home, it will be difficult for the teacher to stop the behavior. Figure 2.1 gives additional examples of positive reinforcement, negative reinforcement, punishment, and extinction.

Schedules of Reinforcement

A schedule of reinforcement is essential when a teacher uses reinforcement as part of the discipline plan. A reinforcement schedule refers to the frequency or timing of the delivery of reinforcement. Reinforcement schedules are important in developing positive behavior patterns. Reinforcement may occur on a continuous or intermittent schedule. When children are reinforced every time they respond, a **continuous schedule** is being used. A continuous schedule is important until an association is made between the desired behavior and the reinforcement.

When a child is reinforced after some occurrences of the desired behavior, but not each time, an **intermittent schedule** is being used. There are two types of intermittent schedules. **Interval schedules of reinforcement** distribute reinforcement based on time. For example, if after five minutes of seat work by the students, a teacher moves through the room and places a reward (gold star, candy, or token) on the student's desk, the teacher would be rewarding the students on an interval schedule. A **ratio schedule of reinforcement** is based on the number of responses rather than the passage of time. If the teacher in the earlier example moved throughout the room placing the reward on the desk of students who have successfully completed five questions, the teacher would be using a ratio schedule. Both interval and ratio schedules can be given on a fixed schedule. In a fixed schedule, students know when the reward will occur, because it is predictable. Report cards are based on a fixed-interval schedule, because students know exactly when grades will be given. Of course, some students would argue that the issuing of report cards is not reinforcement but punishment!

The last type of reinforcement is a **variable schedule**, in which the giving of the reward is varied, so that no patterns can be established. A variable-interval schedule would be one in which students do not know how much time must pass before they will be rewarded. In a variable-ratio schedule, the reward may come after the student has completed five problems or it may not come until the student has completed twenty questions (Zirpoli & Melloy, 1997). The unpredictability of the schedule keeps the student focused and on task. Figure 2.2 provides an illustration of the types of schedules of reinforcement.

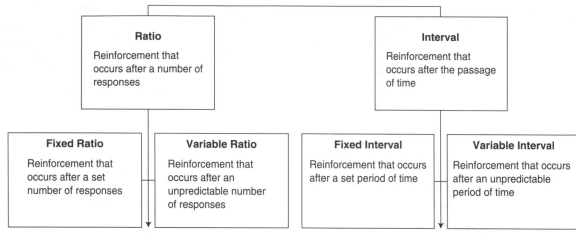

FIGURE 2-2   Schedules of Reinforcement

Types of Reinforcement

One of the criticisms of behavioral strategies is the emphasis on extrinsic reward, because many people believe that children should behave in appropriate ways just for the intrinsic value of the behavior. Kazdin (1975) suggests that with extrinsic reinforcers, "there is no 'real' change in the behavior of the person who is reinforced. The person is just being 'bought' or 'bribed' to perform a particular behavior" (p. 49). Advocates of behavioral strategies counter by suggesting that extrinsic reinforcement is the primary reason for *all* behavior and that those who criticize behavior-modification techniques are being extrinsically rewarded for their criticism!

There are two categories of extrinsic reinforcers: primary (unconditioned) and secondary (conditioned). **Primary reinforcements** satisfy the biological needs or drives of a student, and their reinforcing value does not have to be explained (Kazdin, 1975). They include such things as food, water, and sleep. However, primary reinforcers may not be reinforcing in all situations. A student who has just had a nap will not find sleep reinforcing. Because primary reinforcers are essential to the well-being of students, many would argue they should not be given or withheld as part of classroom management.

The reinforcements used most often in the classroom are **secondary reinforcements**. Not reinforcing in themselves, secondary reinforcements get their power from the significance attached to them by students. A secondary reinforcement can be in the form of a tangible object, approval or attention from another, or being allowed to participate in a preferred activity. A tangible reinforcer can be any object coveted by the student, such as money, certificates, stickers, pencils, games, and personal items. The type of tangible reinforcers selected is important, because what will work for young children (stickers, trinkets, toys) may have little reinforcing value for middle school or high school students. In many classrooms, tangible reinforcements are earned through the collections of tokens. A **token reinforcer** has no intrinsic reinforcing properties; its

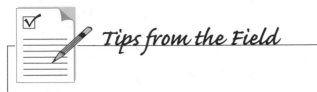

Tips from the Field

My drama class produced a videotape of class rules and behavior. I assigned a different rule to a group of two or three students. They had to write, practice, and perform a skit demonstrating appropriate and inappropriate behavior. My drama students had a great time producing the skits, and the video will be a fun way to review the rules in all of my classes.

In Memory of
Barbara Keihle
Language Arts Teacher
Nestucca High School
Cloverdale, OR

value is based on the tangible object or desired activity for which it can be exchanged. Through tokens, students receive immediate reinforcement in the form of a check, chip, or voucher that can be traded for reinforcement at a future date. The use of token economy and other forms of tangible reinforcers have been studied extensively in their relation to student behavior and have been found to modify student behavior (Skiba, 1983). However, as Zirpoli and Melloy (1997) stress, a token economy will not work if the child is too young to understand the exchange value or if the child has a zero token balance at the exchange period.

Social reinforcers are the behaviors of other people (teachers, parents, peers, and administrators) that increase desired behaviors. They include compliments, praise, facial expressions, physical contact, and attention. Skiba (1983) notes that for social reinforcers to be effective they must be given only when the desired behavior is exhibited, they must vary, and they must be spontaneous. The advantages of using social reinforcers are that they are easy to use, inexpensive, readily available, and do not interrupt the flow of instruction.

Activity reinforcers offer rewards by allowing the student to participate in preferred activities, and are another natural and easily dispensable reward for desirable behavior. Appropriate activity reinforcers include extra time on the computer, leadership roles in class activities or sports, and eligibility to operate audiovisual equipment. David Premack (1959) did extensive research on the concept that participation in preferred activities can be used to reinforce participation in less-desired activities. This concept is known as the **Premack Principle**. Activity reinforcers carry many of the same advantages as social reinforcers. However, because they must often be delayed and not presented immediately to the student, the delay in timing may mean that a student does not understand the connection between behavior and activity. This is especially true for young children.

WORKING WITH INDIVIDUAL STUDENTS

When behaviorists began researching the connection between behavior and reinforcement, the research focused on individuals rather than on groups of people. Behavioral strategies are most effective with individuals. Two strategies, shaping and behavior modification, are especially useful in helping teachers to modify the behavior of individual students.

Shaping is used to teach new behaviors and skills and refers to the reinforcement of successive approximations of a terminal behavior. For example, if a child were learning the alphabet, one would not wait until the child could recite the entire alphabet before reinforcing the child. Instead, parents and teachers clap their hands when a young child manages to remember the first few letters. As the child becomes more confident, the reward is withheld until more letters are recited. Eventually, reinforcement (cheers, hugs, smiley faces, or applause) is withheld until the entire alphabet is recited. Just as rewarding approximate behaviors can work with learning the alphabet, it can also work as a child learns new behaviors. If Min Lee has never managed to spend an hour in class without leaving her seat, it may be necessary for the teacher to praise Min Lee when she has managed to remain in her seat for ten minutes. Later, the reinforcement should be withheld until Min Lee can stay in her seat for a longer period of time. Eventually, through shaping, Min Lee's behavior should match that of her classmates.

Behavior Modification involves systematically applying behavioral principles in an effort to change specific behaviors in an individual. Eggen and Kauchak (2001) note that because the term *behavior modification* may have a negative connotation, the term **applied behavior analysis** is often used instead. The goal of behavior modification is to make long-term changes in the behavior of students and should not be used for the modification of minor classroom disruptions (Kazdin, 1975). The initial goal is to change the immediate behavior with the ultimate goal of maintaining the change after the program is terminated. The case study of David at the end of this chapter is an example of a behavior-modification program.

Danforth and Boyle (2000) suggest that before a behavior-modification program can be put in place, the teacher must determine the following:

- What is the specific behavior that is problematic? What is the behavior targeted for observation, measurement, or modification? The target behavior is the behavior identified by the teacher as the behavior that must be changed. This requires careful analysis of the behavior. A student's wiggling in his seat may be the result of a splinter in his chair. In this case, a behavior-modification program would be a waste of the teacher's time and a frustration to the student.
- What is the baseline rate of current behavior? Collection of the baseline data gives the standard against which the success of the behavior-management program will be judged and allows for goal setting by the teacher and the student (Wielkiewicz, 1986).
- What are the behavioral goals? Behavior-change goals based on observation and analysis of current behavior should be stated in specific terms that are clearly observable and measurable (Zirpoli & Melloy, 1997).

- What are the events or actions that tend to trigger undesired behaviors? Are there conditions that precede a behavior and influence the probability of misbehaviors (Smith & Misra, 1992)? When teachers can control these triggers, they can minimize disruptive behaviors in the classroom.
- What would be rewarding to the student? It is important that the reward be something acceptable to both the child and the teacher. If the reinforcer is not something desired by the student, there will be no change in the behavior. If the reinforcer is something the teacher cannot give because it is inappropriate, too costly, or too time consuming, another reinforcer will have to be found.
- Who can systematically and consistently provide the rewards, and how can this be arranged? A behavior-modification program will not be successful if the teacher cannot measure the target behavior for changes and consistently and systematically provide the rewards. Often this is difficult in a classroom of twenty or thirty children. In this case, another adult may be needed to provide the reinforcer, or the student's behavior may need to be modified in a less formal manner.

STRENGTHS AND WEAKNESSES OF THE BEHAVIORAL MODEL

Behavioral strategies are widely used in schools. In many cases, teachers are not aware that they are using researched methods, because the techniques seem a natural way of interacting with children, and advocates for behavior strategies would argue that this naturalness is precisely the strength of programs using a behavioral approach. Other strengths include:

- Behavioral strategies work. A hundred years of research has shown that behaviors can be taught, changed, modified, or corrected. Doyle (1990) stresses that the techniques derived from laboratory studies of contingencies of reinforcement have been researched extensively and advocated widely in discipline strategies. Controlled studies, often in special settings, have indicated that behavior-analysis techniques are remarkably successful.
- The use of behavioral strategies forces the teacher to be more aware of what is going on in the classroom. In many cases, the teacher becomes a more objective and precise observer of student behavior (Whitman & Whitman, 1971).
- A behavioral program increases the likelihood that the teacher will be consistent in treatment of students. It gives teachers a systematic plan for dealing with discipline problems.
- Behavior-management strategies provide all children a chance to be "good." For many students with behavioral disabilities, this may be their first opportunity to receive consistent reinforcement (Whitman & Whitman, 1971).

Critics of behavioral strategies cite philosophical and practical reasons for their objections to its use. Many find such programs to be manipulative and controlling and think they teach children to work for rewards rather than for the intrinsic satisfaction that comes with doing a good job. Other weaknesses cited include:

- The concept of ignoring undesirable behavior while praising desired behaviors is impractical for individual classroom teachers who lack the assistance of independent observers and support personnel and who work with large groups of students.
- Teachers are less likely to examine their own teaching methods or other classroom factors as possible causes of students' unproductive behavior. Savage (1999) suggests that teachers using behavioral strategies are less likely to blame classroom problems on poor teaching methods, poor interpersonal skills, or inappropriate exercise of teacher authority. They also may not recognize that the student's behavior is an attempt to cope with boredom, anxiety, or anger.
- Behavioral strategies can be harmful if used by insensitive and unethical teachers and administrators. The result may be a hatred of school.
- Teaching children to avoid certain behaviors because they will be punished is not the same as teaching that the behaviors are wrong, immoral, or unethical. Kohn (1996) suggests that rewards only manipulate students; they do nothing to help children become kind or caring people.
- One student's reward may be another student's punishment. In a classroom of twenty to thirty students, it is difficult to find rewards that will appeal to every student.

BEHAVIOR MANAGEMENT IN THE CLASSROOM
Scenario

Third-grade teacher Amy Collins is puzzled by David Brower's behavior. Every few minutes, David is out of his seat, going to the tissue box, the trashcan, or to the pencil sharpener. Ms. Collins has told the students that they do not need to request permission to do these things, but only David abuses the privilege.

Sometimes, David will stand beside his desk, rummaging through his books and belongings, and at other times, he just stands at his desk, lost in thought. When Ms. Collins tells David to return to his seat, he quickly does so and never complains. David's constant roaming is becoming a problem for both Ms. Collins and the other students, who are distracted by his behavior and who feel that they, too, should be allowed to roam about the classroom constantly. During the past week, she punished David for his excessive out-of-seat behavior by giving him extra work and not allowing him to have recess; neither had any impact.

Ms. Collins talked to David's second-grade teacher about his behavior, but Ms. Smith couldn't remember David being a problem in her classroom. Ms. Smith suggested that Ms. Collins's expectations were too high. Concerned that she was making too much of David's misbehavior, Ms. Collins asked the school guidance counselor to observe her class and give her suggestions. The guidance counselor was amazed that during the two hours she observed the classroom, David was out of his seat twenty-seven times. The average number of times the other students left their seats during that same time period was three times.

Working with the guidance counselor and David's mother, Ms. Collins developed a plan to shape David's behavior. Ms. Brower told Ms. Collins that David had been begging for a new pair of skates for several weeks. They decided that they would allow David to work for the skates by changing his out-of-seat behavior.

After school, David, his mother, the guidance counselor, and Ms. Collins met to talk about David's misbehavior. When Ms. Collins told David that he was out of his seat forty-three times the day before, David agreed that this seemed excessive. When asked why he thought he was out of his seat so much, David just shrugged. Ms. Collins asked if David was willing to work on staying in his seat more, and he quickly agreed.

Together, a plan was developed. With forty-three as a baseline, they agreed that for the next week, David would be out of his seat no more than thirty-five times a day. Each day Ms. Collins would send home a note telling how many times David had left his seat. Each day he met his goal, he would earn a point toward earning his skates. When he earned thirty points, he would earn the skates. They also agreed that they would reduce the times he could be out of his seat once David had earned five points. This reduction would continue until he was out of seat no more than ten times a day, the average number of times his classmates were out of their seats during a day.

The first day, David exceeded his goal and only left his seat thirty times. He was pleased with the note sent to his parents by Ms. Collins. Unfortunately, the second day, he forgot and did not meet his goal. After a few days, however, David's parents were receiving positive notes most days. It took seven weeks for David to meet his goal and to earn his skates. During that time, David became aware of his behavior and never returned to constant classroom roaming.

SUMMARY

Behavioral approaches to classroom management have their roots in the work of Pavlov (1849–1936), Watson (1878–1958), Thorndike (1874–1949), and Skinner (1904–1990). Based on the concept known as the Law of Effect, the premise is that rewarded behaviors will be repeated, and unrewarded behaviors will cease. Therefore, according to behaviorists, all behaviors—good and bad, appropriate and inappropriate—are learned and maintained by reinforcement. Therefore, the systematic application of reinforcement is the basis of behavioral techniques and is the foundation of many of the classroom models presented in this text.

KEY TERMINOLOGY

Definitions for these terms appear in the glossary:

Behavior modification
Behavioral techniques
Consequences
Continuous schedule of reinforcement
Exclusionary time–out

Extinction
Intermittent schedule of reinforcement
Interval schedule of reinforcement
Law of Effect
Negative reinforcement

Nonseclusionary time–out

Positive reinforcement

Premack Principle

Presentation punishment

Primary reinforcements

Punishment

Ratio schedule of reinforcement

Removal punishment

Seclusionary time–out

Secondary reinforcements

Shaping

Social reinforcers

Token reinforcer

Variable schedule of reinforcement

CHAPTER ACTIVITIES

Reflecting on the Theory

1. Eleventh-grade history teacher Chris Bilyeu is having a problem with his fifth-period class. At the beginning of the semester, a few students were tardy for class. He thought it best to ignore the students and to continue with his lectures. Now, almost half the students in his fifth-period class are tardy, and many are five to ten minutes late for class.

   How would you handle this situation? How can the behavioral approaches presented in this chapter be used to resolve this problem?

2. In the scenario provided at the end of this chapter, Ms. Collins was successful in changing David's behavior. Consider the following:

   a. If the shaping activity had not worked with David, what might have been some of the reasons?

   b. Would you be comfortable using this method? Why or why not?

   c. What are the drawbacks to this method?

3. Give a classroom example of each of the following:

   Positive reinforcement
   Negative reinforcement
   Removal punishment
   Ratio reinforcement
   Variable reinforcement
   Interval reinforcement
   Fixed reinforcement
   Extinction

4. What is meant by a token economy? How is a token economy used in the classroom?

5. Are there types of students or students of certain grade levels who might not respond to behavior-management techniques? Explain why.

Developing Your Portfolio

1. In the chapter-opening scenario, Ms. Johnson designed a reward plan for her class. Design your own plan for rewarding individual students and for rewarding the entire class. How will you reward your students for appropriate behavior?

Developing Your Personal Philosophy of Classroom Management

1. One of the criticisms of behavioral strategies is the emphasis on extrinsic rewards. Do you think there is too much emphasis on extrinsic rewards in classrooms today?
2. Would you be comfortable using a behavioral approach to classroom management in your classroom? Why or why not? Are there some strategies that you will definitely incorporate into your classroom-management plan?

CHAPTER REFERENCES

Alberto, P. A, & Troutman, A. C. (2002). *Applied behavior analysis for teachers: Influencing student performance (*6th ed.*).* Upper Saddle River, NJ: Merrill/Prentice Hall.

Biehler, R. F., & Snowman, J. (1990). *Psychology applied to teaching* (6th ed.). Boston: Houghton Mifflin Co.

Danforth, S., & Boyle, J. R. (2000). *Cases in behavior management.* Upper Saddle River, NJ: Merrill/Prentice Hall.

Doyle, W. (1990). Classroom management techniques. In O.C. Moles (Ed.), *Student Discipline Strategies: Research and Practice.* Albany: State University of New York Press.

Eggen, P., & Kauchak, D. (2001). *Educational psychology: Windows on classrooms* (5th ed.). Upper Saddle River, NJ: Merrill/Prentice Hall.

Jones, V. F., & Jones, L. S. (2001). *Comprehensive classroom management* (6th ed.). Boston: Allyn & Bacon.

Kazdin, A. E. (1975). *Behavior modification in applied settings.* Homewood, IL: The Dorsey Press.

Kohn, A. (1996). *Beyond discipline: From compliance to community.* Alexandria, VA: Association for Supervision and Curriculum Development.

Morris, R. C. (1996). Contrasting disciplinary models in education. *Thresholds in Education, 22,* 7–13.

Premack, D. (1959). Toward empirical behavior laws: I. Positive reinforcement. *Psychological Review, 66,* 219–233.

Savage, T. V. (1999). *Teaching self-control through management and discipline* (2nd ed.). Boston: Allyn & Bacon.

Skiba, R. J. (1983). *Classroom behavior management: A review of the literature.* Monograph No. 21. St. Paul: University of Minnesota Center for Research on Learning Disabilities.

Skinner, B. F. (1954). The science of learning and the art of teaching. *Harvard Educational Review, 24*, 86–97.

Skinner, B. F. (1968). *The technology of teaching.* New York: Appleton-Century–Crofts.

Smith, M. A., & Misra, A. (1992). A comprehensive management system for students in regular classroom. *The Elementary School Journal, 92*, 353–371.

Walker, J. E., & Shea, T.M. (1999). *Behavior Management: A practical approach for educators* (7th ed.). Upper Saddle River, NJ: Merrill/Prentice Hall.

Whitman, M., & Whitman, J. (1971). Behavior modification in the classroom. *Psychology in the Schools, 8*, 176–186.

Wielkiewicz, R. M. (1986). *Behavior management in the schools.* New York: Pergamon Press.

Zirpoli, T. J., & Melloy, K. J. (1997). *Behavior management: Applications for teachers and parents* (2nd ed.). Upper Saddle River, NJ: Merrill/Prentice Hall.

Chapter 3

Assertive Discipline

Objectives

Chapter 3 prepares preservice teachers to meet INTASC standards #5 (Motivation and Management), #9 (Reflective Practitioner), and #10 (School and Community) by helping them to:

- understand the basic principles behind Assertive Discipline.
- evaluate the rights of teachers and the rights of students.
- determine the role of administrators and parents in supporting rule enforcement.
- determine the appropriate consequences for misbehavior.
- establish appropriate reward systems for individual students and for classwide recognition.
- learn techniques for the effective use of Assertive Discipline in the classroom.

Scenario

Preservice teacher Helen Garcia has been assigned to observe fifth-grade teacher Marilyn Conner. During her first day of observation, Helen was intrigued by
Ms. Conner's discipline plan and thought it was one she would like to use. At the front of the classroom was a large poster outlining Ms. Conner's rules and consequences. The rules for Ms. Conner's class are:

- Come to class prepared.
- Stay on-task during instruction.
- No speaking out of turn.
- Keep hands, feet, and objects to yourself.
- No teasing or bullying.

The consequences for misbehavior are:

First Offense:	Receive a warning.
Second Offense:	Lose ten minutes of recess/play time.
Third Offense:	Lose fifteen minutes of recess/play time plus write in behavior journal.
Fourth Offense:	Teacher will call parents.
Fifth Offense:	Be referred to the principal.

On a white board beside the list of rules and consequences were twenty-four magnetic nametags with the name of each student in the class written on a plate. These nametags were lined up along one edge of the board. Across the top of the board were the words *First Offense, Second Offense, Third Offense, Fourth Offense,* and *Fifth Offense.* Unfortunately, before Helen could ask Ms. Conner how she used the nametags, class began.

During the first few minutes of class, Jonathan raised his hand and told Ms. Conner that he had forgotten his pencil. Without stopping her instruction, Ms. Conner pointed to the white board and the box of sharpened pencils on a table below the board. Without discussion, Jonathan placed his magnetic nametag under the category First Offense and took a pencil. Jonathan went back to work, and Ms. Conner continued her instruction.

All went well until mid-morning, when Ms. Conner noticed two girls passing a note. As she took the note from the girls, she pointed to the white board, and both girls moved their nametags to the First Offense category.

Later in the day, Ms. Conner noticed Jonathan drawing rather than doing his assignment. Ms. Conner told him to move his nametag to the Second Offense category. Later, when the class went to the playground, Jonathan had to stay in the library and finish his assignment. When ten minutes had passed, he was allowed to join his classmates.

During the remainder of the day, two other students received warnings, but no student went beyond the Second Offense category. Helen also noticed that the entire class was reinforced for good behavior. When the music teacher complimented the students on their good behavior during class, Ms. Conner told the class they had earned a marble. All the students applauded as the marble dropped into a jar among what appeared to be hundreds of other marbles.

By the end of the day, Helen was eager to find out about the marble jar and the magnetic plates on the board. "Would you mind telling me about your classroom-management plan? I thought it really worked well."

"Well, it is certainly nothing new," Ms. Conner explained as she straightened the desks. "I first saw this procedure when I did my student teaching. My cooperating teacher said she had learned the method at a conference on classroom management. However, I've changed a few things about how I manage behavior. She had the students write their names on the board and then put a check behind their name for each infraction of the rules. I found the magnetic nametags at an office supply store, and they work well. Other teachers in this school are doing variations of this same concept. For example, Ms. Frazier, next door, still has students write their names on the board, and Mr. Rader keeps a clipboard for each day with the students' names and makes checks in it. I don't like that method as well, because he has to tell the student that they are getting a check."

"Will Jonathan start tomorrow with his name in the Second Offense category, or does he begin fresh?"

"No, I move the plates back after each day. Everyone starts with a clean slate each day. However, I do keep a record of what happened each day. Let me show you." Ms. Conner retrieved a notebook that contained records sheets for each student. "Each sheet contains a record for a month. I will record the problems that Jonathan had today. If I need to contact his parents, I can tell them about his behavior over a period of time. This notebook assures that I have an accurate record of each student's behavior."

Helen looked at her watch and realized that she was keeping Ms. Conner, "I didn't mean to keep you so long. This has been a great day for me; I really learned a lot. I hope you won't mind if I steal a few ideas."

"Not at all; that's what good teachers do. And you're welcome to come back anytime. You were a big help today."

INTRODUCTION

Although Ms. Conner may not know the origin or name of her discipline plan, she is actually using the basic concepts of a classroom-management program, **Assertive Discipline,** developed by Lee and Marlene Canter in the early 1970s. Since that time, Assertive Discipline has become as common to classrooms as chalk and pencils. This model or variations of this model are used throughout the United States.

Unlike the discipline models developed outside the classroom in the 1950s and 1960s, Assertive Discipline was developed to solve the problems of actual teachers. Lee and Marlene Canter realized that many of the problems found in classrooms were based on the failure of teachers to be assertive in having their needs met, resulting in many teachers feeling overwhelmed and powerless. Using theories and principles from assertiveness training and behavior modification, the Canters developed Assertive Discipline, which allows teachers to meet their needs by systematically applying behavioral strategies to classroom situations.

In 1989, Canter noted that he and his staff had trained 750,000 teachers. Since that time hundreds of thousands have read the numerous books published by Canter and Associates, attended workshops, and watched videos on the principles of Assertive Discipline. Through these means, teachers have been introduced to the following basic principles of Assertive Discipline:

- Teachers have the right to teach and to expect students to behave.
- Teachers must develop consistent and firm rules.
- Teachers must identify consequences to be used when students choose to misbehave.
- Teachers must provide positive consequences for appropriate student behavior.
- Teachers must create classroom plans to provide negative and positive consequences for behavior.
- Teachers must seek and expect support from parents and administrators.

Unlike much of educational literature that focuses on the needs of students, Canter and Canter (1976, 1992) emphasize the wants, needs, and rights of the teacher. Canter and Canter stress that teachers have the right to:

- Establish classroom structure, rules, procedures, and routines that clearly define the limits of acceptable and unacceptable student behavior.
- Determine and request appropriate behavior from students, so that the teacher's needs can be met while encouraging the positive social and educational development of the child.
- Ask for assistance and support from parents and the school administration.
- Teach students to consistently follow rules and directions throughout the school day and school year.

Although the Canters did not overlook the rights of children, the emphasis of such rights centered around supporting the teacher's ability to control the classroom. According to Canter and Canter (1976, 1992), students' rights include:

- The right to know the behavior expected of them by the teacher.
- The right to have firm and consistent limits established, so that they can eliminate inappropriate self-disruptive behaviors.
- The right to have consistent encouragement, so that they will be motivated to interact appropriately.
- The right to know the consequences of inappropriate behavior.
- The right to be taught acceptable and responsible behavior.

Tips from the Field

The Internet is a powerful tool in classroom management. From my website, I can receive and send e-mails from my students and their parents. I have my classroom rules and consequences posted. I created a monthly calendar, so that parents know of upcoming events. At the beginning of the each week, I post my homework. If a student misses class, the student or his her parent can easily find the material missed. I have been amazed at how the Internet has increased my ability to communicate with parents and students.

Michael Mosley
Grade 7 Social Studies Teacher
Kenwood Middle School
Clarksville, TN

THE ASSERTIVE TEACHER

In 1976, Canter and Canter suggested that it is the teacher's response style that sets the tone of the classroom. The teacher's style will impact each student's self-esteem and success. They identified three basic response styles used by teachers when interacting with students: nonassertive, hostile, and assertive. The nonassertive and hostile styles are reactive in nature; the assertive style is proactive in nature.

Nonassertive teachers fail to make their needs or wants known and allow students to take advantage of them. Nonassertive teachers appear wishy-washy, which confuses students because they do not know what to expect. Nonassertive teachers threaten, but students know there will be no follow-through. Therefore, aggressive students run the class, and less aggressive students are frustrated, because their rights are constantly violated. Nonassertive teachers feel frustrated and have a good deal of inner hostility toward the students. They burn out quickly and either leave the teaching profession or suffer a career filled with unhappiness.

Hostile teachers respond in a manner that disregards the needs and feelings of students and, in many cases, violates students' rights. Their responses to students are negative, condescending, sarcastic, or hostile. Too often they make unprofessional comments about a student in front of the student, the student's peers, and other teachers. When behavior must be corrected, the consequences are overly severe or physical. Hostile teachers describe the classroom as a battleground, and when they win, which they often do, they do so because students are afraid.

Assertive teachers clearly and firmly express their needs. They have positive expectations of students, and this is reflected in their words and actions. Because they say what they mean and mean what they say, students know the limits in the classroom. When they must respond to inappropriate behavior, they are consistent and fair. Because students are not required to play guessing games with the teacher, and because they consider the teacher as fair, the teacher is respected and the teacher's expectations are met.

Consider the following responses by teacher Michael Collins:

Mr. Collins teaches eleventh-grade world history, and his fourth-period class is a challenge, because students go to lunch midway through the class. After lunch, Mr. Collins struggles to regain the students' attention and his momentum. Today, when Mr. Collins returns to the classroom after lunch, four girls are sitting on the tops of their desks engaged in an animated conversation about the events that took place at the ballgame the evening before. Vivian, a cheerleader, has the girls mesmerized with her account of post-game romance. Standing in the front of the class, Mr. Collins says, "Ladies, it is time to begin."

Vivian, giving Mr. Collins her most charming smile says, "Can't you wait just a minute? I'm almost finished."

Mr. Collins, the **nonassertive teacher**, responds, "Well, how much longer will you be?"

Mr. Collins, the **hostile teacher**, responds, "Don't try your beauty-queen charm on me. I don't care how cute you are, it won't work on me. Now get your butt in your seat and your book on your desk."

Mr. Collins, the **assertive teacher**, responds, "You can finish after class. Now, I believe we were discussing the rise of Communism before we left for lunch."

ROADBLOCKS TO DISCIPLINE

Canter and Canter (1976, 1992) acknowledge that no teacher is assertive in all situations. They state that the biggest "roadblock" teachers face in being assertive is their own negative expectations of their ability to deal effectively with students. According to the Canters, teachers assume that there are too many factors outside the control of the teacher impacting student behavior and limiting the teacher's ability to control the classroom. Teachers cite such issues as heredity, home situations, emotional problems, peer pressure, poor parenting, and poverty as critical factors influencing behaviors over which they have no control. However, Canter and Canter stress that if teachers accept that such factors limit the ability to maintain classroom control, they will expect to have little control. Lee and Marlene Canter also discourage teachers from looking at their own behaviors that might be leading to the student's misbehavior; they suggest that such questioning will result in "guilt, anxiety, and frustration" (Canter & Canter, 1976, p. 5).

If teachers expect all students to behave appropriately and believe they have the ability to maintain classroom control, control will exist. Canter and Canter encourage teachers to give up the idea that some students *can't* behave and recognize that some students *choose* not to behave. As Canter and Canter (1976) stress, "If you feel the child can't behave, or you can't influence him to behave, there is little or nothing you can, or will, do to change his behavior" (p. 51). However, when students and teachers see misbehavior as a choice, such choices can be controlled. Assertive teachers require students to choose appropriate behaviors or face the consequences for not doing so.

THE ASSERTIVE-DISCIPLINE PLAN

Canter and Canter (1976, 1992) stress that planning is essential to good teaching and to good discipline. Without a plan, teachers will have to choose an appropriate consequence at the moment of misbehavior. In the stress of the moment, the teacher may be unfair and inconsistent and may respond differently to students from different socioeconomic, ethnic, or racial backgrounds (Canter, 1989). Planning assures that students' rights are protected and that all students are treated fairly and consistently.

An effective plan must be in place the first day of class. To help guide a teacher in developing an individual classroom discipline plan, the following questions should be addressed:

- What behaviors does the teacher want students to eliminate or display?
- What negative consequences will be appropriate for the students?
- What positive consequences will be appropriate for the students?
- How can appropriate and inappropriate behaviors be tracked?

STEPS IN DEVELOPING THE PLAN

The **first step** in development of the discipline plan is to seek approval from the administration and to plan for notification of parents. This is critical, because the application of consequences will require the support of both the school's administration and the students' parents. Without their support, the plan will fail. Many teachers are hesitant to involve administrators and parents because, according to Canter and Canter (1992), there is a myth that a competent teacher will not need such assistance. They stress, to the contrary, that *no* teacher is capable of working with each and every student *without* support.

The **second step** is the establishment of classroom rules. Canter and Canter give the following guidelines for rule development:

- Rules must be observable. Whether a student has observed or violated a rule should not be debatable. Rules such as "Be nice" or "Always do your best" are too open for interpretation to be enforced.
- Rules should be enforceable throughout the day. A rule such as "Students will not carry on conversations during work time" is inappropriate when the teacher divides the students into groups with instructions to work together. Rules that apply only during certain situations will confuse students and be ineffective.
- Rules should be age appropriate. A rule such as "All cell phones and pagers are forbidden" would be as inappropriate for first-graders as "Only 12-inch voices in the hallways" is for twelfth-graders.
- Rules should cover typical discipline situations. If the teacher plans to punish students for being tardy, "Come to class on time" must be one of the rules.
- Rules must teach appropriate classroom behavior. A rule such "Don't hit, kick, or touch anyone else with your hands, your feet, or any other object" is designed to teach younger children appropriate school behavior.

The creation of classroom rules establishes the boundaries for classroom interactions and provides a sense of security for students.

Assertive Discipline is often referred to by teachers as the "Marble in the Jar" plan. When the model was first introduced, Canter (1979) suggested that teachers drop a marble in a large jar whenever the class demonstrated good behavior. When the jar was full, the class could be rewarded by a party, extra free time, a movie, or a field trip. This focus on providing positive reinforcement is the **third step** in developing a discipline plan. Canter and Canter (1992) stress that such reinforcement is needed when one realizes that 90 percent of teachers' comments to students regarding their behavior are negative. Positive reinforcement is important, because it creates a more productive classroom environment, reduces the frequency of problem behaviors, and maximizes the teacher's influence over students.

The discipline plan should include both individual and classwide recognition. Individual recognition can be done in a variety of ways. Praising students is the easiest and most fundamental way to positively recognize appropriate behavior. Positive notes or phone calls to parents should be a regular part of the reinforcement plan. Other reinforcements can include special privileges (computer time, being the classroom assistant, homework passes), awards, certificates, or tangible items.

Canter and Canter (1976, 1992) also recommend classwide recognition, and state that such recognition: (1) works well because of peer pressure, (2) is effective when working on a specific problem, and (3) should be implemented as needed rather than all year long. With classwide recognition, the class works together to earn points for a classwide reward. In addition to collecting marbles in a jar, classes may earn points on the board, collect letters to a special word, or bank play money as a way to earn the reward.

The **fourth step** in the discipline plan is to provide consequences for those students who choose to disobey the rules of the class. When this happens, Canter and Canter (1976, 1992) emphasize that the teacher must be prepared to deal with misbehavior calmly and quickly. If the teacher has planned ahead, there will be a clear course of action to follow. This will prevent a knee-jerk reaction to situations and allow the teacher to be consistent in the treatment of students. The effective use of consequences includes selecting appropriate consequences, developing a hierarchy of consequences based on the number of times rules are broken, and devising a tracking system for recording behaviors.

Canter and Canter give the following guidelines for selecting consequences:

- There should be no more than five consequences.
- Consequences must be something the students dislike, but they must never be physically or psychologically harmful. Canter and Canter never advocate corporal punishment.
- Consequences do not have to be severe to be effective. For 70 percent of students, a simple warning is sufficient. For another 20 percent who may need more than a warning, the consequences the teacher chooses do not have to be severe to be effective. Canter and Canter (1992) estimate that only 10 percent of students will cause real problems, and consequences should not be designed for this group. Instead, the Severity Clause (explained later) should be used with this population of students.
- Negative consequences should be applied *every* time a student chooses to behave inappropriately.

A consequence might be time-out, which is isolation from the other students. This isolation can occur in or out of the classroom. For secondary students, being required to stay after class and miss crucial time with their peers is an effective consequence. Having students write in a behavior journal is an often-used and especially effective consequence, because it helps students focus on what they did and what they could have done differently. In a behavior journal, students write accounts of their misbehavior, the reasons they broke the rules, and what they should have done instead. Finally, the removal of a favored activity (recess, computer time) is an effective consequence. If the student's inappropriate behavior continues or escalates, parents or the principal must become involved. According to the Canters, the consequences need not be severe to be effective; their value lies in students knowing that they will occur each time a rule is broken.

Consequences should be applied through a **discipline hierarchy**. The hierarchy should begin with a warning, and with each infraction of a class or school rule, the consequences

Tips from the Field

Consistency and structure are two management tools to use. On day one, rules and consequences must be discussed and revisited daily and sometimes multi-daily, for the first few days of school. You'll find that you have to review them during the year as well (as the need arises). Students need to have boundaries and some will push the limit. But stand with firm but fair hands and remind them of the rules, always ask them if they have made the right choice and what they could have done differently in order to have made the right choice.

Kim Russell
Grade 7 Teacher
Vidor Junior High
Vidor, TX

escalate. By the fourth infraction, parents should be contacted. If the misbehavior continues, the student should be sent to the principal.

For the hierarchy to work, teachers must have a system for keeping track of student misbehavior. In 1976, the Canters suggested that the first time a rule is broken, the student's name is written on the board. This constitutes a warning. When a rule is broken for a second time, or if a different rule is broken, a check is placed behind the student's name, and the consequence for a second offense is applied. If misbehavior continues, consequences are applied for each check mark earned. This continues until the student is required to go to the principal. The use of names and checks on the chalkboard was considered to be essential to Assertive Discipline. Canter and Canter originally used the check method to eliminate the need to stop the lesson and issue verbal reprimands. However, some parents and teachers considered this method humiliating to students. The Canters (1992) now suggest using a clipboard, classroom-management log, or color-coded cards to track behavior. Regardless of the method used, the Canters stress that each day students should begin with a clean slate, and misbehaviors are not carried over from the day before.

Because classrooms will have a small percentage of students for which warnings and progression of consequences will not be effective, the **fifth step** in your discipline plan should be a **Severity Plan**. In cases of severe misbehavior that places students or the teacher in danger or prevents instruction from taking place, the student should not receive a warning or progress through the hierarchy. Instead, severe misbehavior requires immediate removal from the classroom and assistance from the school's administration. A sample discipline plan appears in Table 3.1.

TABLE 3.1   *Sample Classroom Discipline Plan*

Ms. Jackson's Third-Grade Classroom-Management Plan

Classroom Rules

Do not talk while the teacher is talking, while other students are contributing, or during tests or quizzes.

Walk quietly and in an orderly way in the hallways.

Don't hit, kick, or touch anyone else with your hands, feet, or other objects.

Bring all needed materials to class.

Don't bring food or drink into the classroom unless given special permission to do so.

Consequences of Breaking Classroom Rules

First Time to Break a Rule:	Warning
Second Time to Break a Rule:	Five minutes in Quiet Corner writing in Behavior Journal
Third Time to Break a Rule:	Ten minutes in Quiet Corner writing in Behavior Journal
Fourth Time to Break a Rule:	Fifteen minutes in Quiet Corner and parents are called
Fifth Time to Break a Rule:	Sent to Principal
Severity Clause:	Sent to Principal

Positive Recognitions:

Individual Rewards

Notes and Phone Calls to Parents

"No homework" passes
Certificates of citizenship

Class Rewards

Points toward party or special field trip

A KINDER, GENTLER CANTER

Responding to criticism by teachers, parents, and administrators, Lee and Marlene Canter presented a softer approach to classroom discipline in their writings of the late 1980s and 1990s. In 1989, Canter expressed concern that both advocates and critics of Assertive Discipline have made its principles sound simplistic and overfocused on providing negative consequences. In *Assertive Discipline: Positive Behavior Management for Today's Classroom*, published in 1992, the Canters note that to be successful, a discipline plan should be built on a foundation of mutual trust and respect. A fundamental change in Assertive Discipline principles of the 1990s is that before focusing on rules, rewards, and consequences, the teacher must build a relationship with students and earn their respect (Canter, 1996). Realizing that children cannot obey rules that they do not understand, Canter and Canter now encourage teachers to teach the rules and procedures at the beginning of the year. Unlike the program outlined in 1976, the Canters suggest that teachers use the discipline

TABLE 3.2   *Significant Changes in the Principles of Assertive Discipline*

Original Program	Changes in Recent Years
Did not mention elements of trust and respect. Stressed development of rules and consequences and means of successful plan.	Discipline plan must be based on trust and respect. Before rules and consequences can be effective, trust and respect must be present (Canter, 1996).
Stressed that all children can behave, and misbehavior is a choice.	Stresses that *most* students can behave when they want to do so (Canter & Canter, 1992). This change acknowledges the inability of some children to follow rules because of emotional, mental, or behavioral disorders.
Stressed that all children *could* behave, not that they must be *taught* to behave.	Teachers must teach the behaviors they expect (Canter, 1989; Canter & Canter, 1992).
Stressed that all off-task behavior was subject to consequences, in that it prevented teachers from providing instruction.	Establishes distinction between disruptive and nondisruptive off-task behavior and suggests alternative means of handling nondisruptive off-task behavior (Canter, 1996; Canter & Canter, 1992).
Suggested writing names on board as ways of dealing with behavior without interrupting instruction.	Behavior should be tracked in a private way in order to not humiliate or embarrass the student (Canter & Canter, 1992).
Provided no discussion of ways to deal with difficult children except for enforcement of severity clause.	More emphasis on ways to deal with difficult students (Canter & Canter, 1992). Change acknowledges that original plan will not work with difficult students.

hierarchy as a guide and warned that the hierarchy should not totally control teacher behavior. Many teachers find this new emphasis confusing, because the foundation of Assertive Discipline was to be consistent and to treat each student equally. Other significant changes to Assertive Discipline are outlined in Table 3.2.

STRENGTHS AND WEAKNESSES OF ASSERTIVE DISCIPLINE

In the thirty years since the introduction of Assertive Discipline, the model has received both criticism and praise. The major strength of Assertive Discipline is its simplicity. This simplicity has been especially helpful for beginning teachers. Once the plan has been developed and approved by the administration, teachers are not required to make choices about how to react to student behaviors; they *know* how they will react to discipline situations. This prevents teachers from responding emotionally or being inconsistent in their responses. Fundamental to the model is the notion that teachers treat all students alike, applying the same standards and expectations for success to all students. Other strengths of Assertive Discipline include:

- Research has shown its effectiveness. In 1989, Canter noted that the results of research on Assertive Discipline have consistently shown that teachers dramatically improve student behavior when they use Assertive Discipline. However, Emmer and Aussiker (1990) reviewed research on the effectiveness of Assertive Discipline and found that its use in the classroom had little or no impact on student behavior and attitudes.

- Assertive Discipline addresses student *behavior* rather than student *character*. When rules are broken, the teacher provides a consequence without making value judgments about the motivation or character of the student.
- The plan requires the support and involvement of administrators and parents. By presenting the discipline plan to parents and administrators before the first day of implementation, teachers are confident that they will have their support.

There is as much criticism of Assertive Discipline as there is praise. Weaknesses of the program include:

- Some suggest that the principles of Assertive Discipline may be counterproductive. For example, McEwan (2000) quoted one student who suggested, "All students in class got to misbehave once, have their names written on the board, and then settle down, so no one faced consequences" (p. 155). Another concern is that students start with a clean slate each day. Some teachers complain that the names of the same students are written on the board day after day, with no real change in their behaviors from one day to the next. Some students may actually find the consequences for misbehavior rewarding, resulting in an increase in inappropriate behavior. These students see having their name on the board, check marks, or turned cards as a status symbol. One middle-school teacher remarked that many of her students enjoyed the recognition of having their names on the board. As she put it, "For some of my students, having your name written on the board is a good thing. They like the chalk, but for them, spray paint would be even better."
- Covaleskie (1992) expressed the opinion of many when he said, "A discipline program cannot be judged merely by asking whether it does a job of keeping children out of trouble in school; being a good person is more than that" (p. 174). He fears that programs such as Assertive Discipline fail to teach students to be truthful or teach them the reasons why they shouldn't lie. Instead, Covaleskie suggests that the lesson learned is to not get *caught* lying.
- Assertive Discipline establishes an authoritarian environment in which students have virtually no rights and are mere recipients of the teacher's demands (Queen, Blackwelder, & Mallen, 1997). Kohn (1996) agrees, and suggests that Assertive Discipline clearly places the blame for the discipline situation on the shoulders of the students: "The problem always rests with the child who doesn't do what he is asked, never with what he has been asked to do" (p. 13).
- Assertive Discipline may only stop behavior for a short period of time and may not translate to other situations or areas. A rule such as "Don't talk when others are talking" may be viewed as a rule for the classroom but not for the auditorium, gym, library, or other classes. Curwin and Mendler (1988) express concerns about such a focus on rules: "When rules are not developed from principles, students learn, for example, to be in their seats when the bell rings without understanding the importance of responsible work habits" (p. 68). Therefore, the effectiveness of

Assertive Discipline would depend on the goals of the teacher. Assertive Discipline may meet the teacher's goal to change behavior for a moment in class but would not meet the goal of changing behavior for a lifetime.

- There is no attempt to find the cause of misbehavior. Palardy (1992, 1996) contends that Assertive Discipline treats the *symptoms*, but not the *causes* of behavior, because it makes no attempt to identify or treat the underlying causes of behavior. He stresses that child abuse, drug abuse, malnourishment, rejection, insecurity, loneliness, and emotional distress—all possible causes of misbehavior—do matter and in many instances can be treated by caring, competent teachers. According to Palardy, if the cause of behavior is not discovered, the behavior will persist. The only question is where, when, and to what extent the behavior will be displayed.
- There is limited opportunity for teacher discretion. It offers only one response when rules are violated and does not account for motivation or reason (Curwin & Mendler, 1988).

Assertive Discipline's success may be the cause of some of its failures. As Canter (1989) notes, Assertive Discipline has become a generic term. Many teachers and administrators have been trained by individuals who did not use or stress all of the principles of Assertive Discipline. Unfortunately, according to Canter, not everyone follows the plan as originally intended.

ASSERTIVE DISCIPLINE IN THE CLASSROOM
Scenario

When June Wong was hired as principal of Henderson Elementary School, she pledged to have the best-disciplined school in the system. After attending a workshop on Assertive Discipline, she spent the summer developing a discipline plan for her school. Before the school year began, she called a meeting of all the teachers in order to explain the plan. Her plan included:

- Schoolwide rules for nonclassroom situations.
- Individual classroom rules to be established by each teacher.
- Individual classroom consequences for a rule infraction.
- Individual and classroom rewards.
- A schoolwide award system.
- Notification of parents of the classroom teacher's rules and of the schoolwide discipline policies.

The schoolwide rules Ms. Wong established included:

- Walk in single file on the yellow line through the hallways.
- No talking in the hallways unless addressed by an adult.
- Use 12-inch voices in the cafeteria.
- Follow all directions from the teachers during drills and alarms.
- Don't tease or bully classmates.

Consequences for infractions of the rules were:

First Offense: Warning.
Second Offense: Ten minutes in detention and writing in behavior journal.
Third Offense: Twenty minutes in detention and writing in behavior journal.
Fourth Offense: Thirty minutes in detention and call to parents.
Fifth Offense: Sent to principal.

Any adult employee of the school could apply a consequence. The adult applying the consequence was to inform the classroom teacher of the schoolwide rule infraction. In addition to the schoolwide rules, each teacher was instructed to establish an individual class list of rules and consequences.

To reward students for good behavior, an afternoon of games and fun was planned for the last day of each six-week period. Throughout the six weeks, students could earn "Fun Bucks" for good behavior. Any adult employee could reward a student for good behavior with "Fun Bucks." Students demonstrating excellent behavior could receive "Fun Bucks" from the cafeteria monitor, the custodian, or the school secretary. A student demonstrating good citizenship by helping a fellow student could be awarded with "Fun Bucks" by the classroom teacher, the custodian, the librarian, or the bus driver. Teachers could also reward students demonstrating good classroom behavior with "Fun Bucks."

Students who were in detention during the six-week period were not allowed to participate in the reward afternoon. Instead, they were required to go to one classroom and continue with their schoolwork. Those allowed to participate could play games, buy prizes with their "Fun Bucks," and win door prizes donated by local businesses.

On the day of the first reward afternoon, Ms. Wong realized she had a problem. First, there were more students who had to remain in the classrooms than were allowed to participate in the reward afternoon. In fact, in some classrooms, *no* students were allowed to participate. Second, one teacher had rewarded her students constantly, and her students had earned more "Fun Bucks" than all the other students combined.

The next day, Ms. Wong called the faculty together to discuss and refine the discipline plan. First, they agreed that students would have to be in detention twice during the six weeks to lose their chance to participate in the reward afternoon. They also discussed and agreed about what behavior was worthy of a reward.

By the end of the second six-week period, Ms. Wong was pleased with her discipline plan. The second reward afternoon was a huge success, with 80 percent of the students in the school participating. When students were in the hall, they quietly walked in a straight line. When she visited classrooms, she found students on-task and well-behaved. The cafeteria was a quiet place with few disturbances. One afternoon, after walking through the building, she returned to the office and told the school secretary, "The building is so quiet, I almost forget there are children in the building. I'm very pleased by what we have accomplished."

SUMMARY

The most widely accepted classroom-management model throughout the 1970s and 1980s was clearly Lee and Marlene Canter's *Assertive Discipline*. This model, or variations of this model, are still used in schools throughout the United States. Using theories and principles from assertiveness training and behavior modification, *Assertive Discipline* has as its premise the right of the teacher to define and enforce standards for student behavior in the classroom. *Assertive Discipline* is a series of actions that are directed at clearly specifying expectations for student behavior.

KEY TERMINOLOGY

Definitions for these terms appear in the glossary:

Assertive Discipline   Hostile teachers
Assertive teachers   Nonassertive teachers
Discipline hierarchy   Severity plan

CHAPTER ACTIVITIES

Reflecting on the Theory

1. Eighth-grade teacher Natalie Cansler is having a problem with one of her students, Cary Kirby. Cary arrives each day without the required materials. Some days he forgets his pencil; other days it is his textbooks. Each day, he requests that he be allowed to return to his locker for some forgotten item. Ms. Cansler feels she is in a no-win situation. If she allows Cary to return to his locker, he loses valuable instructional time. If she refuses, he spends the hour unable to do his work.

   How could the principles of Assertive Discipline be used to change Cary's behavior?

2. In the scenario at the beginning of the chapter, Ms. Conner punished Jonathan for not having a pencil but then allowed him to select a pencil from a box of sharpened pencils. Did allowing Jonathan to take a pencil encourage Jonathan to forget his pencil in the future? Would you have given Jonathan a pencil or made him do without? Why?

3. Think of a teacher you consider "assertive." What are the behaviors that this teacher displays?

4. Are there types of students or students of certain grade levels who might not respond to Assertive Discipline techniques? Explain your reasoning.

5. The end of the chapter describes the discipline at Henderson Elementary School. Would you be comfortable working in a school that has adopted a plan such as Henderson Elementary School? Why or why not?

Developing Your Portfolio

1. Canter and Canter suggest that teachers predetermine the consequences for rule violation. What consequences will you have for inappropriate behavior? Will you establish a discipline hierarchy? Why?

Developing Your Personal Philosophy of Classroom Management

1. Would you be comfortable using Assertive Discipline as your classroom-management approach? Why or why not? Are there some strategies from Assertive Discipline that you will definitely incorporate into your classroom-management plan? Why?
2. Canter and Canter suggest that students "choose" to misbehave. Do you agree? Are students who misbehave choosing to violate the classroom rules, or are there other factors that might be impacting students' behavior? If so, what might they be?

RESOURCES FOR FURTHER STUDY

Further information about Assertive Discipline and resources for its use in the classroom can be found by contacting:

Canter and Associates
P.O. Box 2113
Santa Monica, CA 90407-2113
800-262-4347
310-95-3221

CHAPTER REFERENCES

Canter, L. (1979). Taking charge of student behavior. *National Elementary Principal, 58,* 33–36.

Canter, L. (1989). Assertive discipline: More than names on the board and marbles in a jar. *Phi Delta Kappan, 71,* 57–61.

Canter, L. (1996). First, the rapport—then, the rules. *Learning, 24,* 12, 14.

Canter, L., & Canter, M. (1976). *Assertive Discipline: A take charge approach for today's educator.* Santa Monica, CA: Canter and Associates.

Canter, L., & Canter, M. (1992). *Assertive Discipline: Positive behavior management for today's classroom.* Santa Monica, CA: Canter and Associates.

Covaleskie, J. F. (1992). Discipline and morality: Beyond rules and consequences. *Educational Forum, 56,* 173–183.

Curwin, R. L., & Mendler, A. N. (1988). Packaged discipline programs: Let the buyer beware. *Educational Leadership, 46*, 68–73.

Emmer, E. T. & Aussiker, A. (1990). School and classroom discipline programs: How well do they work? In O.C. Moles (Ed.), *Student discipline strategies*. Albany, NY: State University of New York Press.

Kohn, A. (1996). *Beyond discipline: From compliance to community*. Alexandria, VA: Association for Supervision and Curriculum Development.

McEwan, B. (2000). *The art of classroom management*. Upper Saddle River, NJ: Merrill/ Prentice Hall.

Palardy, J. M. (1992). Three instances of myopia among teachers in public schooling. *Journal of Instructional Psychology, 19*, 49–53.

Palardy, J. M. (1996). Taking another look at behavior modification and assertive discipline. *NASSP Bulletin, 80*, 66–71.

Queen, J. A., Blackwelder, B. B., & Mallen L.P. (1997). *Responsible classroom management for teachers and students*. Upper Saddle River, NJ: Merrill/Prentice Hall.

Chapter 4

Positive Classroom Discipline

Objectives

Chapter 4 prepares preservice teachers to meet INTASC standards #5 (Motivation and Management), #6 (Communication), and #9 (Reflective Practitioner) by helping them to:

- understand the basic principles behind Positive Classroom Discipline.
- understanding the impact of nonverbal communication in setting limits in the classroom.
- learn techniques for the effective use of Positive Classroom Discipline in the classroom.
- evaluate classroom seating arrangements in maintaining appropriate classroom control.
- evaluate the relationship between instruction and classroom management.

Scenarios

Juan Morales is whispering to his friend Dion when he realizes the class has become unusually quiet. Turning toward the front of the class, he sees that Mr. McAdams had stopped talking and is giving him "The Look." "The Look" is famous throughout Miller High School, and Mr. McAdams has perfected the ability to stare so intently that students immediately stop whatever they are doing. Unable to maintain eye contact with Mr. McAdams, Juan picks up his pencil and turns his attention to the work on his desk. When Mr. McAdams is confident that Juan has turned in his seat and is now focused on the assigned work, he leans over to help another student.

As veteran sixth-grade teacher James Evans's class takes turns reading the chapter from their history text, two girls in the back of the room pass a note. As Doug reads the next paragraph, Mr. Evans moves to the back of the room and stands directly in front of the girls. He stands there until both girls turn to face him and begin to read silently from their book. When Doug reaches the end of paragraph, he says, "Thank you, Doug." Then, putting his finger on the spot where she should begin reading, he motions for one of the note-passing girls to read the next paragraph. As she reads, he moves away from the girls and takes his position behind another student who needs a reminder to stay on task.

Each week, the students in Marian Boyd's fifth-grade class can earn time for what Ms. Boyd calls the PAT (Preferred Activity Time). On Monday, Ms. Boyd announces that on Friday the class will have a PAT if they earn 30 minutes of free time during the week. After much discussion, the class decides that they want to play their favorite review game as their PAT. Excited, they start to work, hoping to earn their PAT. During the afternoon, Ms. Boyd gives the students two minutes to put up their dictionaries, get out their math homework, and sharpen their pencils. When the two minutes is over, Ms. Boyd takes out a stopwatch and keeps track of the additional time it takes for everyone to get back in their seats and to be ready for math. She then subtracts the extra minutes it took to complete the task from the time allowed for Friday's PAT. The next day, Ms. Boyd gives the students five minutes to go to the bathroom as they return from lunch. When two girls take an additional two minutes, this time is subtracted for the PAT. Later in the week, Jamell is reading a comic book instead of finishing his seatwork. Without saying a word, Ms. Boyd takes out the stopwatch and starts tracking the time that Jamell is wasting. When several of the students notice what is happening, they tell Jamell to put the comic book away and to get back to work. At the end of the week, the class had twenty-five minutes left for their PAT and happily spent the time playing their favorite review game.

INTRODUCTION

The three teachers described in the preceding paragraphs have two things in common. First, each is using negative reinforcement to manage their classroom. In each case, the teacher is using something the students find aversive (receiving the look, being in a student's space, losing time for preferred activities) until the students return to their work. In addition, these three teachers are using techniques that are the basis of Fredric Jones's **Positive Classroom Management** approach.

Fredric Jones (1987, 2001) began investigating effective classroom-management techniques in the early 1970s. After spending thousands of hours observing both effective and ineffective classroom managers, Jones found that instruction can occur only in a well-controlled classroom and that teachers with poor classroom control can lose up to 50 percent of instructional time. In cases in which teachers must choose to discipline or to continue with instruction, Jones stresses that they must always choose to discipline.

Jones (1979) suggests that the major discipline problem in the classroom is not hostile defiance by a few students. According to Jones, the greatest discipline problem is the massive amount of time wasted by the majority of students. Jones found that in the average classroom, 80 percent of all disruptions are nothing more than students talking to their neighbors. Students wandering around the room cause another 15 percent of disruptions. Most of the remaining problems are minor disruptions, such as pencil tapping, note passing, or playing with an object. These disruptions are not severe and seem insignificant. However, it is hard enough to manage one child who is misbehaving, but when there are two misbehaving students, the drain on the teacher's skill and energy are squared. If there is a third child involved, this skill and energy drain is cubed. Simultaneously teaching and maintaining order in a class of twenty requires tremendous skill and energy. The lack of either skill or energy will result in a stressed teacher and a tremendous loss of instructional time.

By using proximity control, negative reinforcement, incentives, and good body language, Jones proposes that classroom control can be maintained and that learning can occur. Jones's theories are grounded in behavioral theory and classroom research at all grade levels. Jones (1987) stresses that to control student behavior, an effective behavior-management program must systematically strengthen desired behavior while weakening inappropriate behavior. Strengthening desired behaviors must go hand in hand with eliminating undesired behavior. Too often, teachers focus on eliminating *undesired* behavior without having a plan to increase the *desired* behavior. However, without a plan to increase desired behav-

whatever replaces inappropriate behavior is left to chance and may actually be another discipline problem. To obtain or strengthen desired behaviors, Jones advocates the use of positive and negative reinforcement. To stop inappropriate behavior, Jones uses a backup system that is punitive in nature.

In Jones's model, the enforcement of classroom standards and the development of co-operative behavior are combined, in order to maximize learning and minimize disruptions. Jones (1987) stresses that an effective classroom-management system must be:

- Positive and affirm the student.
- Economical. Jones uses the term *cheap* to describe systems that are practical and simple, require little paper work, and are easy to use. Cheap systems are designed to reduce the teacher's workload.
- Self-eliminating. An effective system will eventually become unneeded, because students will be trained to act appropriately. If the plan does not become self-eliminating, then it is either the wrong plan or is self-perpetuating. Self-perpetuating plans have built-in flaws; they actually reinforce unwanted behavior and feed the problem.
- Low-key, supportive, and almost invisible.

Positive Classroom Discipline focuses on the management of group behavior. The model consists of four main components:

1. Classroom structure
2. Limit Setting
3. Responsibility Training
4. Backup Systems

CLASSROOM STRUCTURE

Jones (1987, 2001) considers classroom structure the centerpiece of classroom management. Preparing the structure of the classroom is a proactive step that prevents the majority of classroom disruptions. Issues to consider in providing structure include arranging the furniture and creating classroom rules and procedures. Consider the following example:

At the end of the first six weeks, Heather Drapper asked her husband to meet in her classroom so they could rearrange the furniture. "I need to move my desk," she explained. "I want no more than eight feet between me and the student sitting farthest from the front of the room." Together they moved her desk and rearranged the students' desks. When they had finished, Heather walked to each desk. She stood in front of each desk and then moved around to stand behind the desk. Satisfied that she could be in any student's space in a matter of seconds, she rewarded her hard-working husband by taking him out to dinner.

In her short time in the classroom, Ms. Drapper has learned that one of the easiest ways to prevent discipline problem is location, location, and location. Jones (2001) stresses that the students who are closest to the teacher are the best behaved. To maintain appropriate control,

Traditional Classroom with Limited Walkways   Jones's Model with Multiple Walkways

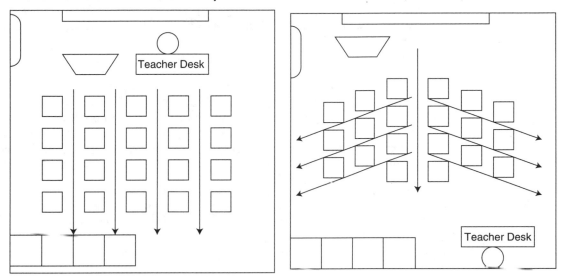

FIGURE 4-1   Effective and Ineffective Classroom Arrangements

teachers must constantly work the crowd by moving throughout the classroom and being at every desk. This method of classroom control is sometimes thought as "management by walking around" or **proximity control**.

The classroom arrangement should allow for maximum teacher mobility, physical proximity to students, and the moment-to-moment accountability of students. There must be walkways, so that teachers can reach each student quickly. The best possible room arrangement is one that puts the least distance and fewest barriers between the teacher and any student in the classroom. See Figure 4.1 for examples of effective and ineffective classroom arrangements.

Jones (2001) suggests that the main problem in most classrooms is the arrangement of furniture. With the traditional arrangement of the desk in the front of the room, the distance from the chalkboard to the students in the front row can be anywhere from eight to thirteen feet. By moving the desk to a corner or to the back of the room, students are moved forward and closer to the area of instruction. Walkways between, in front of, and behind desks should be created. Like Ms. Drapper, teachers should measure the time it takes to get to each student.

The location of overheads and teacher centers with computers and monitors creates additional problems. Because of the need for this equipment to be centrally located for maximum viewing by all students, they are typically placed at the front of the classroom. In some cases, teachers become trapped behind a table of electronic equipment. Jones suggests that teachers move out and allow students to operate the equipment. Being the "overhead/computer operator" is rewarding to the student selected for the task, and it allows the teacher to work the crowd in the back of the room.

Tips from the Field

I believe in the power of "The Look." In my class, the students have an expression that goes, "When the eyebrows go up, it's going to get rough." Fortunately, each class tells the students in the next class this expression. Therefore, whenever students misbehave, all that is necessary for me to do is to arch my eyebrows and the students immediately stop whatever they are doing. "The Look" is a critical skill in classroom management.

Larry Bader
Grade 5 Teacher
Putman County Elementary School
Eatonton, GA

One of the most proactive things a teacher can do to structure the classroom is to establish classroom rules and procedures. Jones (1987, 2001) describes general rules as these dealing with broad classes of behavior and that are best stated in positive rather than negative languages. He stresses that effective classroom rules are: (a) limited in number, usually no more than five to eight, (b) enforceable quickly and consistently, (c) simple and clear, and (d) posted for all to see.

Procedures and routines are the techniques for doing the predictable things that occur normally throughout a school day. Teachers should spend time teaching the procedures and routines expected in their classes. Jones (2001) suggests that the teachers of the best-run classrooms spend most of the first two weeks of the semester teaching their procedures and routines. In the following example, Bridget Campbell's third-grade class has an effective routine for the beginning of each day:

As Bridget Campbell arranges the materials she will use throughout the day, her students begin to arrive. Taking a second to greet each student, Ms. Campbell answers individual questions and checks to make sure the pencil jar is full of sharpened pencils. As the students enter, they pull a card from an envelope on which their name is written. These envelopes are part of a large display on the bulletin board next to the door. They then place the card in one of two boxes, one marked "buying lunch" and the other marked "bringing lunch from home." The students know that they are then to put away their coats and backpacks and go immediately to their desks. Once seated, students are to place their homework on the right-hand corner and to begin working on the daily review. While the students work on the daily review, Ms. Campbell checks attendance by seeing whose card is still in its envelope. She then counts the cards in the "buying lunch" box and e-mails both the attendance and lunch reports to the office. When finished, she walks by each desk, checking to see whether homework has been completed. In just a few minutes, the class begins as Ms. Campbell discusses the daily review.

LIMIT SETTING

"Rules define limits, but they do not establish limits" (Jones, 1987, p. 81). The establishment of rules is only the beginning of effective classroom management. To create limits in the classroom, Jones proposes a method, **Limit Setting**, through which teachers systematically teach students that they mean business. Through the teacher's interpersonal power, physical presence, and emotional tone, the message is sent to the students that the teacher's rules are for real. Limit Setting, according to Jones, goes beyond telling the class the rules: it is training them to follow the rules.

Limit Setting is rule enforcement. It is consistently disallowing infractions of the basic classroom rules. However, Jones (1987, 2001) asserts that Limit Setting is not punitive, because it is done in a quick, low-key but decisive fashion that avoids embarrassing students. The training that takes place during Limit Setting is done with the body, not the mouth. Jones (1996) stresses that body language is the all-important medium through which teachers convey assertiveness. In Limit Setting, the teacher is assertive but never aggressive, because the object of Limit Setting is to calm the students and to get them back on task.

Jones's research (1979) shows that the training of students through Limit Setting techniques eliminates 70 to 95 percent of the disruptions in the regular classroom. Limit Setting consists of the following six steps:

Step One: Eyes in the Back of Your Head   Step one requires the "withitness" described by Kounin (1970). The teacher must be aware of everything that is going on in the classroom at all times. The teacher must catch disruptions as soon as they begin and respond immediately. Disruptions such as talking to one's neighbor are fun and self-rewarding. Ignoring the behavior will not make it go away, because the student may be rewarded for misbehaving by the student's peers.

Step Two: Terminate Instruction   The teacher must immediately terminate instruction to deal with the disruptive behavior. If the teacher does not, Jones stresses, students will have learned that the teacher places greater importance on instruction than on discipline. If the teacher does not take action, the amount of inappropriate behavior will continue until the teacher is forced to stop instruction.

Step Three: Turn, Look, and Say the Student's Name   The turn is the teacher's emotional response to inappropriate behavior. Before turning, the teacher should take a relaxing breath. Being calm, Jones stresses, is the key to effective Limit Setting. To appear calm and relaxed, hands should remain down by the side and the jaw should be slack. Waving hands show frustration, and the mouth will show distress if it is not slack. Face the student squarely, and say his or her name in a firm tone. Look the student in the eye and maintain unwavering eye contact.

Has the disruptive behavior stopped and has the student returned to work? The teacher should look at the student's knees and feet to determine compliance. According to Jones, the knees and feet tell the entire story. If they are facing the front of the room, the teacher can assume the inappropriate behavior has been stopped. If the feet and knees are not turned squarely in the chair, the teacher has only achieved pseudo-compliance. Unless the student has turned squarely in the desk, the student plans to

Jones stresses that the body language of the teacher sends a clear message to students and prevents many misbehaviors from escalating.

return to what he or she was doing as soon as the teacher's back is turned. Other pseudocompliance techniques include pretending to read or to write.

Step Four: Walk to the Edge of the Student's Desk   If the student does not turn around square in his or her seat, Jones advises the teacher to move toward the student at a deliberate pace until the teacher's leg is touching the edge of the desk. In a relaxed, calm manner, the teacher makes eye contact. Jones stresses that the teacher should remain at the edge of the desk until the student turns squarely in the desk. When the student returns to work, the teacher should watch for a few minutes, thank the student, and then move away.

Step Five: Prompt   If the student did not return to work after the teacher stood at the student's desk for several minutes, the teacher should lean over at the waist until his or her weight is on one palm. Getting eyeball to eyeball with the student, the student should be given a prompt—a message that tells the student what to do next. The prompt might be moving work around in front of the student, pointing to the work to be done, or verbally telling the student to turn around and to begin to work. Once the student has complied, the teacher should thank the student and then move away.

Step Six: Palms   If the student does not comply during Step Five, the teacher should lean slowly across the desk and place both palms flat on the far side of the desk on either side of the student. The teacher should remain eyeball to eyeball with the student until the student complies. When the student complies, the teacher thanks the student and moves away.

Step Seven: Camping Out in Front   If the student has been backtalking during this encounter, Jones stresses that Step Six should be continued and the teacher should "camp out" until the student complies. Jones (1987) describes the golden rule of dealing with backtalk as "doing nothing"—"waiting out" the student. When the student stops talking, the teacher should give a prompt, wait until the student complies, and then move away. Jones stresses that the teacher should never move out until confident that the student has begun to work.

Step Eight: Camping Out from Behind   If backtalk involves more than one student, camping out in back may be more effective. The teacher should use the wide walkways and move around the desks to stand directly between the students. Leaning on the table of the first student, as described in Step Five, blocks the view of the second student. The teacher should totally ignore the second student and establish eye contact with the first student. Then the teacher should wait until the first student is back on target. Only when the first student is working is it time to focus on the second student.

Why does Limit Setting work? It works because students want the teacher out of their space. In order to have the teacher move away, almost all students stop the inappropriate behavior and return to their work. It works because Limit Setting uses behavioral research that shows that negative reinforcement increases desired behavior.

Jones (1987) stresses that Limit Setting shouldn't be necessary throughout the year. During what he calls the **"acquisition phase"** (when the students are first learning the classroom rules), the teacher may need to use Limit Setting several times a day. But Jones promises that once students realize that the teacher intends to enforce the rules and is consistent in this enforcement, Limit Setting will be needed less and less.

There are limitations to Limit Setting and Jones (1987, 2001) acknowledges that it will not work in all situations. Jones provides the following limitations of Limit Setting:

- If the teacher cannot be calm and shows anger and frustration, the effectiveness of Limit Setting is weakened. Calm is strength in Limit Setting.
- If the teacher has a poor relationship with the students, they may not return to work as a challenge to the teacher's authority. For Limit Setting to be effective, students have to trust that the teacher will move away when they return to work.
- If the teacher moves away too quickly, students may learn that only pseudocompliance is needed to get the teacher out of their space.
- If the teacher is trapped behind a desk or teacher center, the ability to move quickly to a student will be lessened. Students then know they have time to get back on task before the teacher can reach them.
- If the lesson is boring or the students have been sitting too long, the interruption created by a Limit Setting episode may be rewarding. Students may then encourage each other to be off task, just to break the monotony of the class.

- If the teacher is not aware of what is going on around the classroom, much behavior that could be solved by Limit Setting will be ignored. Inappropriate behavior will increase, because students will realize that no one is watching.
- If the entire class is off task, standing by one desk will do little to solve the situation.
- If the student is agitated or physically aggressive, moving into the student's space may be viewed as a threat. Teachers need to know their students well enough to read when Limit Setting will work and when it will not.

RESPONSIBILITY TRAINING

Classroom management is, as the name implies, management of the class. To be effective, rewards or incentives must be a group system rather than a collection of individual incentive systems (Jones, 1987). To generate consistently good behavior from all class members, Jones proposes that teachers devise a complex, formal incentive system that utilizes (1) bonuses and (2) penalties. Essential are (1) group rewards and (2) group accountability. **Responsibility Training** is such a group incentive program, in which the philosophy is "One for all and all for one." The heart of Responsibility Training is the accountability students have for and to each other. Responsibility Training takes the teacher out of the enforcer, or nagging parent, role.

Basic to Responsibility Training are incentives. Incentives are used to increase productivity and to encourage students to follow classroom rules. In recent years there has been criticism of incentives and rewards, because they have been viewed as bribes. Jones (2001) notes that a proactive incentive system (such as Responsibility Training) is an exchange that is established in advance and is, therefore, not a bribe. It is planned as a normal part of the day. However, a reactive system is established in the heat of the moment and should be considered a bribe.

Incentive systems can be simple or complex. A simple incentive system provides a reinforcer in exchange for a specified behavior. Jones (1979) notes that incentive systems must have three parts: a task, a reward, and a system of accountability. One of Jones's (1987, 2001) favorite incentive programs is what he calls **"Grandmama's Rule."** Just as Grandmama told her grandchildren that they had to finish their dinner before they could have dessert, in Responsibility Training students are told that they must complete a required task in order to earn **Preferred Activity Time (PAT)**. "Grandmama's Rule" is the juxtaposition of two activities: (a) the things students *have* to do and (b) the things the students *want* to do.

Preferred activities can be any educational activity students like to do. Jones (2001) suggests that these activities be readily available, easy to use, represent a reasonable amount of prep time for the teacher, and serve an educational purpose. PATs can be whatever activities students like and might include centers, games, and videos.

The success of PATs depends on students working together to earn the PAT. The group earns time for the PAT when *every* member of the class is productive and the group loses time when *any* member of the class is off task. Jones (2001) suggests that in most classrooms, the peer group reinforces deviant behavior. With Responsibility Training, the teacher uses the power of the peer group to control class behavior.

Tips from the Field

After seven years of teaching in both public and private schools, I have learned that if students respect you and know in their hearts that you show them respect, management will fall into place. Respect and consistency are the keys. This respect builds from the minute they walk into the door. By showing them that you respect them enough not to degrade or yell at them in front of their peers, they will respect you. I can't advise consistency enough. Our students cry for structure and consistency, as they come from homes that we can only imagine the terror they live through each day.

Bridget Cantrell
Grade 3 Teacher
Santa Fe Trail Elementary School
Independence, MO

In some situations, an individual student's behavior will cause the entire class to lose the reward. When that occurs, Jones (2001) suggests that the teacher remove the student from Responsibility Training and use **Omission Training** to change the student's behavior. Omission Training is the name given to an incentive program system that rewards the omission, or avoidance, of unwanted behavior. In Omission Training, the teacher rewards the individual student for behaving appropriately for a certain period of time. To increase the likelihood of success, the class is also rewarded when the student is on task. Therefore, the student has an opportunity to become a class hero and be accepted by the class, and the class helps the student learn new behavior.

The establishment of an Omission Training program requires that the teacher:

- Remove the defiant student from Responsibility Training so the class is no longer being punished for the student's inappropriate behavior.
- Talk to the student in a nonpublic place about the student's behavior.
- Establish an individual reward program for the student.
- Announce to the class that the student is now on an individual program. However, when the student earns time or a reward, the reward is shared with the entire class.
- Withdraw the student from Omission Training as the student learns appropriate behavior and is more accepted by the group.

For over twenty years, Jones has trained teachers to successfully use Responsibility Training and Omission Training to change student behavior. In the majority of classrooms, the system works well. However, he has found that in some classes a clique in the class will reinforce their own deviant behavior and are immune to peer pressure. He also stresses that the PATs must change often, because reinforcement satiation is the eternal enemy of any incentive system.

BACKUP SYSTEM

Although Jones (1987, 2001) proposes that most inappropriate behavior will be stopped through Limit Setting and Responsibility Training, a few students will force the use of negative sanctions. Jones's **Backup System** is a systematic, hierarchic organization of negative sanctions. He suggests the use of the Backup System when there is an obnoxious incident or a repeat disruptor who does not respond to Limit Setting or Responsibility Training.

The Backup System is composed of three levels: small backup responses, medium backup responses, and large backup responses. Table 4.1 provides examples of consequences at each level. As students work up the levels, the consequences become more severe, and more professional assistance is involved.

Small backup responses are the first line of defense in the classroom. They are done privately, and in many cases the other students have no knowledge that they are being administered. Small backup responses are communications rather than sanctions. The objectives of the small backup system are (a) to inform students that they are entering the Backup System and (b) to invite students to return to their work.

Medium backup responses are more public. They can include being sent to time–out or having the student's name placed on the board. Medium responses are more punitive than corrective.

Large backup responses require help from outside the classroom and the involvement of at least two professionals. Sending students to the office, assigning detention, and suspending a student are the most common examples.

Corporal punishment is never advocated by Jones. Jones (1987) states that of all the discipline techniques in existence, corporal punishment has the fewest assets and the greatest number of liabilities.

TABLE 4.1   *Examples of Responses in Jones's Backup System*

Small Backup Responses	Medium Backup Responses	Large Backup Responses
Private–Between Student and Teacher	Public Within the Classroom	Public and Requires Two Professionals
Speaking Privately to Student	Assigning Time–out in Classroom	Sending Student to the Office
Catching the Student's Eye	Assigning Time–out in Colleague's Room	Sending Student to In-School Suspension
Putting Finger to Lips	Warning Student Publicly	Requiring Student to Attend Saturday School
Pulling Parent's Address Card	Sending Student to the Hall	Calling Police
	Holding Conference with Parent	Giving Detention
	Requiring Student to Stay After School	Expelling Student

SUMMARY OF THE FOUR-STEP MODEL

Jones (1987, 2001) proposes a four-component model that includes Classroom Structure, Limit Setting, Responsibility Training, and Backup Systems. He suggests that teachers be proactive by establishing classroom limits through classroom rules and procedures. When these rules and procedures are challenged, Limit Setting is the first line of defense against typical disruptions in the classroom. However, Limit Setting is mild social punishment and, as such, is incomplete. A reward system must be established to promote desired behavior. Responsibility Training provides balance by establishing such a reward system. In cases in which the first three components do not stop inappropriate behavior, Backup Systems must be in place. However, Jones (1987) cautions teachers to extract as much management as possible from Classroom Structure, Limit Setting, and Responsibility Training before moving to punitive backup responses.

FREDISMS

Since Jones wrote his first book in 1987, teachers have to come to appreciate what Jones has to say about classroom management as much as they appreciate his classroom-management system. His quotes have become famous and are called "Fredisms." Below are some of the favorite Fredisms:

"It takes one fool to backtalk. It takes two fools to make a conversation out of it" (Jones, 1996, p. 24).

"If the technology of discipline management could be likened to an animal, then corporal punishment would surely be its ass end" (Jones, 1987, p. 344).

"Almost every form of classroom disruption is its own reward. Being self-reinforcing, disruptions are self-perpetuating" (Jones, 1987, p. 33).

"Every student in your class has a Ph.D. in teacher management" (Jones, 1987, p. 34).

"Discipline management is an indoor sport. Basketball players know how to fake and poker players know how to bluff. Students know how to do both at the same time" (Jones, 2001, p. 193).

"Goofing off is its own reward. Goofing off is always the easy, pleasurable alternative to being on the ball" (Jones, 1987, p. 241).

"A roomful of students will always have more tricks up their sleeves than you will have in your bag of tricks. Bag of tricks represents to me the antithesis of a modern profession with an empirically-based technology of professional practice" (Jones, 1987, p. 320).

STRENGTHS AND WEAKNESSES OF POSITIVE CLASSROOM DISCIPLINE

Perhaps Jones's Positive Classroom Discipline's greatest strength lies in the fact that it is grounded in behavioral research. As stated in Chapter 2, behavioral theory is backed by a hundred years of research that shows that a student's behavior can be changed by reward and punishment.

An additional strength is that Jones specifies a set of steps or activities to follow when dealing with discipline problems. This provides a structure for the actions of teachers. Jones (1987) stresses that "knowing how to" in addition to "knowing about" is critical for teacher success in controlling a classroom.

Morris (1996) suggests that an additional strength is that Jones encourages teachers, administrators, and parents to work together to combat discipline problems.

There are, however, numerous weaknesses in the Jones discipline plan. Some of these weaknesses are:

- Middle and high school students may become aggressive in response to the "in your face" approach. This approach may force a confrontation that neither the teacher nor the student wants.
- Student independence is not encouraged. Jones's model is one of absolute teacher control, with few student choices (Morris, 1996). Such absolute control can be seen in Jones's definition of Responsibility Training. "Responsibility training is an advanced type of time incentive that gets almost any student to do almost anything you want her or him to do when you want it done to your standards as a result of having asked only once" (Jones, 1987, p. 160).
- The use of students to keep fellow classmates in lines can create problems rather than solve them. Resentment and revenge may be the result.
- Jones's insistence that instruction should be stopped when discipline problems arise may actually create problems in some classrooms. Some students may encourage each other to disrupt the class just so instruction will cease.

POSITIVE CLASSROOM DISCIPLINE IN THE CLASSROOM
Scenario

While part of the class works on math-review problems, fifth-grade teacher Janie Jandrokovic asks several students who are struggling with their vocabulary words to move to the computers so they can work on their words. As she helps a student load the software, she notices Zack passing a CD to Garrett. Stopping what she is doing, Ms. Jandrokovic turns to face the two boys. Caught, Garrett shoves the CD under his desk and pretends to work on his math. Upset that Garrett has kept his CD, Zack shoves him and says, "Give it back."

Garrett motions to let Zack know that Ms. Jandrokovic is watching, hoping that Zack will leave him alone and return to work. Unfortunately, Zack is more concerned about his CD than he is with his teacher. "I said give it back," he repeats.

Ms. Jandrokovic walks to the boys and moving behind Garrett and Zack, she stands between the boys. She leans down and sticks out her hand, indicating to Garrett that he is to place the CD in her hand. Seeing this, Zack exclaims, "Hey, you can't take that; it's mine. You give it back."

Ignoring Zack, Ms. Jandrokovic continues to lean down between the two boys blocking Zack from view. Once she has been given the CD, she motions for Garrett to begin his math problems. The entire time she is dealing with Garrett, Zack keeps up a continuous stream of backtalk. "I want my CD back. Just because you can't afford CDs for your own children, doesn't mean you should take mine. You wait until I tell my Dad. It's not right to take my things."

Ms. Jandrokovic ignores Zack until Garrett has been at work for a few minutes. Placing her hand on Garrett's shoulder, she says, "Thank you, Garrett." Then turning to Zack, she leans one arm on his desk and makes eye contact.

"You just wait until my folks hear that you stole my CD. Boy, are you going to be in trouble. You can't take my things," Zack continues. Realizing that Ms. Jandrokovic isn't going to argue back and plans to continue staring at him, he gives up and picks up his pencil.

Ms. Jandrokovic continues to stand by Zack's desk until he quits arguing and works three math problems. She then thanks Zack for getting back to work and returns to the computer station to finish loading the software.

When the class returns from gym a few hours later, Ms. Jandrokovic pulls Zack aside. When all the students have entered the classroom, Ms. Jandrokovic tells Zack, "I called your mother while you were in gym to tell her about the CD. She is coming to school this afternoon so the three of us can discuss your behavior. You are to stay in class this afternoon, and your mother will meet with us as soon as school is dismissed."

SUMMARY

Fredric Jones's discipline model, *Positive Classroom Management*, proposes that instruction can only occur in a well-controlled classroom. Therefore, he advocates that discipline must occur before instruction can begin. By using proximity control, negative reinforcement, incentives, and good body language, Jones proposes that classroom control can be maintained and learning can occur. Jones's theories are grounded in behavioral theory and classroom research at all grade levels. *Positive Classroom Discipline* consists of four main components: Classroom Structure, Limit Setting, Responsibility Training, and Backup Systems.

KEY TERMINOLOGY

Definitions for these terms appear in the glossary:

Acquisition phase	Positive Classroom Management
Backup System	Proximity control
Grandmama's Rule	Preferred Activity Time (PAT)
Limit Setting	Responsibility Training
Omission Training	

CHAPTER ACTIVITIES

Reflecting on the Theory

1. Fifth-grade teacher Angela Pruitt is dealing with one of the most common classroom problems; talkative students. Three girls constantly disrupt the class by talking. Ms. Pruitt has moved the girls so that they sit apart from each other, but they still manage to waste time talking, passing notes, and giggling over something one of them has said.
   How would Fredric Jones tell Ms. Pruitt to handle this situation?
2. Both Canter and Jones give suggestions for rule formation. How are the approaches similar? How do they differ?
3. What are the similarities and differences in Jones's approach to the techniques described in the chapter on behaviorism (Chapter 2)?
4. Do you agree with the way that Ms. Jandrokovic handled the situation with Zack and Garrett? What would you have done differently?

Developing Your Portfolio

1. Jones believes that classroom arrangement is important to the success of classroom management. Analyze a classroom in which you have observed for the following:

   a. teacher mobility
   b. physical proximity to students
   c. moment-to-moment accountability of students
   d. walkways and aisles
   e. barriers between the teacher and any student in the classroom.

Developing Your Personal Philosophy of Classroom Management

1. Jones's model has been called an "in your face" approach? Are there types of students or students of certain grade levels who might not respond to Jones's techniques? Would you be comfortable using this approach? Why?
2. Jones suggests that instruction should be terminated when discipline is needed and if the teacher must choose between discipline and instruction, discipline should come first. Do you agree or disagree? Why?
3. With Jones's approach, the group earns time for the PAT when every member of the class is productive, and the group loses time when any member of the class is off task. Do you agree with this philosophy? Why?

RESOURCES FOR FURTHER STUDY

Further information about Positive Classroom Discipline and resources for its use in the classroom can be found by contacting:

Fredric H. Jones & Associates, Inc.
103 Quarry Lane
Santa Cruz, CA 95060
(831) 425-8222
(831) 426-8222

CHAPTER REFERENCES

Jones, F. (1979). The gentle art of classroom discipline. *National Elementary Principal, 58*, 26–32.

Jones, F. (1987). *Positive classroom discipline.* New York: McGraw-Hill.

Jones, F. (1996). Did not! Did, too! *Learning, 24*, 26.

Jones, F. (2001). *Tools for teaching.* Santa Cruz, CA: Fredric H. Jones & Associates, Inc.

Kounin, J. S. (1970). *Discipline and group management in classroom.* New York: Holt, Rinehart, and Winston.

Morris, R. C. (1996). Contrasting disciplinary models in education. *Thresholds in Education, 22*, 7–13.

Cooperative Discipline

Objectives

Chapter 5 prepares preservice teachers to meet INTASC standards #2 (Student Development), #5 (Motivation and Management), #8 (Assessment), and #9 (Reflective Practitioner) by helping them to:

- use knowledge about human behavior drawn from the research of Adler, Dreikurs, Albert, and Nelsen to develop strategies for classroom management.
- understand the motives for student behavior.
- learn to assess the social structure of the classroom through the use of a sociogram.
- evaluate research concerning the use of consequences as an alternative to traditional punishment.
- learn strategies for applying natural and logical consequences in the classroom.
- understand the basic principles of Cooperative Discipline.

Scenario

At the end of her first year of teaching, third-grade teacher Sara Prabhu spent a few days reflecting on what she wanted to do differently the next year. Although she planned to change the physical setup of her classroom and revise several of her teaching strategies, the area she felt that needed the most improvement was her classroom-management plan.

When Sara began teaching, she adopted the discipline plan her cooperating teacher had used during Sara's student-teaching experience. This plan required the establishment of classroom rules and consequences. Throughout each day, students turned cards as they violated classroom rules. As more and more cards were turned, the consequences became more severe. After using this model for a year, however, Sara was frustrated and felt there were many flaws in her plan. The most critical flaw was that the consequences were not tied to the misbehavior or the motive for the misbehavior. Because Sara saw little connection between the behavior and the consequence, she was sure her students failed to see the connection as well.

During the summer, Sara was determined to find a classroom-management plan that better fit her teaching style and personal philosophy. She read numerous books and articles on classroom management and finally found an article written in the early 1970s on the use of logical consequences. Intrigued, she read the works of Rudolf Dreikurs. Dreikurs's model made sense to her, because the consequence for misbehavior was directly tied to the misbehavior. She felt certain that by using logical consequences, her students would see the relationship between their behavior and their punishment.

When school began, Sara waited until she met with the class before developing the classroom rules. After a discussion of what would make their classroom run smoothly, the class agreed upon a set of rules. They established no consequences, because consequences were to be based on the behavior and on the motive for the misbehavior. A few days into the term, the lunchroom monitor told Sara that a group of her students had failed to clean their table and had left it too messy for other students to use.

Thinking of the appropriate logical consequence for such behavior, Sara sent the students to the cafeteria to clean the table and to apologize to the cafeteria staff. During the weeks that followed, Sara often had to struggle to find an appropriate logical consequence for each misbehavior but remained confident that students were learning from the consequences rather than simply feeling punished.

INTRODUCTION

The last chapter in this section on Classroom Management as Discipline focuses on the work of Rudolf Dreikurs. Since the late 1960s and 1970s, many teachers, like Sara Prabhu, have adopted Dreikurs's model, **Logical Consequences**. When developed, Logical Consequences represented a shift from a behavioral focus on discipline to a more humanistic approach, using the concept that the motivation and goals of student behavior must be considered in the development of a discipline plan. However, Dreikurs stressed that understanding the motivation behind behavior does not negate the need for appropriate consequences for misbehavior. Therefore, a major focus of Logical Consequences is to control student behavior.

Expanding Dreikurs's discipline concepts, Linda Albert and Jane Nelsen have provided a more current twist to Dreikurs's original theory. Dreikurs, Albert, and Nelsen all stress that it is important to understand why students behave in a particular way. Through this understanding, teachers can develop strategies to handle particular problems (Morris, 1996). The premise behind Logical Consequences, however, is not just to control behavior but also to assist students in taking responsibility for their actions and behaviors.

Dreikurs based many of the concepts of Logical Consequences on the work of a Viennese psychiatrist, Alfred Adler, who proposed that all behavior has a purpose (Dreikurs & Loren, 1968). According to Adler (1958), each individual act by a student is goal-driven. Unlike behavioral theorists, Adler did not see students as passively reacting to what is happening to them. Adler suggested that students are actively interacting with the environment and, even more importantly, that a student's behavior is a product of the student's appraisal and perception of the situation. Unfortunately, this appraisal is often subjective, biased, or inaccurate; but to students, perceptions and assumptions are reality and are therefore not questioned. Consider the following example:

> Because Cynthia's ninth-grade teacher asked students to work problems on the board, Cynthia always dreaded going to math class. Because she was overweight, Cynthia hated going to the board, knowing her classmates were staring at her. Today, she was assigned a problem that she hadn't been able to work the night before. Standing in front of the board, she felt her face redden as she struggled with the problem. She kept her face to the board, praying the answer would emerge. Then she heard laughing coming from the back of the room. Assuming the class was laughing at her, she turned and yelled, "I hate all of you. I hate this class." She ran from the room before she could learn that the class was actually laughing at a late-arriving student who was trying to sneak into the classroom without being seen by the teacher.

Adler's premise is that all people are social beings, and the need to belong or to be accepted is a basic human motivation (Dreikurs & Loren, 1968). Every action of a student is an endeavor to find a place in the social structure of the classroom. Ideally, students discover that contributing to the welfare of the group is the best way to gain and maintain acceptance by others. Unfortunately, this is not always the case. Dreikurs suggests that the reason for this failure is that children are excellent observers but poor interpreters. According to Dreikurs, students watch all that goes on around them but often make incorrect assumptions. All too frequently, their assumptions prevent students from understanding which actions would help them to be accepted by the class. To help students find their place in the class and, ultimately, in society, Albert (1996) noted that teachers must understand the following:

- Students choose their behavior. Teachers have the power to influence, not control, student choices. She suggested that some students have a choosing disability rather than a physical or learning disability.
- The ultimate goal of student behavior is to fulfill the psychological and emotional need to belong.
- Students misbehave to achieve one of four goals.

GOALS OF MISBEHAVIOR

Dreikurs and Loren (1968) stress, "All misbehavior is the result of a child's mistaken assumption about the way he can find a place and gain status" (p. 36). It is not the cause of a particular action but the overall goal of the student that explains student behavior. A student's behavior makes sense only when the teacher understands the student's goal, but asking students why they did something wrong may be useless (Dreikurs & Cassel, 1990). Based on Adler's original theory, Dreikurs identified four student goals:

1. To seek attention
2. To gain power
3. To seek revenge for some perceived injustice
4. To avoid failure

The most common goal for children is **attention-seeking**. Students often have the mistaken idea that they have self-worth only when attention is paid to them (Dreikurs & Cassel, 1990; Dreikurs & Loren, 1968). Although all children want and need attention, Dreikurs stresses that it becomes a problem when the goal of attention-seeking behavior is not to learn or to cooperate but to elevate the personal power of the student. For these children, being ignored is intolerable. In order to be noticed by the teacher or their peers, they are willing to accept punishment, pain, and humiliation.

Attention seeking plays out in numerous ways, some constructive and some destructive. In the passive form of attention seeking, the child may appear to be a model child and in some cases is the teacher's pet. Unfortunately, the demand for attention becomes stronger and stronger. When no longer satisfied with small amounts of attention, the student becomes a nuisance, a show-off, or the class clown. The attention-seeking student will constantly ask questions, not for information but for attention. All of these behaviors are designed to keep the teacher and fellow students focused on the attention-seeking student (Dreikurs & Cassel, 1990; Dreikurs & Loren, 1968).

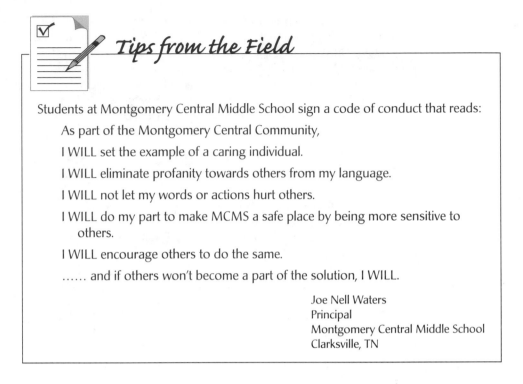

Tips from the Field

Students at Montgomery Central Middle School sign a code of conduct that reads:

As part of the Montgomery Central Community,

I WILL set the example of a caring individual.

I WILL eliminate profanity towards others from my language.

I WILL not let my words or actions hurt others.

I WILL do my part to make MCMS a safe place by being more sensitive to others.

I WILL encourage others to do the same.

...... and if others won't become a part of the solution, I WILL.

> Joe Nell Waters
> Principal
> Montgomery Central Middle School
> Clarksville, TN

Albert (1996) notes that there is a silver lining to attention-seeking behavior, in that the student wants a relationship with the teacher. Therefore, the teacher can redirect inappropriate behavior, so that the child gets attention in a more appropriate manner.

Albert (1996) states, "Young people don't lose their temper; they use it" (p. 41). This accurately describes the student who is **power seeking**. When the teacher tries to stop or redirect one of these students, a power struggle between the student and the teacher can ensue. In this situation, the student is trying to control the adult rather than get attention. The power-seeking student wants to be the boss and will contradict, lie, have a temper tantrum, or question the teacher's ability. Older students often have verbal tantrums and use what Albert (1996) calls the "lawyer syndrome" in which they drill the teacher as if the teacher were on the witness stand. Some power-seeking students are more passive. They are "sneaky," with their words representing one thing and their actions another.

Although the teacher may feel physically or professionally threatened, it is important that the teacher not engage in a power struggle with the student. As Dreikurs and Loren (1968) note, "Once the battle has been joined, the child has already won it" (p. 38). Although power-seeking students can be extremely frustrating, Albert (1996) stresses that these students do have positive characteristics of leadership ability, assertiveness, and independent thinking, which can be redirected into more appropriate action.

Revenge-seeking behavior is the result of a long series of discouragements, in which the student has decided that there is no way to acquire the attention or power desired, and that revenge will make up for the lack of belonging. Although the teacher and other students may be the target of a student's anger or pain, the cause of this anger and pain may actually be the result of personal circumstances, such as a broken home, parental unemployment, or racial prejudice (Albert, 1996).

Revenge-seeking students think everyone is against them. They think that teachers and fellow students are unfair to them, disregard their feelings, and hurt them. They are convinced that no one likes them, and because of this belief, they provoke others to a point at which relationships with the teacher and classmates are destroyed (Dreikurs & Cassel, 1990; Dreikurs & Loren, 1968).

Students who feel beaten seek to retaliate. Revenge-seeking students are so deeply discouraged that they believe that only by hurting others can they find a place in the social atmosphere of the school. These students often threaten teachers and classmates. They can be the *victims* of a bully, or they can *become* the bully. Many harbor feelings that are manifested in violence toward themselves or others.

Revenge-seeking students know what the teacher holds dear and do what it takes to violate those values. Feeling personally attacked, the teacher feels hurt, disappointment, and dislike for the student. The behavior of these students often borders on the pathological and requires intervention from professionals. Therefore, it is important that teachers not retaliate or become emotionally upset. Only through an attitude of understanding and assistance can these students be helped.

Failure-avoiding students expect only failure and defeat, and after a while, these students simply give up. Feeling they cannot either achieve academically or find a place in the social structure of the class, they withdraw. Eventually, they sit alone and shrug off attempts by the teacher to help. Dreikurs, Grunwald, and Pepper (1982) describe these students as extremely discouraged and defeated. They may refuse to try, because:

- They are overly ambitious and fear they cannot do as well as they want to.
- They are competitive and fear they can't do as well as others do.
- They feel pressured by parents and teachers and incapable of meeting their expectations.
- They fear they will fail if they try.

Albert (1996) notes that a student who is avoiding failure rarely distracts or disrupts the classroom. Instead, the student sleeps or daydreams quietly throughout the class. The teacher may find it hard to determine whether the student *cannot* do the work or if the student *will not* do the work. Dreikurs and Cassel (1990) note that the student's discouragement is contagious, and soon the teacher feels helpless to reach the student. Often, the student is left alone to withdraw further from the teacher and other classmates.

Nelsen (1987) identified two clues to identifying mistaken goals. First, teachers should evaluate their reactions to students' misbehaviors. If the teacher feels irritated or annoyed, the student's goal is to get attention. If the teacher feels threatened, the student is displaying power-seeking behavior. If the teacher is hurt by the student's behavior, the student is probably seeking revenge. Finally, if the teacher feels inadequately prepared to help the student, the student is displaying failure avoidance.

The second clue is the child's response to the teacher's intervention. Attention-seeking students will stop their annoying behaviors for a short time if they receive attention from the teacher. The power-seeking student will continue to misbehave and may verbally defy the teacher. The revenge-seeking student's misbehavior will intensify when the teacher attempts to stop the behavior. Failure-avoiding students refuse to respond and withdraw further, hoping to be left alone. Consider the behavior of students in the following example:

> After Ms. Brentner gave the directions to the class, she allowed the class to start on their homework during the last fifteen minutes of class. Walking around the room to make sure everyone understood her directions, she noticed Garrett staring off into space. Placing her hand on Garrett's shoulder, she said, "Garrett, you need to start to work."

> **Attention-seeking Garrett** looks up at Ms. Brentner, smiles, and begins his work.

> **Power-seeking Garrett** responds by loudly announcing, "This is stupid. It is the same stuff we did yesterday. Why do we have to do the same thing over and over again?"

> **Revenge-seeking Garrett** violently jerks away from Ms. Brentner's touch and shouts, "Get your stinky hands off me. I don't need your help."

> **Failure-avoiding Garrett** keeps his head down and looks at the paper on his desk. Speaking barely above a whisper, he says, "I can't. I don't understand how to do this."

Nelsen (1987) notes that it is much harder to discover the goal for behavior after students enter their preteens. Although more teens display the mistaken goal of power or revenge than younger students, other factors are at play as well. Peer pressure is extremely important to teenagers, and Nelsen suggests that seeking peer approval is an additional goal for students. Teenagers also have the mistaken goal of excitement and will often misbehave "just for the fun of it."

REACTING TO STUDENT BEHAVIOR

Dinkmeyer and Dinkmeyer (1976) stress that to effectively work with students, teachers need to understand the goals of the students' behaviors. To do this, the teacher must work to determine the real issues underlying behavior. Table 5.1 further explains how to determine these goals.

Dreikurs and Cassel (1990) advise that the teacher's reaction to misbehavior should be related to the goal for the behavior. For attention-seeking students, reinforcement should occur only when these students are acting appropriately. Often these students are not aware of how annoying their antics have become and will try to correct their behavior when the teacher talks to them about the situation. In some cases, the teacher can provide a signal that indicates that the behavior needs to stop. Unfortunately, the teacher and the attention-seeking student are not alone in the class, and classmates may give the student the attention he or she seeks. When this occurs, the student may stop trying to get the attention of the teacher and act out even more.

Dreikurs and Loren (1968) note that when dealing with a power-seeking student, the first requirement is disinvolvement. Because there is no reinforcement for the student if power is not contested, it is critical that the teacher not engage the student in a power struggle. The teacher should

TABLE 5.1   *The Four Mistaken Goals of Students*

Mistaken Goal	Student's Belief	Example of Student's Behaviors	Teacher's Reaction to Behavior	Student's Reaction to Intervention by Teacher
Attention-Seeking	The student feels part of class only when getting attention from the teacher or other students	Constantly demands attention Desires to be teacher's pet Shows off Becomes the class clown	Annoyance/Irritation	Stops momentarily but then resumes
Power-Seeking	The student feels part of the class when controlling the teacher or other students	Contradicts Lies Has temper tantrums Questions teacher's authority or knowledge	Professionally threatened	Continues to verbally or physically defy the teacher
Revenge-Seeking	The student feels left out of the social structure, so strikes out at classmates or teacher	Is aggressive toward teacher or classmates Becomes a bully Threatens teachers or classmates	Hurt	Intensifies behavior
Failure-Avoiding	The student feels incapable of achieving socially or academically and no longer tries	Sleeps or daydreams through class Attempts to be invisible	Inadequate to help student	Withdraws further from teacher or classmates

Source: Dreikurs, Grunwald, and Pepper (1982); Nelsen (1981).

avoid a direct confrontation. Because neither the student nor the teacher wants to lose face, discussion of the student's behavior should take place in private. When the teacher's power is challenged, it is best for the teacher to allow a cooling-off period. After both the teacher and the student have had an opportunity to become calmer, they can discuss the student's misbehavior. It is important that students are allowed to have their say. Many times this will defuse the situation because for many students, having their *say* is as important as having their *way*.

Albert (1996) stresses that power seeking can be reduced when students are allowed a voice in the classroom. She advocates granting legitimate power by involving students in decision making. When students can have a choice, they feel they have power. When students have real responsibility they are less likely to strive for power in destructive ways.

For dealing with revenge-seeking students, it is important that teachers try to build a caring relationship. This begins by talking with the student about the behavior. In some cases, students aren't aware that they are taking out their frustrations on the teacher. In other cases, the students know exactly what they are doing and must not be allowed to physically or psychologically hurt other students or the teacher. Regardless of the motive or reasons for the behavior, revenge-seeking students must be required to return, repair, or replace any damaged objects (Albert, 1995).

In dealing with students seeking to avoid failure, the teacher should try to determine the cause of the problem. Albert (1995) suggests that teachers modify the instructional methods, provide additional tutoring, encourage the student to use positive self-talk, and teach new strategies to use when the students wants to quit trying.

CONSEQUENCES OF MISBEHAVIOR

Dreikurs rejects the use of punishment, because he feels that students associate the punishment not with their own actions but with those of their punisher (Queen, Blackwelder, & Mallen, 1997). He further suggests that the only students who respond well to punishment are the ones who do not need it, the ones for whom reasoning would be enough. Nelsen (1987) agrees that too often punishment creates what she calls the four R's of punishment: resentment, revenge, rebellion, and retreat.

Rather than punishment, Dreikurs advocates a method that advances the social order. Dreikurs, Grunwald, and Pepper (1982) note that the social order consists of a body of rules that must be learned and followed in order for a classroom to be a caring place in which students can learn and grow. To learn responsibility, students must experience the consequences of behavior in order to preserve the "social order." The teacher is the representative of the social order, the person who imposes consequences for failing to respect the established rule.

The idea that the consequence must fit the crime is the key to Dreikurs's system (Kohn, 1996). Every act has a consequence; some occur naturally, and some are teacher-imposed. **Natural consequences** are the results of ill-advised acts. They are the result of the evolution of events and take place without adult interference. Meyerhoff (1996) notes that there is no need for a teacher to provide natural consequences, because they will occur even without the teacher's intervention. It is the teacher's job, however, to make sure that the natural consequences of a student's behavior are not physically or psychologically harmful to the student.

Logical consequences are teacher-arranged rather than being the obvious result of the student's own acts (Meyerhoff, 1996). It is important that these consequences are related to the student's actions and are discussed with the student. If the consequences are not understood and accepted by the student, the student may consider the consequences as punishment rather than as a logical result to the student's own behavior. Unfortunately, logical consequences are not always readily apparent or easily devised, but when used appropriately, they can have tremendous power, in that they help students to learn accountability for their choices (Nelsen, Lott, and Glenn, 1997).

If logical consequences are used as a threat or imposed in anger, then they become punishment. To avoid consequences being viewed as a punishment, Dreikurs and Loren (1968) provided the following criteria distinguishing logical consequences from punishment:

- Logical consequences express the reality of what happens in society when one breaks a law or rule. They are tied to the social order, because they represent the rules of living, which all human beings must learn in order to function in society. Punishment, on the other hand, only expresses the personal power of the teacher and the authority a teacher has over students.
- Logical consequences are tied directly to the misbehavior. Punishments rarely are.
- Logical consequences involve no element of moral judgment; punishment inevitably does. Logical consequences distinguish between the deed and the doer.

Tips from the Field

To help my students feel a part of the class, we have classroom careers that rotate each week. Some of the careers include:

Courier: Serves as the teacher's messenger to deliver items to the office.

Game Show Host: Assists teacher in drawing of names, prizes, and reading questions.

Horticulturist: Takes care of the classroom plants.

Lunch Monitor: Takes daily lunch count, hands out lunch tickets.

Paper Passer: Passes out new assignments.

Technologist: Responsible for keeping the computer area neat and shutting down computers at the end of the day.

Krisanda Venosdale
Grade 4 Teacher
Monroe School
St. Louis, MO

- Logical consequences are concerned only with what will happen now. Punishments are tied to the past.
- Logical consequences are applied in a nonthreatening manner. Often, there is anger in punishment.
- Logical consequences present choices for the student. Punishment demands compliance. When a teacher employs a logical-consequences approach, the student must be given the option of stopping inappropriate behavior or face the consequences of the misbehavior (Dinkmeyer and Dinkmeyer, 1976).

HELPING STUDENTS CONNECT

Albert (1996) advises that providing consequences will not prevent students from misbehaving in the future if the consequences are not accompanied by encouragement techniques that build self-esteem and strengthen the student's motivation to cooperate and learn. It is important, according to Albert, that students are made to feel that they are capable, connected, and can contribute.

Students can be made to feel capable by creating a classroom in which it is acceptable to make mistakes. The teacher needs to ensure that everyone can be successful by providing work appropriate for various learning styles and skill levels. The emphasis should be on completing work in a satisfactory manner and on continuous improvement.

Students need to believe that they can develop positive relationships with teachers and fellow classmates. To help students connect, Albert (1995) suggests that teachers:

Allowing students to work together increases the feeling of community within the classroom.

- Accept all students and encourage tolerance of diversity.
- Give attention to students by listening and showing interest in their activities outside of class.
- Show appreciation of students' kindnesses and good work through praise, phone calls, or written notes to parents.
- Use affirmation statements that are specific about a student's positive qualities.
- Build affectionate relationships with simple acts of kindness.

Teachers should also help students realize they need to contribute to the welfare of their classmates and to the positive atmosphere of the class. Allowing students to have leadership roles within the class can promote this awareness. Nelsen, Lott, and Glenn (1997) advocate the use of class meetings for that purpose. They suggest that class meetings can be the place in which true dialogue and problem solving can begin. Class meetings should be held to discuss problems and issues of concern for the entire class.

Rather than using traditional classroom rules, Albert (1996) advocates the use of a class-room code of conduct. She suggests that students see classroom rules as adult-driven. Codes of

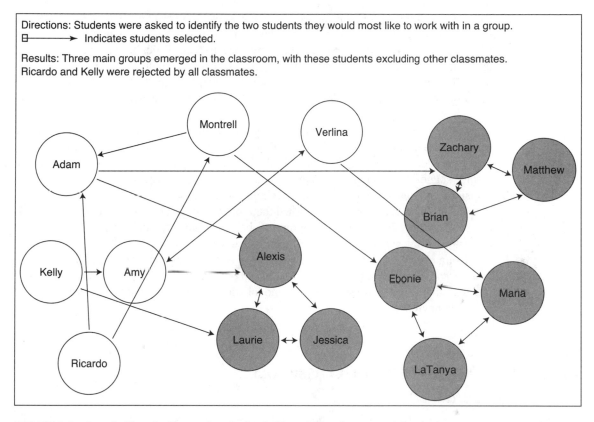

Directions: Students were asked to identify the two students they would most like to work with in a group.
⊟——→ Indicates students selected.

Results: Three main groups emerged in the classroom, with these students excluding other classmates. Ricardo and Kelly were rejected by all classmates.

FIGURE 5-1   Sample Class Sociogram Fourth-Grade Class, Miller Elementary School

conduct provide a framework for how everyone in the class, *including the teacher*, will interact and treat each other. With a code of conduct, students are held accountable for their behavior at all times. A code of conduct allows students to feel they have a voice in how the class will act.

Dreikurs recognized that a classroom is a social setting in which students act and behave in their own unique ways. It is the teacher's role to integrate all of the diverse personalities within the class and to stimulate the democratic processes (Dreikurs & Cassel, 1990). To determine the social climate of a classroom, Dreikurs suggests the use of a sociometric test. **Sociometry** is the study of the relationships among people. Through **sociometric tests**, the teacher can understand and integrate subgroups in the class, integrate the isolated, and improve the relationship and social interactions. The results can influence the seating plan of the classroom, the grouping of students for projects or enterprise, the formation of committees, and the understanding of cliques and leaders. See Figure 5.1 for an example of how a sociogram can visually display a class structure.

STRENGTHS AND WEAKNESSES OF COOPERATIVE DISCIPLINE

Many see Dreikurs's Logical Consequences and the later variations of Dreikurs's theories by Albert and Nelsen as a positive way of promoting communication and respect between and students. They suggest that the model promotes autonomy by allowing students to take responsibility for their actions and choices. However, the model is not without its critics.

One criticism is that first-year teachers may have a difficult time identifying and understanding students' motives for misbehavior, because children often send false or mixed signals (Morris, 1996). Queen, Blackwelder, and Mallen (1997) contend that within the context of a classroom, it is impossible for even a veteran teacher to determine the goal of each child's behavior.

Kohn (1996) also questions Dreikurs's idea that student behavior is a choice. He states, "Adults who blithely insist that children choose to misbehave are rather like politicians who declare that people have only themselves to blame for being poor" (p. 17). He further suggests that such a concept removes the need for teachers to consider their own decisions and classroom demands in creating problem students.

Even after teachers have established the motives for misbehavior, it may still be difficult to know how to respond to inappropriate behavior. Unfortunately, there is not always a natural or a logical consequence to fit the misbehavior.

Kohn (1996) calls logical consequences "punishment lite." He states that it is difficult to differentiate between punishment and logical consequences and questions whether there is a real difference between Dreikurs's model and other models that promote punishment for misbehavior.

COOPERATIVE DISCIPLINE IN THE CLASSROOM
Scenario

When Erica McCaslin began her first year of teaching sixth grade at Bracey Middle School, she decided to use Cooperative Discipline as her classroom-management model. Rather than establishing a set of classroom rules, she allowed the students to spend the first few days of school establishing a classroom code. Dividing the class into groups, each group wrote what they thought the code should be. After putting all the codes on the board, parts from several were incorporated and the class agreed on the following class code:

> We, Ms. McCaslin's sixth-grade class, believe that all students should be treated with dignity and courtesy. We believe that we have the responsibility of helping everyone learn, and we will do nothing that prevents Ms. McCaslin from teaching or anyone from learning. We will show respect for each other, our teacher, our classroom, and the school.

Each student in the class signed the code of conduct and a copy was posted above the whiteboard.

The class agreed that if a problem developed between a student and Ms. McCaslin, Ms. McCaslin would handle the situation and provide the consequence for misbehavior. If a problem developed between two students, the students would be sent to a classroom tribunal who would decide the consequences. So that all students would have a chance to serve on the tribunal, three students are picked each month to serve as the tribunal, and no student can serve twice until all students have had an opportunity to serve.

During the first month, Ms. McCaslin had several opportunities to see how well her plan was working. When Bethany failed to finish her assignment, Ms. McCaslin decided that Bethany would miss the opportunity to attend the assembly and would remain in the classroom to finish her work. When Jamal broke the aquarium when he leaned back in his chair, the tribunal decided he would have to pay to replace the aquarium. Jamal's parents agreed that Jamal would have to contribute three dollars a week from his spending money to the replacement of the aquarium. When Nick pulled the chair from under Kristin, causing her to fall to the floor, the tribunal decided that Nick would have to spend one hour in time–out writing a letter of apology to Kristin.

Although Ms. McCaslin sometimes found it difficult to find an appropriate consequence for each misbehavior, she felt the plan helped students make the connection between their behavior and the consequence of their behavior.

SUMMARY

Rudolf Dreikurs's Logical Consequences and Linda Albert's Cooperative Discipline are the last models presented with a focus on control. When developed, Logical Consequences represented a shift from a behavioral focus on discipline to a more humanistic approach based on the concept that the motivation and goals of student behavior must be considered in the development of a discipline plan. Expanding Dreikurs's discipline concepts, Linda Albert proposes a cooperative approach to help students connect, contribute, and feel capable. Based on Adler's original theory, Dreikurs and Albert identified four student goals: (1) to seek attention, (2) to gain power, (3) to seek revenge for some perceived injustice, and (4) to avoid failure. The idea that the consequence must fit the crime is the key to their theories, in that every act has a consequence; some occur naturally, and some are teacher imposed.

KEY TERMINOLOGY

Definitions for these terms appear in the glossary:

Attention-seeking students	Power-seeking students
Failure-avoiding students	Revenge-seeking students
Logical consequences	Sociometric tests
Natural consequences	Sociometry

CHAPTER ACTIVITIES

Reflecting on the Theory

1. As Mr. Hoernschemeyer prepared to leave his seventh-grade class, he noticed that someone had carved the letters "JK" into a desk. Since Jack Kelly occupied the desk each sixth period, it was not difficult for Mr. Hoernschemeyer to guess who had damaged the desk.

What should Mr. Hoernschemeyer do now? How can he apply the principles of *Logical Consequences* to resolving this situation?

2. In the opening scenario, Ms. Prabhu designed consequences based on the misbehaviors and the students' motives for them. Do you agree with this method for determining the appropriate consequence for misbehavior? What problems might this method create in a classroom?

3. Kohn suggests that logical consequences are just "punishment lite" and that they are just punishments with a less offensive name. Do you agree, or are logical consequences different from punishment?

Developing Your Portfolio

1. Describe five typical classroom misbehaviors. Describe a natural consequence, a logical consequence, and a typical punishment that might be used for each.

2. Observe the behaviors of three students. Describe the behaviors of these students. How does the teacher react to their behaviors? How do the students react to the teacher's intervention? Based on your observations, classify the students' behaviors as attention-seeking, power-seeking, revenge-seeking, or failure-avoiding.

Developing Your Personal Philosophy of Classroom Management

1. Would you be comfortable using Cooperative Discipline as your classroom-management approach? Why or why not? Are there some strategies that you will definitely incorporate into your classroom-management plan?

2. Many consider a strength of Assertive Discipline is the consistency with which punishment is administered. Cooperative Discipline theory provides for a more individual approach to discipline. Which do you consider to be more critical—to be consistent or to deal with students as individuals?

RESOURCES FOR FURTHER STUDY

Further information about Cooperative Discipline and resources for its use in the classroom can be found by contacting:

Dr. Linda Albert
8503 N. 29th Street
Tampa, FL 33604
813-931-4183 (Phone)
813-935-4571 (Fax)

CHAPTER REFERENCES

Adler, A. (1958). *What life should mean to you.* New York: Capricorn.
Albert, L. (1995). Discipline: Is it a dirty word? *Learning, 24,* 43–46.

Albert, L. (1996). *Cooperative discipline*. Circle Pines, Minnesota: American Guidance Service.

Dinkmeyer, D., & Dinkmeyer, D., Jr. (1976). Logical consequences: A key to the reduction of disciplinary problems. *Phi Delta Kappan, 57*, 664–666.

Dreikurs, R., and Cassel, P. (1990). *Discipline without tears* (2nd ed.). New York: Dutton.

Dreikurs, R., Grunwald, B. B., & Pepper, F. C. (1982). *Maintaining sanity in the classroom*. New York: HarperCollins.

Dreikurs, R., & Loren, G. (1968). *A new approach to discipline: Logical consequences.* New York: Hawthorn Books.

Kohn, A. (1996). *Beyond discipline: From compliance to community*. Alexandria, VA: Association for Supervision and Curriculum Development.

Meyerhoff, M. K. (1996). Natural and logical consequences. *Pediatrics for Parents, 16*, 8–10.

Morris, R. C. (1996). Contrasting disciplinary models in education. *Thresholds in Education, 22*, 7–13.

Nelsen, J. (1987). *Positive discipline*. New York: Ballantine Books.

Nelsen, J., Lott, L., & Glenn, S. (1997). *Positive discipline in the classroom* (2nd ed.). Rocklin, CA: Prima Publishing.

Queen, J. A., Blackwelder, B. B, & Mallen, L. P. (1997). *Responsible classroom management for teachers and students.* Upper Saddle River, NJ: Merrill/Prentice Hall.

Part

II

Classroom Management as a System

Four models that emphasize a systems approach to classroom management are presented in Part II: Classroom Management as a System. The changing theories of William Glasser are the focus of Chapter 6. Chapter 7 presents Richard Curwin and Allen Mendler's model, Discipline with Dignity. Chapter 8 focuses on building communities and provides the theories of Haim Ginott and Alfie Kohn. The research of Carolyn Evertson is the foundation of her model, Classroom Organization and Management Program (COMP). Her model is presented in Chapter 9. The models presented in Part II: Classroom Management as a System share the following characteristics:

- Classroom management is systematic.
- Classroom management and instruction are interwoven.
- Teachers and students share the responsibility for managing classroom behaviors.
- Rule development is a joint effort between students and teachers.
- A range of consequences should be provided to meet the diverse needs of students.
- Students must be taught appropriate behavior.
- The focus is on *prevention* of misbehavior rather than *reacting* to discipline problems.
- Planning is essential to effective classroom management.
- Classroom communities provide a safe, caring learning environment.
- Teachers should *teach* the rules and procedures of the classroom rather than assuming that students understand their meaning.

Chapter 6

Reality Therapy and Choice Theory

Objectives

Chapter 6 prepares preservice teachers to meet INTASC standards #1 (Content Pedagogy), #2 (Student Development), #5 (Motivation and Management), and #9 (Reflective Practitioner) by helping them to:

- use knowledge about human behavior drawn from Reality Therapy, Control Theory, and Choice Theory to develop strategies for classroom management.
- recognize basic human needs and understand how the desire to meet these needs impact student behavior.
- learn techniques for applying Reality Therapy/Choice Theory in the classroom.
- learn the essential elements of a Quality School.
- determine whether they will incorporate Glasser's concepts for classroom management into their personal discipline plan.
- evaluate the curriculum for relevance for students' lives.
- learn to use classroom meetings to manage curriculum and discipline problems.

Scenario

Eleventh-grade teacher Jason Stewart had just started going over notes with his history class when the door opened and Jamelia came in the room. Stopping, he motioned toward the hallway, "Jamelia, may I see you in the hall for a moment?"

Closing the door behind him, he asked, "Jamelia, what were you doing?"

Shrugging and grinning slightly, Jamelia responded, "I was coming to class, that's all."

Working hard to not give in to his impatience, Mr. Stewart asked, "Well, I don't typically ask students coming to class to come to the hall, do I? So, what were you doing that made me stop class and ask to speak to you in the hall?"

Holding her hands up in a sign of surrender, she joked, "I know, I know. I was late. I'm sorry. I'll try to be on time from now on."

"Jamelia, this is the third time this week you have come to class late. Something has to change. Do you want to tell me why your lateness upsets me?"

Leaning against a locker and hoping no one would see her in the hall, Jamelia said softly, "Because it is against a rule."

"Well, that's true, but coming to class on time is a rule for a reason. Jamelia, I don't want to take any more time discussing this issue. We both need to get back in class. Since you drive to school, why don't you come by this afternoon before you leave? When you come, be prepared to tell me two things. One, I want you to tell me why I have a rule about arriving to class on time. Two, I want you to have a plan so that we can avoid this problem in the future."

A few minutes after 3:00, Jamelia appeared in Mr. Stewart's door. "I'm sorry about this morning. I'll try to not be late again. I know that when I'm late it disrupts the entire class when I enter the room." Mr. Stewart waited, so Jamelia added, "Plus, I miss important information. But it really isn't my fault. I just can't get here in the five minutes between classes."

Motioning for Jamelia to take the seat pulled beside his desk, Mr. Stewart asked, "Why? If everyone else can get here, why can't you?"

"Well, I have homeroom over in Ms. Henderson's class in the B hallway. Then I have senior English with Mr. Frank in this wing. After English, I have gym. That means I either have to carry my history notebook and book through three periods or I have to go back to B hallway to my locker between gym and this class. By the time I leave the gym, go to the B hallway to my locker, and come all the way back over here, I'm late. If I take all my books to gym class, I have no place to put them. My gym locker will barely hold my clothes and my English book. I can't get the materials for your class in it as well. So, now do you understand why I'm late every day? I'm trying to get from gym to B hallway and then to your class in five minutes."

"I understand, but your lateness is still unacceptable. There has to be a solution. Could we get a locker for you in this hallway?"

"I'm afraid that would just make me late to my afternoon classes. After fourth period, all my classes are in the B hallway. Could I store my history book and notebook in here while I go to gym? I could bring them by on my way to English class and then I could come here after gym class without going to my locker. Would you mind storing my things?"

"No, that would be fine. In fact," he said looking around the room and walking to a cabinet behind his desk, "you could put them in here. Come in between your homeroom and English class and put your books in this cabinet. Then you can come straight from gym class and be here on time." Mr. Stewart extended his hand to Jamelia, "I'm proud of you. I think you have developed a good plan."

Jamelia shook his hand, "Thanks for helping me, and thanks for understanding my problem."

INTRODUCTION

In helping Jamelia develop a plan for solving her behavior problem, Mr. Stewart is using one of William Glasser's basic concepts for classroom management. Glasser maintains that it is a fundamental role of the teacher to help students learn to make good choices in the classroom and in life.

In 1965, William Glasser wrote *Reality Therapy* in which he challenged the widely accepted perception of behavior as externally driven and contended that all behavior is internally motivated. Reality therapy is driven by the following principles:

- Individuals are responsible for their own behavior. Behavior is not seen as a by-product of society, heredity, or an individual's past.
- Individuals can change and live more effective lives when given guidance and support.
- Individuals behave in certain ways in order to mold their environment to match their own inner pictures of what they want (Wubbolding, 1988).

In 1969, Glasser's *Schools Without Failure* documented the application of reality therapy to school situations. School failure, Glasser (1997b) contends, is the result of students

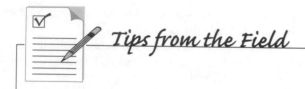

Tips from the Field

I keep track of responsible student conduct by assembling a 3-ring notebook and placing one page per student inside at the beginning of the year. On the first day of school, I show the students their blank page and challenge them to keep it blank for the whole school year. Here's how it works. When a student breaks one of our rules, that student must go to the behavior notebook and write a brief account of what transpired. If I agree with the assessment, I sign it and date it. This page is sent home with the report card at the end of the marking period. A big point is made of the fresh start for all at the beginning of the next marking period. If a student has a blank page all year, I send home the original blank page with a heartwarming note of praise for good behavior all year long.

Maribeth Petery
Grade 4 Teacher
Clay Elementary School
Ephrata, PA

and teachers accepting the notion that behavior is externally manipulated and therefore outside the control of the student. This belief results in teachers spending too much of their time trying to control and manipulate students rather than helping students understand the choices they are making. However, Glasser stresses that students will only feel safe to make these choices if school is seen as a "good place" where all people, especially the adults, are caring and courteous.

Throughout the years, William Glasser has remained current by adapting his original model outlined in *Schools Without Failure* to the changing needs of students. In the 1970s, Glasser adapted the concepts of **control theory** to his approach to education. Glasser called his approach control theory, because it proposes that the only behavior one can control is one's own. Control theory is "a descriptive term because we try to control our own behavior so that what we choose to do is the most need-satisfying thing we do at the time" (Glasser, 1992b, p. 44).

Since 1986, Glasser (1988, 1997a) has used the term **choice theory** rather than "control theory" for his approach. He changed the name in order to avoid confusion about who has the control in decision making—students or teachers. Choice theory has a more positive tone and reaffirms that individuals control their own behavior rather than being pawns to external stimuli. Today, Glasser provides a system of classroom management using a preventative approach.

The premise of choice theory is that all human behavior is generated by what goes on inside the behaving person. According to Glasser (1984, 1996) all behaviors—logical or illogical, appropriate or inappropriate—satisfy powerful needs within the person. Therefore, students are genetically driven to meet the following four needs:

1. *The need to belong.* For students, this includes being around their peers and being accepted by other significant people in their lives. Students must feel they belong, have friends, and are involved with the class and the teacher.
2. *The need for power.* This need is so strong that Glasser (as cited in Gough, 1987) states, "I believe that the need for power is the core—the absolute core—of almost all school problems" (p. 658). Power comes from feeling important, being recognized for accomplishments and skills, and feeling competent.
3. *The need for freedom.* Students have the need to make choices and to have a degree of independence. This need is met by allowing students to use creative and problem-solving skills to make choices.
4. *The need for fun.* Too often overlooked as a basic human need, students need to take pleasure in what they are doing. Classrooms need to be places in which learning is mixed with laughter. This need can be met by providing students an opportunity to learn something motivating or interesting.

GLASSER'S PLAN FOR CLASSROOM MANAGEMENT

According to Glasser, school will only be a satisfying place and students will only be successful if they fulfill their need for belonging, power, freedom, and fun within the school environment. When these needs are not met, students spend their time avoiding school or behaving in a way that creates problems for both the student and the teacher. For example:

When fifth-grader Keith Garrett wasn't allowed to join in a game of kickball, he grabbed the ball and threw it over the playground fence. When his classmates complained, he taunted them by laughing, "I guess no one will play now."

When tenth-grader Zachary Spivey started playing in a local band, he promised his parents that his grades wouldn't drop. But as the band became more popular and gained recognition, Zach had to choose between studying and practicing with the band. For Zach, studying material he had no interest in and couldn't imagine using in real life was less important than helping the band succeed.

Most of the eighth-graders at Sullivan Middle School hated going to Mr. Glanz's class. Each day they did the same thing. After a five-minute review of the questions from the day before, students were told to read a chapter from the book and to answer a new set of questions. Deciding to end the boredom in the class, Kenny passed a note instructing his classmates to drop their books on the floor at 10:45. Exactly at 10:45 an explosion of books hitting the floor relieved the boredom of another day in social studies.

While going over her classroom rules, third-grade teacher Lori Coltrap announced that the students would have assigned seats not only in the classroom but in the lunchroom as well. When the boys in the class discover that the arrangement provided for an equal number of boys and girls at each lunch table, they were unhappy and protested that they were being treated unfairly. Later in the day, the lunch monitor told Ms. Coltrap that her class was unruly and that several of the boys in the class threw food at the girls sitting across from them.

Because most behavior problems, like the ones described here, are viewed by Glasser as a result of a deficiency in meeting students' basic needs, Rich (1979) describes Glasser's classroom-management approach as a deficiency model. According to Glasser, the emphasis of most classroom-management plans is misplaced. As he notes, "We are far too concerned with discipline, with how to 'make' students follow rules, and not enough concerned with providing the satisfying education that would make our over concern with discipline unnecessary" (Glasser, 1988, p. 12).

However, Glasser does not place all responsibility for meeting students' needs on the teacher or the school. Ultimately, he stresses, students are responsible for fulfilling their own needs, for controlling their own behavior, and for making their own choices. However, students cannot make responsible choices unless they are strongly and emotionally involved with those who can.

Glasser makes a distinction between punishment and discipline. Punishment, which Glasser views as behavioral in nature, begins and ends with trying to force students to follow the rules by inflicting pain if they refuse. Punishments, ranging from criticizing, nagging, and complaining to actual abuse and violence, are destructive to the relationship between student and teacher (Glasser, 1997b).

Discipline, in contrast, asks students to evaluate and take responsibility for their actions (Rich, 1979). Discipline may *seem* like punishment, because it involves the sanctions of the loss of either freedom or privileges until the student makes a plan for changing behavior. Unlike punishment, however, discipline allows the student some control over the situation. When a sanction is given, it is only for the time it takes to agree to work out a way to follow the rules (Glasser, 1984). Glasser (1969) states that the keystone of discipline is for a child to make a value judgment and a commitment to change.

In order to promote student responsibility and to teach students to make appropriate choices, Glasser (1977) created the following ten-step discipline plan:

1. When a discipline situation occurs, the teacher should spend time thinking about the student's behavior. It is important to determine how the teacher might be contributing to the inappropriate behavior. A careful analysis of the student's behavior could identify triggers that can be easily eliminated.
2. The teacher should determine how such behaviors have been handled in the past. If those interventions have not been working, they should be abandoned.
3. The teacher should work to prevent behavior problems in two ways. First, classwork should be relevant and interesting. Second, it is important to establish a positive relationship with students. Students and teachers who care and respect each other avoid explosive situations.
4. The teacher should ask the student, "What are you doing?" This is a much more important question than "Why are you doing what you are doing?" because most students will shrug or respond that they don't know. When students are required to tell what they are doing, they must stop and think about their actions. Thinking about an act can help the student take ownership of the problem. This alone may stop the behavior from occurring in the future.

5. If the problem persists, the teacher must have a conference with the student. In some ways, the conference solves the problem, because the student is given the attention that he or she wants and may need. During the conference, the teacher should ask, "Is what you are doing against the rules? What should you be doing? Is what you are doing helping you or the class?" Glasser (1969) stresses that students must make value judgments about what they are doing. Until they realize that what they are doing is wrong, they must suffer the consequences of their behavior.

6. In Reality Therapy, the student is asked to plot a better course of behavior by developing a plan. The plan must be more than an agreement to stop. It must be a plan of positive action. Rich (1979) notes that the teacher should help the student develop the plan, and once a student makes a commitment to change, the teacher should accept no excuse for failing to do so.

7. If the preceding steps do not work, the student should be isolated with a time–out. This time–out should occur inside the classroom. While in time–out, the student cannot participate in the activities of the classroom until he or she has revised the plan or written a new plan to prevent further problems.

8. If the problem persists or if the student disrupts while in the classroom time–out, in-school suspension is the next step. Although the teacher is expected to demonstrate extreme patience with the student, the teacher also has the obligation to teach the other students. A student who cannot manage appropriate behavior after steps 1–7 have been applied should go to in-school suspension. Glasser suggests that in-school suspension be located in a comfortable, nonpunitive environment staffed by someone whose primary goal is to help the student devise a plan for returning to class. "Whether it happens early in elementary school or in the last part of high school, the first time a student disrupts enough to be asked to leave the class is a crucial point in that student's school career" (Glasser, 1992b, p. 143). Because what happens during in-school suspension can make or break a child, it is critical that the person in charge of in-school suspension be a caring person who has the student's best interest at heart.

9. If the student is out of control and cannot be contained in an in-school suspension room, the parents must be notified and the child removed from the school. However, Glasser (1977) stresses that this removal by the parents is for one day only. Parents and students should be told, "Tomorrow is a new day" (p. 63).

10. In the rare event that steps 1–9 do not prevent the student from being a disruption or danger to other members of the school, the student must stay home permanently or be referred to a community agency better equipped to meet the student's needs.

Although this ten-step plan was the foundation of Glasser's early work and has been used by teachers for over twenty years, Glasser (1998) now rejects his ten-step plan. He feels that discipline programs like the one he created simply do not work. He stresses that there are no quick fixes; the only good solutions to discipline problems are systematic and long term. Teachers should also be careful not to depend on any discipline program that demands that they do something to or for students to get them to stop behaving unsatisfactorily in class. Only a discipline program that is also concerned with classroom satisfaction

TABLE 6.1   *Glasser's Elements of Effective Discipline*

- Effective Discipline Takes Place in an Atmosphere of Trust and Mutual Respect
- Effective Discipline is Never Coercive
- Effective Discipline is Not Punishment
- Effective Discipline Recognizes the Difference Between a Discipline Problem and a Discipline Incident
- Effective Discipline Involves Caring Adults Helping Students Change Their Behaviors
- Effective Discipline Helps Students Meet Their Needs
- Effective Discipline Helps Students Make Appropriate Choices
- Effective Discipline Teaches Personal Responsibility
- Effective Discipline Deals with Students' Present Behaviors, Not Their Past
- Effective Discipline Requires Students to Make Value Judgments About Their Behaviors
- Effective Discipline Involves Helping Students Plan for Behavioral Change
- Effective Discipline Means Never Giving Up on a Student

will work. Glasser now focuses on changing schools and classrooms rather than on changing students. Table 6.1 outlines the elements of effective discipline according to Glasser.

THE QUALITY SCHOOL

Glasser stresses that classroom and school discipline plans would be unnecessary if students' needs are met in what he calls a **Quality School**. Although Glasser does not guarantee the elimination of all discipline incidents, he promises that in a Quality School, in which relationships are based upon trust and respect, discipline problems will be greatly reduced. Glasser has outlined his criteria for a Quality School in numerous articles and two texts, *The Quality School* and *The Quality School Teacher.* The basic components for a Quality School are:

- Students, teachers, administrators, and parents are taught Choice Theory. Through this training, students recognize their needs and appropriate means for meeting those needs. Teachers learn to be noncoercive and provide guidance and counseling to students.
- Staff and students work together to develop the rules for their school. Together they establish the class rules, and everyone signs an agreement to accept the rules. As a result, threats and punishments are eliminated.
- Regular class meetings are held to decide how to best conduct the business of school. In an interview with Brandt (1988), Glasser stressed that the cause of 95 percent of discipline problems in schools is the fact that students feel that no one will listen to them. By having regular classroom meetings in which problems

are aired, the majority of discipline situations are eliminated. Glasser first described the importance of whole-class meetings in 1969 when he stated that a nonjudgmental discussion about what is important and relevant to students provides a stable bridge across the gap between school and life. Three types of classroom meetings are advocated: problem-solving meetings, in which the goal is to solve a classroom problem; open-ended meetings, in which any intellectually important subjects can be discussed; and education-diagnostic meetings, in which students discuss how well they understand the curriculum.

- Teachers are viewed as facilitators. Teachers give real-life meaning to what they are teaching and help connect the material to students' lives. Orderly classes are taught in a way that is psychologically satisfying to the student. In a Quality School, there is no busywork and no compulsory homework.

- The curriculum has meaning. Too often, students find much of the curriculum not worth the effort it takes to learn the material. In the Quality School, students work on the useful skills of speaking and listening, reading and writing, and problem solving.

- Students take responsibility for evaluating their own work. Starting in kindergarten, teachers teach students how to strive for quality work.

- Grades are viewed as less important than learning. As long as students want to try to improve their grades, students are given an opportunity to complete work. Students keep working until their self-evaluations and their teacher's evaluations reach the level of quality desired (Glasser, 1969). No student should be labeled a failure through the use of the grading system.

- Teachers are not pressured to prepare students for standardized tests. All tests are open book. Questions are written or oral. There is no requirement to memorize facts.

- The school notifies parents only to tell them positive things. Discipline incidents are manage without involving parents. The burden of solving problems is on the student rather than on the parents.

- Discipline problems and disruptive students disappear in a Quality School. However, as students and teachers move to an acceptance of the Quality School as a reality, time–out is provided for those students who disrupt the classroom. There the students receive counseling and are encouraged to develop a plan for improving their behavior. In a Quality School, the door is kept open for a positive relationship between student and teacher. As Glasser stresses in *The Quality School*, "A Quality School is a need-satisfying school, and because it is, it is never coercive" (1992b, p. 278).

REALITY THERAPY/CONTROL THEORY IN THE CLASSROOM

Scenario

Principal Terrance Aguilar knew it was going to be an interesting day when veteran bus driver Evelyn Rawlins walked in with six of Marshall Middle School's best students in tow.

Class meetings provide a way for students to resolve classroom conflicts before they escalate.

Explaining that there had been an incident on the bus, she left the students with Mr. Aguilar. Instructing the students to wait in the office until after the morning announcements, Mr. Aguilar busied himself with the morning routine. When classes had begun, he ushered the six students into the conference room and told them to have a seat.

"Ms. Rawlins has told me some of what transpired on the bus this morning. I want to hear your side. Now here are the ground rules. Only one of you can talk at a time. If you want to speak, raise your hand and wait until I call on you. Each of you will be given a chance to give your version of the incident. Who would like to start?"

Two arms flew up, belonging to Dennis Lowell and Dana McMahan. Pointing to Dana, Mr. Aguilar said, "I understand that you have had property destroyed, so I will begin with you. Tell me what you saw."

"April and I were sitting in the back of the bus and talking when Dennis came back, grabbed my notebook, and threw it out the bus window. I hadn't said anything to him or done anything to him to make him do that." Tears started to stream down her face, "Now all my notes and my homework from last night are gone."

Turning to Dennis, Mr. Aguilar asked, "Is that true? Did you throw her notebook out the window."

Head down, Dennis responded, "Yes, Sir. I'm really sorry. It was a stupid thing to do, but Lori said Dana had put a note that April had written about me in her notebook. The guys were laughing at me, and it just made me mad." Turning to Dana he said, "I'm really sorry. I just didn't think."

Five hands went up, and Mr. Aguilar motioned for April to speak. "It wasn't a note about him. Last night my mother told me I could pick one friend to go to the Torpedo concert. I wanted to take both Dana and Lori and knew that one of them would be mad if I took the other one. So, I wrote a note to Dana telling her that I wanted her to go with me and that she wasn't to tell Lori about the concert. When Lori saw Dana reading a note, she wanted to see it. Dana put it in her notebook and told her it wasn't any of her business. The next thing we knew, she went to the front of the bus and told Dennis I'd written a love note about him. She knew that wasn't true. She was just being mean."

"Lori, why did you tell Dennis that April had written a note about him."

"I was mad. They had some big secret and left me out." Turning to April, she said, "If you had just told me the truth, I would have understood."

Without waiting to be recognized, April sighed, "*Sure* you would. I know you better than that. You can be mean, and today proves that. You aren't my friend anymore."

"April, I'm really sorry. What I did was mean. I know that. Please don't say you won't be my friend again."

Turning to Adam and Rodney who were being very quiet, Mr. Aguilar asked, "And what is your part in this? Why were you brought in?"

Adam looked at Rodney and then answered, "Well, we were teasing Dennis. Then when he grabbed the notebook, we kind of encouraged him to throw the notebook out the window. It seemed like a good idea at the time, but now I can see it was stupid. We didn't think about Dana losing all her notes and her homework. I'm really sorry Dana, and Dennis, I'm sorry we were teasing you."

"Rodney, how about you? Do you have anything to say?"

Rodney looked shocked that he was called on. "Well, I guess I'm sorry that I teased Dennis."

Mr. Aguilar took a deep breath, "Well, let's see if I understand everything. April's mother told April she could take one friend to the Torpedo concert. April didn't want to hurt Lori's feelings by not inviting her, so she wrote Dana a note and told her that she wanted her to go but that she wasn't to tell Lori. Lori saw Dana reading the note and wanted to know what was in the note. When Dana wouldn't tell her, Lori went up to the front of the bus and told Dennis that Dana had a note about him in her notebook. Then, you two," he said, pointing to Rodney and Adam, "started to tease Dennis. Dennis got mad, went back and grabbed Dana's notebook, and threw it out the bus window. Have I missed anything?"

Rodney decided to add to the story, "Well, Dana started to scream, and everyone started to yell at each other. Ms. Rawlins stopped the bus and made us all take our seats. She wouldn't let Dana off the bus to look for her notebook. Instead she brought us all to you."

"Well, this is what I want us to do. We are all going to sit quietly for five minutes. During that time I want each of you to decide what you need to do to help resolve this situation and to make sure nothing like this happens again. I'll let you know when your five minutes are up."

As the students thought through their options, Mr. Aguilar assessed the group. All were good students, and all had had some part in creating the situation. He noticed that all three girls were crying and that all the boys were looking at the floor. He hoped that the five minutes would seem like a very long time to all of them.

"All right, our five minutes are up. Who wants to go first?"

Dennis quickly raised his hand. "I feel terrible about Dana's notebook. I would like to call my mother so she can drive me back to look for the notebook. Maybe her papers are still there. I will buy her a new notebook just like the one I threw out the window. Dana and I have pre-algebra together, so I will make a copy of my notes for her." He stopped, and then he added, "And I will write a note apologizing to Ms. Rawlins."

"Dana, what do you say to that?"

"That would make me feel better. I am worried about my notes from my classes and homework for today. I'm sorry I hurt Lori's feelings. And I think I need to apologize to Ms. Rawlins, too."

April raised her hand. "I should have just told Lori I was taking Dana instead of being sneaky. It is better to be honest. Lori, I'm sorry if we hurt your feelings, and I still want to be your friend. I have English and Social Studies with Dana, so she can copy my notes. I will also write a note of apology to Ms. Rawlins."

Lori had started to cry. "I shouldn't have told Dennis what I did. I knew the note wasn't about him. I just wanted to hurt Dana and April. April, Dana, and Dennis, I'm sorry for what I did. I will also apologize to Ms. Rawlins."

Adam raised his hand. "I have Science with Dana. I will make a copy of my Science notes for her. I'm sorry I teased Dennis, and I'm sorry I caused a problem on the bus. I will also apologize to Ms. Rawlins."

"Well, Rodney, that leaves you. What have you learned from this experience and what is your plan?"

"Like I said before, I shouldn't have teased Dennis. I, too, will apologize to Ms. Rawlins. I guess I've learned how things can get out of hand really fast."

"Good; I think we have a plan. Dana, I will ask your teachers to either not count your homework today or to let you have another day to get it done. If Dennis doesn't find your notebook and your notes, I think we have a plan to replace your property. Are you comfortable with everything?"

"Yes, sir. I just don't want April and Lori to be mad at me."

In unison the two girls said, "We aren't mad."

Standing, Mr. Aguilar said, "I'm pleased with how you have resolved this situation, and I hope all of you have learned how fast saying something that's not true can cause a problem. Now, all of you except Dennis should go to class. Dennis, I will take you to the office so you can call your mother."

STRENGTHS AND WEAKNESSES OF REALITY THERAPY/CHOICE THEORY

As one of the first to provide an alternative to traditional behavioral approaches for managing a classroom, Glasser's models have been met with both criticism and praise. Many applauded the emphasis on self-discipline over punishment. Rich (1979) described Glasser's ten

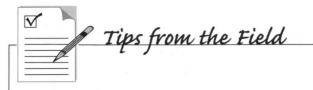

Tips from the Field

For the past 4 years I've worked as a GED English instructor in an alternative school. I found the following strategies effective with this group of students.

1. Give students respect. Most young men hate the word *boy* and *son*. Call them by their name, or even better, call them Mr. X (last name).
2. Tell the truth as you see it. Make sure they understand that the truth is a form of respect.
3. Teach what a sincere, honest apology is and when it is acceptable. Be sure to offer one every time you mess up, and do it publicly before the wronged student.
4. Train students in how to handle themselves when a principal/security officer/teacher is upset with them. This is a wonderful skill and helps at-risk students to get out of trouble.
5. Defend, congratulate, and apologize to students in public. Counsel, irritate, and castigate in private.

Marjory W. Thash
Grades 7–12 Teacher
East Central Alternative School
Union, MS

steps for classroom management as structured and organized and felt they gave new teachers a detailed map to follow. Perhaps the most positive element of Glasser's approach is that it stresses a positive, trusting atmosphere between teachers and students.

However, the application of Reality Therapy and Choice Theory to classrooms has not been without its criticisms. Part of the confusion about some elements of Glasser's approach has to do with the various names given to his theories and practices. Many of the elements of Reality Therapy, Control Theory, Choice Theory, and the Quality School are difficult to understand, and it is difficult to understand which elements have been discarded as Glasser modified his approach.

Many argue that Glasser overlooks some of the serious problems students have by suggesting that they simply *choose* to act or respond in certain ways. Neither Glasser's original ten-step plan nor the elements of the Quality School provide a means for helping students overcome a history of abuse, depression, or behavioral disability. Morris (1996) questions teachers' abilities to meet the needs of each student within a classroom. For example, if a student steals food from a classmate because the student is hungry, having the students devise a plan for not stealing food overlooks the real problem. Some students may not be emotionally, developmentally, or psychologically able to solve many of their problems.

Extensive training for teachers is required for the elements of the Quality School to function as Glasser describes. In addition, all teachers within a school would have to agree philosophically with Glasser's theories. Such agreement would be hard to find in the typical public school.

Finally, little guidance is given in Quality School for dealing with discipline situations. Comments like "Care" and "Never give up" provide little practical guidance to a teacher who is struggling to meet the needs of twenty to thirty students.

SUMMARY

In 1965, William Glasser wrote **Reality Therapy**. Although the name of his model has changed from *Reality Therapy* to *Control Theory* to *Choice Theory*, his basic concept that all behavior is internally motivated has not changed. Central to his theories is the belief that the role of the teacher is to help students make good choices by connecting student behavior to the associated consequences of that behavior. Glasser's early principles were operationalized through class meetings, clear specifications of rules, the use of plans or contracts, and a series of steps designed to guide the teacher's actions when dealing with problem behavior. Glasser has adapted his models to the changing American student through the concept of the Quality School, in which relationships are based upon trust and respect, and discipline problems are eliminated.

KEY TERMINOLOGY

Definitions for these terms appear in the glossary:

Choice Theory	Quality School
Control Theory	Reality Therapy

CHAPTER ACTIVITIES

Reflecting on the Theory

1. Seventh-grade social studies teacher Deborah Schwartz couldn't believe her eyes as she watched straight-A student Gretchen Smith cheating from a piece of paper she had hidden in the sleeve of her sweater. Confronting Gretchen, Ms. Schwartz confiscated the note on which the test's answers were written. Gretchen started to cry and explained that she hadn't had time to study. She begged Ms. Schwartz to let her take the test again.

   What suggestions would Glasser give Ms. Schwartz for dealing with Gretchen? Explain your reasoning.

2. Glasser makes a distinction between discipline and punishment. Do you consider these separate concepts or just different names for the same thing? Explain.
3. Both Dreikurs and Glasser address meeting students' needs. Compare the student needs outlined in their theories.
4. In the first scenario, Mr. Stewart asked several questions of Jamelia in order to help her develop a plan to change her behavior. What questions were asked? Were you comfortable with the plan developed? Why or why not?

Developing Your Portfolio

1. Describe four discipline situations you have observed. Consider the causes of these situations. Analyze each situation to determine whether it was a result of:

   - unmet needs of the student
   - ineffective curriculum
   - poor teaching strategies
   - some other factor

2. Glasser describes four basic human needs that must be met for school to be a "good place." How will you meet these needs in your classroom?

Developing Your Personal Philosophy of Classroom Management

1. Table 6.1 provides an analysis of Glasser's elements of effective discipline. Review these elements. Which match your personal philosophy of classroom management? Which would you reject? Why?
2. What strategies from Reality Therapy/Choice Theory would you incorporate into your classroom-management plan?
3. Review the components of a Quality School. Which of these components match your personal philosophy of classroom management? Which would you reject? Why?

RESOURCES FOR FURTHER STUDY

Further information about Reality Therapy/Choice Theory and resources for its use in the classroom can be found by contacting:

The William Glasser Institute
22024 Lassen Street
Suite 118
Chatsworth, CA 91311
(800) 899-0688
(818) 700-8000 (fax)

Chapter References

Brandt, R. (1988). On student's needs and team learning: A conversation with William Glasser. *Educational Leadership, 45,* 38–44.

Glasser, W. (1965). *Reality therapy: A new approach to psychiatry.* New York: Harper and Row.

Glasser, W. (1969). *Schools without failure.* New York: Harper and Row.

Glasser, W. (1977). 10 steps to good discipline. *Today's Education, 66,* 60–63.

Glasser, W. (1984). *Control theory: A new explanation of how we control our lives.* New York: Harper and Row.

Glasser, W. (1986). Discipline is not the problem: Control theory in the classroom. *Theory into Practice, 24,* 241–246.

Glasser, W. (1988). *Choice theory in the classroom.* New York: HarperPerennial.

Glasser, W. (1992a). The quality school curriculum. *Phi Delta Kappan, 73,* 690–694.

Glasser, W. (1992b). *The quality school: Managing students without coercion.* (2nd ed.). New York: HarperCollins.

Glasser, W. (1993). *The quality school teacher.* New York: HarperPerennial.

Glasser, W. (1996). The theory of choice. *Learning, 25,* 20–22.

Glasser, W. (1997a). Choice theory and student success. *Education Digest, 63,* 16–21.

Glasser, W. (1997b). A new look at school failure and school success. *Phi Delta Kappan, 78,* 597–602.

Glasser, W. (1998). *Choice theory: A new psychology of personal freedom.* New York: HarperCollins.

Gough, P. B. (1987). The key to improving schools: An interview with William Glasser. *Phi Delta Kappan, 68,* 656–662.

Morris, R. C. (1996). Contrasting disciplinary models in education. *Thresholds in Education, 22,* 7–13.

Rich, J. M. (1979). How effective are their strategies to discipline? *NASSP Bulletin, 63,* 19–26.

Wubbolding, R. E. (1988). *Using reality therapy.* New York: Harper and Row.

Chapter 7

Discipline with Dignity

Objectives

Chapter 7 prepares preservice teachers to meet INTASC standards #4 (Instructional Strategies), #5 (Motivation and Management), and #9 (Reflective Practitioner) by helping them to:

- understand the basic principles behind Discipline with Dignity.
- maintain student dignity while dealing with discipline situations.
- learn a systematic approach to classroom management.
- evaluate the needs of teachers and students.
- evaluate the impact of teaching style and strategies on discipline.
- determine the appropriate consequences for misbehavior.
- prevent situations requiring discipline from occurring.
- learn strategies for dealing with students with the potential for violence and aggression.

Scenario

A heated debate is going on at West Creek Elementary School. For over a week, a committee charged with establishing a schoolwide discipline plan has been meeting, and each day, the meeting has ended with more disagreement than agreement. The principal of West Creek directed the group to establish a list of rules and consequences that will be used consistently by each teacher in the school. Unfortunately, the discipline committee has discovered that few teachers agree as to what the rules should be and what the consequences should be if the rules are broken.

"All right," says Heather Jarman, chair of the committee, "I think we have finally agreed on our first rule, 'All homework will be due the day after it is assigned'."

Leaning back in his chair, Drew Austin asks, "Then are we also going to have a rule that all teachers have to return the graded homework the day after it is turned in?"

Frustrated after a week of chairing a committee that appeared to be accomplishing nothing, Heather snaps back, "No, Drew. Our job is not to make rules for the teachers. Our job is to make rules for our students, and I could use your help in getting this accomplished. Now, what should be the consequence for not having homework?"

Adopting a more serious tone, Drew suggests, "Homework not turned in on time will receive a grade of zero."

Veteran teacher Shelby Gibson sighs, "I have students who *never* do their homework. They are already getting a zero and could care less. I don't think giving zeros will motivate these students. We need to take away something they want—like recess."

"OK, I will revise my suggestion. The consequence for missing homework should be that students not having homework will miss recess to complete the work."

First-year teacher Emily Caldarelli spoke up. "So if I understand what we are a saying, all students should have the same consequence. If I have two children who come without their homework, they should both miss recess. What if one is a child who *never* does his homework and the other is a child who didn't do his homework for the first time because of some emergency? Should they be punished in the same way?"

"Why, yes, of course they should both miss recess. They broke a rule. Didn't you understand our charge? Mr. Evans wants consistent rules and consequences for all classes and all students. You can't treat children differently."

Shaking her head in disbelief, Emily countered, "But I treat children differently every day. I have children for whom I adapt instruction because they have a learning disability. I try to adapt to different learning styles. In fact, I'm evaluated on how well I individualize instruction! Yet when it comes to discipline, I'm told I should treat children like they are made by cookie cutters. What we are doing doesn't seem right."

INTRODUCTION

Emily Caldarelli is not alone in her concern that when it comes to discipline, children are treated as if they are cookie-cutter cutouts. For over twenty years, Allen Mendler and Richard Curwin have stressed that a "one size fits all" policy for classroom management is ineffective and inherently unfair. After writing their first book *The Discipline Book*, in 1980, Curwin and Mendler gained national recognition with the publication of *Discipline with Dignity* in 1988. While staying current by constantly updating their research and adapting their books to meet the changing needs of students and teachers, Curwin and Mendler have remained true to their belief that effective discipline comes from the heart and soul of an individual teacher and should not be a generic "one size fits all" program.

Several principles are central to the theory behind **Discipline with Dignity** (Curwin & Mendler, 1988a). The most fundamental of these principles is the idea that everyone in the school setting is to be treated with dignity. This means that students are treated with the same dignity that is granted teachers, administrators, and staff. Curwin and Mendler propose that effective discipline can occur only when decisions for managing student behavior are based on a schoolwide core value system that maintains the dignity of each student in all situations.

Central to treating individuals with dignity is the creation of a school environment in which the needs of both students and teachers are met. Table 7.1 provides a list of the fundamental needs of teachers and students. However, Curwin and Mendler (1980) state that the needs of students and teachers fall into one of four sets of needs:

1. *Personal identity*, which can be met through a positive self-image.
2. *Connectedness*, which can be met through a sense of positive affiliation with others.
3. *Power*, which can be met by having a sense of control over one's own life.
4. *Achievement*, which can be met by being enabled to achieve academically.

Discipline problems develop within the classroom when the needs of an individual student, a group of students, or the teacher are not fulfilled. Curwin and Mendler (1980) stress that discipline problems do not occur in a vacuum; they are part of a total classroom environment, and can be prevented when the classroom is an environment in which both individual and group needs can be met with minimum conflict.

In many cases, Curwin and Mendler (1988a) argue that a discipline problem is a means of conveying to the teacher that something is wrong in the classroom. They suggest

TABLE 7.1   *Identified Needs of Students and Teachers*

Needs of Students	Needs of Teachers
Peer approval	Peer respect
Teacher approval	Administrative respect and support
Academic success	A feeling that students are learning
Social success	The authority to run classroom without interference
Popularity	A safe school environment
A voice in school life	A voice in the running of the school
A fair and just environment	A feeling of worth and importance
A feeling of worth and importance	A fair relationship with the administration
A feeling of belonging	A good living and job security
A positive relationship between school and home	Respect by students
A feeling that the school will take care of them	
Skills and knowledge for career success	

that when discipline problems occur, teachers should look at their own role in creating the problem. It may be that the problem is the result of how the teacher interacts with students or the way in which the teacher conducts the class. Many teachers create minor discipline irritations, such as out-of-seat behavior, foot stomping, pencil tapping, and talking, by ignoring the attention span of students or by failing to vary the way information is presented. In *Discipline with Dignity*, teachers are encouraged to look at their own actions as critically as they look at those of their students.

Curwin and Mendler (1980) view classroom management as a process that evolves in an individual classroom, based on the needs of a specific teacher and his or her students. They do not support one system of classroom management or advocate a particular approach but rather provide a framework within which teachers can develop their own style of classroom management by helping them to recognize and accept feelings, to develop their awareness of themselves and their students, and to establish a classroom structure for dealing with discipline problems when they do occur.

Finally, Curwin and Mendler (1988b) suggest that the job of a teacher includes dealing with student behavior as well as teaching their subject matter. The teacher's goal should not be to eliminate all forms of misbehavior, because students need opportunities to test limits, but rather to help students make appropriate choices and decisions.

In fact, they suggest that discipline is not the critical issue that many believe it is because of what they call the **80-15-5 Principle.** In each classroom, Curwin and Mendler (1988b) propose that there are three groups of students. In the first group, 80 percent of the students rarely break rules or violate principles. The second group is made up of the 15 percent of students who break rules on a somewhat regular basis. The final 5 percent are chronic rule breakers and are generally out of control most of the time. The trick of a good

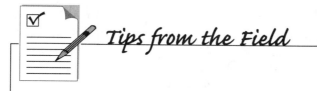

Tips from the Field

In order to make sure that students work with different classmates each time we work in groups, I have developed a unique way to divide students. I determined that typically I would want students to work in groups of 3, 4, 5, or 6. I then selected a symbol to represent different size groups. For example, I used a diamond, heart, club, and spade to represent my 4 student groups. I used the numbers 1, 2, 3, 4, 5, 6 for my six student groups. I used a circle, square, and triangle for my three student groups. I then put these symbols on index cards. I made enough cards to distribute cards to all students. Then when I want to divide my students into four groups, I pass out the index cards in random order. I then tell all students with a diamond on their card to form a group. This assures that my groups are always changing and that all students have a chance to work together.

> Alva Suggs
> Preservice Teacher
> Austin Peay State University
> Clarksville, TN

discipline plan, according to Curwin and Mendler, is to control the 15 percent of students who regularly break rules without alienating or overly regulating the 80 percent who rarely do so, and without backing the 5 percent of chronic rule breakers into a corner.

THREE-DIMENSIONAL PLAN

In order to meet the needs of all students, Curwin and Mendler (1980, 1988a, 1988b) recommend the creation of a three-dimensional discipline plan that focuses on preventing discipline problems from occurring. However, the plan provides actions for when problems do occur and resolves the more serious discipline issues of the 5 percent of students who are chronic discipline problems. The three-dimensional plan is an integration of many discipline approaches and includes elements from Skinner, Jones, Dreikurs, Canter, and Glasser. However, Curwin and Mendler's focus is on maintaining student dignity and teaching responsible behavior.

Unlike models that focus on teaching obedience, the cornerstone of Curwin and Mendler's model is the teaching of personal responsibility. The goal is to teach students to make wise decisions by allowing them to make choices and mistakes in a safe environment. "Teaching responsibility requires motivating students to want to change, teaching them decision-making skills, and providing them with new skills for better behavior" (Curwin & Mendler, 2000, p. 17). In Curwin and Mendler's three-dimensional plan, teachers and students work together to develop the discipline plan.

Prevention

The prevention component of Curwin and Mendler's three-dimensional plan is designed to minimize or prevent classroom problems from occurring by providing structure and direction in the classroom while accommodating the daily issues that arise. The heart of the prevention dimension is the establishment and implementation of social contracts. The **social contract** is a system for managing the classroom and is designed to enhance human interaction in the classroom. Social contracts give students a sense of ownership by involving them in the creation of classroom rules and regulations. Curwin and Mendler (1988a) stress that teachers who exclude students from classroom policy making run the risk of widespread dissatisfaction with rules that students perceive as arbitrary and unfair. When students have a part in the creation of the guidelines they will live by, they feel empowered.

The successful contract begins with the establishment of **classroom principles** that represent the value system of the classroom. Principles, unlike rules, cannot be enforced. Principles define attitudes and expectations for long-term behavioral growth (Curwin & Mendler, 1988b). Although students must be involved in the creation of classroom principles, the process begins with teachers carefully considering their own values in order to determine how they want to manage their classrooms, how they want to treat their students, and how they want students to treat each other. This self-analysis is essential. Curwin and Mendler (1988b) found little difference in the effectiveness of teachers who were permissive, authoritarian, or moderate. The difference lies in how aware teachers are about their own beliefs concerning how a classroom should be managed. Each individual teacher has a different tolerance for noise, movement, humor, and classroom activity. Trying to conduct the class in a way that is not congruent with the teacher's personality and preferred methods will result in increased agitation and anxiety for both students and the teacher.

Once the classroom principles have been established, specific rules, driven by those principles, must be developed. The teacher begins by providing **"flag rules,"** which are nonnegotiable (Curwin & Mendler, 1984). These rules represent the value system of the teacher. Once the flag rules are presented, the students develop rules for each other and for the teacher. Mendler and Curwin (1983) state that rules are critical to successful classroom management, because unclear limits lead to discipline situations.

Consider how the personalities and teaching styles of the teachers on South Hamilton Middle School's sixth-grade team differ:

> The teachers on the Bronco team at South Hamilton Middle School are a very diverse group. Second-year Social Studies teacher Jody Brundage enjoys a lively active classroom. Primarily utilizing cooperative learning groups, she considers herself a facilitator rather than a teacher. Science teacher Catherine Dobrowolski is very structured in her classroom. Always wearing a white lab coat, she encourages her students to use what she calls quiet professionalism as they conduct experiments. Math teacher Garry Guier uses a traditional approach to teaching. In his class, students have assigned seats and spend much of each hour listening to Mr. Guier present material using the overhead projector. Finally, Language Arts teacher Gabriel Quintero considers his classroom a stage and his students his audience. Each day he fascinates his students by dressing as the characters they

are studying, reciting long pieces from plays, and doing anything necessary to maintain their attention. Although each teacher is different in personality and teaching style, the hundred students who make up the Bronco team easily adjust as they move from teacher to teacher, because the teachers on the Bronco team all agreed that there would be clear rules and regulations for each classroom. The rules might be different for each classroom, but students are aware of the limits and the consequences for misbehavior.

Once the students have developed a list of rules, the class votes on the rules. The rules should have at least 75 percent agreement before a suggested rule becomes a classroom rule. This process is important, because it gives ownership of the rules by all the class.

It is important to establish consequences for each rule established by the class. Although the enforcement of these consequences falls in the second dimension of the three-dimension plan, *action*, the creation of the consequences occurs during the *prevention* phase (Curwin & Mendler, 1980). Mendler and Curwin (1983) note that too often teachers wait until a rule is broken before thinking of a consequence. Students need to know the consequences for breaking each rule so they can make suitable choices and become effective decision makers.

Curwin and Mendler (1988a) suggest that a **range of consequences** be established for each rule. Unlike theorists who suggest that the consequences be sequential in their application, Curwin and Mendler recommend that a consequence be selected from the established list based on the needs of individual students. A student who purposely disobeys a rule may have a harsher consequence than a student who accidentally breaks the rule. Curwin and Mendler (1984) emphasize that in all cases, consequences should be instructional rather than punitive and should be regarded as natural and logical extensions of the rules.

The purpose of consequences is to teach students that misbehavior produces effects. Effective consequences are clear and specific, have a range of alternatives, are natural and logical, preserve the student's dignity, and are related to the rule (Curwin & Mendler, 1988b). Consider how Jody Brundage from the Bronco team helped her class establish consequences:

> "Now that we have established our rules, we need to establish a list of consequences for breaking the rules. We need a range of consequences. For example, the consequence might be less severe if someone does something the first time than it would be if a student repeatedly breaks a rule. All right, let's think of our first rule, 'We will not touch each other without permission.' What consequences do you think we should have for this rule?"
>
> Lauren's hand goes up, "If it were an accident, like they just bumped into someone, I think the student should just apologize."
>
> "Yes, but what if they meant to do it," Demari stressed, "I think something else should happen. They need to be punished."
>
> "Maybe they should go to the office," another student added.
>
> After several suggestions were given, the class voted on the consequences they thought best for the first rule. Ms. Brundage said, "So, our list of consequences for breaking our first rule will be:

Student apologizes to classmate.
Student is sent to office.
Student's parents are called.
Student is given in-school suspension.

Are we all in agreement?"

Once the students have created the list of rules and consequences and 75 percent of the students have agreed to them, the class reviews all of the rules and consequences to ensure that there are no misunderstandings. This can be done in many ways, but Curwin and Mendler suggest that one effective way is to actually test for understanding. Once established, parents and administrators are notified of the classroom rules. Curwin and Mendler (1988a) stress that the established list of rules and consequences need to be revised throughout the year to determine whether they are working effectively and whether they need to be changed to meet the changing needs of the classroom.

Action

The action dimension of Curwin and Mendler's three-dimensional plan serves two purposes:

1. When a discipline problem occurs, something must be done to stop the problem.
2. Dealing with the problem quickly and effectively prevents minor problems from escalating.

The first step in the action dimension is to implement the consequences associated with rule violation. However, Curwin and Mendler (1988a) stress that *how* a consequence is implemented is at least as important as the consequence. Tone of voice, proximity to the student, body posture, use of contact, and other nonverbal gestures determine the effectiveness of a consequence as much, or more, than the actual content of the consequence. Curwin and Mendler provide nine principles to guide in the implementation of consequences:

1. *Be consistent.* A consequence from the approved list must be implemented each time a rule is broken. The consequence may be a simple reminder of the rule, but students must realize that the teacher is aware that a rule has been broken. Consistency creates order and predictability in the classroom and shows that the teacher honors the social contract and expects the students to do so as well.
2. *Remind the student which rule has been broken.* Lecturing, scolding, and making the student feel guilty are unnecessary. These tactics only escalate the problem by generating anger and hostile feelings.
3. *Use the power of proximity control.* The teacher should move toward the student. Typically, this is enough to gain the student's attention and stop inappropriate behavior. This will assure all students that the teacher is aware of everything that happens in the classroom. However, the age and personality of the student should be considered with proximity control. For some students, an invasion of personal space is considered a threat and will escalate rather than de-escalate the situation.
4. *Make direct eye contact when delivering the consequence.* Much can be delivered by this unspoken message. However, the teacher must be aware of cultural differences.

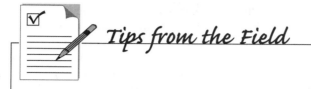

Tips from the Field

Some unruly students suffer from family discord and divorce, parents with drug and alcohol problems, neglect or abuse, serious lack of self-confidence and self-esteem, and personal emotional problems. Sometimes having a personal talk early in the year can uncover what's bothering a student. Take the time early in the year to develop a relationship with your students—get to know them. Often these young people don't want to be disruptive, and understanding their problems can often decrease unacceptable behaviors.

Alison Standing
Behaviour Management Teacher
Churchill State School
Churchill, Ipswich
Australia

In some cultures, a lowering of the eyes is a sign of respect. A student should not be forced to behave in a manner that is uncomfortable or counter to cultural norms.

5. *Use a soft voice.* Shouting and yelling are signs of a lack of control. The softer the tone, the more impact it will have on students.

6. *Acknowledge appropriate behavior.* Too often, the only students who get attention from the teacher are those acting out. Mendler (1997) cited research showing that teachers fail to recognize 95 percent of appropriate behavior. Therefore, finding ways to acknowledge desired behavior should not be hard if teachers pay attention.

7. *Do not embarrass students in front of their peers.* Part of treating students with dignity is allowing them to save face in front of their peers. Speaking quietly to a student or asking a student to step outside the classroom may prevent the escalation of the situation by not forcing a public confrontation.

8. *Do not give a consequence when angry.* It is important to be calm and to model the appropriate way to handle emotionally-charged situations. An overly aggressive delivery will create hostility, resentment, and fear. Teachers who lose self-control fail to model the very behavior they desire in their students.

9. *Do not accept excuses, bargaining, or whining.* Implement the consequence as directly and expeditiously as possible.

Although the manner in which consequences are delivered impacts their effectiveness, Curwin and Mendler (1988a) noted other reasons teachers fail to provide appropriate consequences. One of the most common reasons is that the consequence has not been established by the teacher nor the students but instead by a schoolwide committee. The teacher may find the consequences too harsh or incongruent with the teacher's belief system. A rule or consequences not valued by the teacher will not be implemented.

The second reason is that rule violations often occur at inconvenient times or places. Students know when the teacher is busy or distracted and will test the teacher during these times. If the teacher fails to deal with inappropriate behavior, incidents will occur more and more often during these times.

Teachers often resent the need to play police officers. Teachers would like to walk to the lounge to enjoy their lunch without having to monitor the halls. They would like to watch a pep rally or assembly without having to be on alert for misbehaving students. Unfortunately, students expect and depend on the adults in a school to react and stop inappropriate behavior. They want teachers to be vigilant. This vigilance makes the school a safer place for all to be.

Resolution

Teachers need a method of managing the 5% of students who won't obey the rules, who do not respond to the established consequences, and who are a danger to themselves and others. The resolution dimension of Curwin and Mendler's three-dimensional plan provides the teacher with techniques for working with these students.

The resolution aspect of the three-dimensional plan involves the establishment of **individual contracts** when the social contract in the classroom fails to work. Such contracts are negotiated with the student to determine the cause of the behavior, the means of preventing misbehavior from occurring in the future, and the needs of the students that can be met by the teacher. In many cases, other school professionals (social workers, guidance counselors, administrators) and the student's parents must be involved in the resolution phase (Curwin & Mendler, 1988a).

The purpose of the individual contracts is to help students identify what they need or want from the class and ways of having their needs met without resorting to disruptive actions that violate the classroom social contract. The establishment of an individual contract requires that the teacher:

- Identify those students who are having trouble following the social contract.
- Get in touch with personal feelings about the student. An effort should be made to eliminate any perceptions or biases held toward the student.
- Arrange a time for a private conversation with the student.
- Develop a plan based on the student's needs, maturity, and ability to follow through with the required action.
- Put the plan in writing so that the student will understand what has been determined.
- Meet with the student to revise the plan if he or she cannot carry it out.
- Provide assistance to make the plan work. Determine what went wrong. Determine what interventions are needed.
- Seek outside help from counselors, parents, administrators, and others if additional assistance is needed.

Curwin and Mendler (2000) state that students cannot learn "the three R's" until they learn the most important "R"—responsibility. The three-dimensional plan teaches responsibility by allowing students to make choices within limits and to face the consequences of their choices.

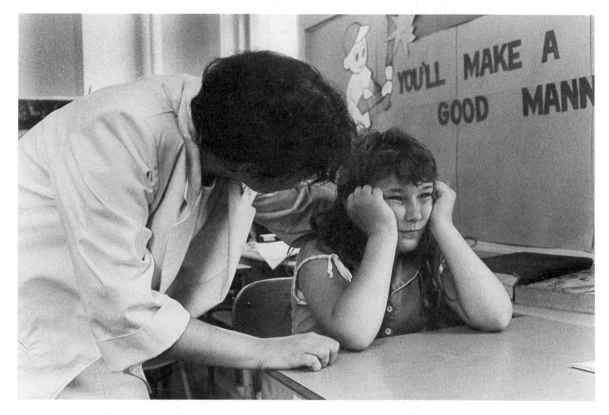

Curwin and Mendler advocate the use of individual contracts with students who continually violate the classroom's social contract.

AS TOUGH AS NECESSARY

In the twenty years since Curwin and Mendler wrote *Discipline with Dignity,* they have trained countless teachers in their methods for managing classrooms. This contact with real students and real teachers has allowed them to stay current as classrooms and students have changed over the past twenty years. In 1997, Curwin and Mendler wrote *As Tough as Necessary* in response to the need of teachers to deal with more violent students and as a response to zero-tolerance policies.

Curwin and Mendler (1999) state that they have zero tolerance for zero tolerance. They stress that teachers, administrators, and parents should have zero tolerance for the idea of doing anything that treats all students the same way. *As Tough as Necessary* provides an alternative to zero tolerance by providing a balance between being strong and being fair. The message in *As Tough as Necessary* is that violence will not be tolerated but that students should not be dealt with in a cookie-cutter fashion. Therefore, in some cases, Curwin and Mendler (1999) agree that the zero-tolerance approach is necessary and that

TABLE 7.2   *General Guidelines for Schools Adopting As Tough as Necessary*

General Guidelines

- School is a place that is safe for everyone
- Differences are resolved through talking, not fighting
- Everyone is responsible for preventing violent behavior
- Everyone cares for and protects one another's person, property, and feelings

Rules Developed from General Guidelines

- No weapons are allowed in school
- Students do not touch one another without permission
- Students report fights or rumors of fights

Source: Curwin, R. L., & Mendler, A. N. (1999). Zero tolerance for zero tolerance. *Phi Delta Kappan, 81,* 119–120.

students may have to be removed from the school in order to provide a safe environment for everyone. In other cases, counseling, parental involvement, and conflict resolution can provide an effective intervention.

Curwin (1995) notes, "Unless we build a humane superhighway that transcends the information superhighway, greed, selfishness, and violence will continue to increase at breakneck speed" (p. 72). To combat the increasingly violent behavior of students, they must be taught:

- Alternatives to violence
- Methods for making effective choices
- Alternative means for expressing anger, frustration, and impatience

Curwin and Mendler (2000) emphasize that violence in schools will not be stopped until students learn the simple lesson that hurting others is wrong. Table 7.2 provides the general guidelines that might be used in a school utilizing the *As Tough as Necessary* principles. Chapter 14 provides additional suggestions for working with students who have the potential for violence.

DISCIPLINE WITH DIGNITY IN THE CLASSROOM

Scenario

After greeting her students on the first day of school, Ms. McBryant asked, "I wonder how many of you noticed that I don't have any rules posted in our classroom? That is because I want you to help me write our classroom rules and procedures. Over the next few days, we are going to establish the rules that you will follow, and you are going to create some rules that I will follow, as well. Now, to begin, we need to think bigger than specific rules; we need to think of some general principles that we want to guide our class."

Noting the confusion on the faces of her students, Ms. McBryant explained, "For example, one of the principles I want for this class is that every student will reach his or her potential. I can't write a rule about that, but I want that principle to guide what I do in the classroom. Now this is what I want you to do. I want you to move your desks so that you are in groups of four. Then, as a group, I want you to think of two or three principles that you think should guide our class. Any questions?"

Later, each group presented the list of principles they had developed. Suggestions included:

Every student is to be respected
All opinions are respected
No one is ridiculed in this class
Every student will be safe
Every student is appreciated

After reviewing all the suggestions, the class agreed to the following statements that summarized their classroom principles:

In Ms. McBryant's class, everyone is treated with respect. This means that all opinions are honored, we help each other learn, and we respect each other's property.

The next day, Ms. McBryant prepared the class to establish the rules that would reinforce the class principles. "Class, now that we have written our classroom principles, we need to develop rules that will determine how our principles are enforced. Now, in a few minutes, I will allow you to develop a list of rules for our class and a list of rules that you think I should follow. However, I have the right to veto any rule that I think will prevent me from doing my job as a teacher. I am also going to give you two rules that are nonnegotiable. These two rules are necessary for our classroom principles to work. My first rule is 'We will not touch each other without permission.' The second rule is 'We will speak in appropriate voices.' Now, let's gather into groups and establish a list of rules."

After each group had developed a list of rules and the class had voted on the rules they would adopt, Ms. McBryant said, "All right, class, I think we have agreed on our classroom rules, and I have combined your list and mine. For you, the rules will be:

We will not touch each other without permission
We will speak in appropriate voices
We will not call each other names
We will not take something that does not belong to us without permission

For me, you have decided that the rules will be:

Ms. McBryant will not give homework over the weekend or during school breaks
Ms. McBryant will not yell at students

I am very proud of you, I think you have developed a list of rules that will make our class run smoothly."

Strengths and Weaknesses of Discipline with Dignity

Perhaps the greatest strength of *Discipline with Dignity* is that it requires teachers to consider their values, their interactions with students, their contributions to discipline situations, and their teaching methods. Another strength is that Curwin and Mendler have used the feedback they have received from classroom teachers to keep the model current as students and classrooms change.

However, the *Discipline with Dignity* approach does have its critics. Blumefeld-Jones (1996) was surprised that Curwin and Mendler would criticize Lee Canter's Assertive Discipline program, because Blumefeld-Jones finds little difference between the two models. He emphasizes that "teacher control is no less central to Curwin and Mendler but is also more subtle since they explicitly argue against such obedience" (p. 14). Kohn (1996) agrees and suggests that *Discipline with Dignity* places too much emphasis on getting students to do what they are *supposed* to do rather than thinking about what they *should* be doing.

Another criticism of *Discipline with Dignity* has been its emphasis on rule development by students. Many teachers view rule development as the role of the teacher and question the idea of students developing rules for the teacher. Others question whether young children are developmentally able to develop rules. Many high school teachers consider the process of rule and consequence development too elementary to use with older students.

Summary

In *Discipline with Dignity*, Richard Curwin and Allen Mendler contend that a "one size fits all" policy for classroom management is ineffective and inherently unfair. They stress that the school environment must meet the needs of each student and teacher by assuring that everyone in the school is treated with dignity. *Discipline with Dignity* is a three-dimensional discipline plan that focuses on preventing discipline problems from occurring. The three elements of this model are prevention, action, and resolution. In the twenty years since Curwin and Mendler wrote *Discipline with Dignity,* their theories have evolved to meet the changing needs of teachers and classrooms. In 1997, Curwin and Mendler wrote *As Tough as Necessary* in response to the need of teachers to deal with more violent students.

Key Terminology

Definitions for these terms appear in the glossary:

80-15-5 Principle	Individual contracts
Classroom principles	Range of consequences
Discipline with Dignity	Social contract
Flag rules	

CHAPTER ACTIVITIES

Reflecting on the Theory

1. In Chapter 3, the following scenario was presented:
   Eighth-grade teacher Natalie Cansler is having a problem with one of her students. Cary Kirby arrives each day without the required materials. Some days he forgets his pencil; other days it is his textbooks. Each day, he asks to return to his locker for some forgotten item. Ms. Cansler feels she is in a no-win situation. If she allows Cary to return to his locker, he loses valuable instructional time. If she refuses, he spends the hour unable to do his work.
   How would Curwin and Mendler suggest that Ms. Cansler deal with Cary's behavior? How does their strategy differ from that of Lee and Marlene Canter?

2. Curwin and Mendler suggest that discipline situations are a fundamental part of the job of a classroom teacher and state, "The teacher's goal should not be to eliminate all forms of misbehavior, because students need opportunities to test limits, but to help students make appropriate choices and decisions." Do you agree or disagree? Why?

3. Curwin and Mendler encourage teachers to avoid a "cookie cutter" approach to discipline. Is there a way to be consistent while meeting the needs of individual students? Explain your reasoning.

4. Curwin and Mendler identify needs of both students and teachers. How will you meet your needs of identity, connectedness, power, and achievement in your role as a classroom teacher?

Developing Your Portfolio

1. Describe your teaching style. What instructional strategies will be common in your classroom? What discipline problems might occur as a result of your style or strategies? How can you eliminate these problems while maintaining your preferred style of teaching?

2. At the end of Chapter 1, you were encouraged to develop a list of the rules you will establish for your classroom. Review the list and change as needed. Develop a "range of consequences" for each of these rules.

Developing Your Personal Philosophy of Classroom Management

1. In the last scenario, Ms. McBryant stated that one of the principles she wanted for her class was for every student to reach his or her potential. What principles will guide your instruction, your interaction with students, and your classroom-management plan?

2. What will be your "flag rules?" Why do you consider these rules nonnegotiable?

3. What strategies from the Discipline with Dignity model will you incorporate into your classroom-management plan?

Resources for Further Study

Further information about Discipline with Dignity and resources for its use in the classroom can be found by contacting:

Discipline Associates
PO Box 20481
Rochester, NY 14602
(800) 772-5277
(585) 427-2659 (fax)

Chapter References

Blumefeld-Jones, D. S. (1996). Conventional systems of classroom discipline. *Journal of Education Thought, 30*, 5–21.

Curwin, R. L. (1995). A humane approach to reducing violence in schools. *Educational Leadership, 52*, 72–75.

Curwin, R. L., & Mendler, A. N. (1980). *The discipline book.* Reston, VA: Reston Publishing.

Curwin, R. L., & Mendler, A. N. (1984). High standards for effective discipline. *Educational Leadership, 41*, 75–76.

Curwin, R. L., & Mendler, A. N. (1988a). *Discipline with dignity.* Alexandria, VA: Association for Supervision and Curriculum Development.

Curwin, R. L., & Mendler, A. N. (1988b). Packaged discipline programs: Let the buyer beware. *Educational Leadership, 46*, 68–71.

Curwin, R. L., & Mendler, A. N. (1997). *As tough as necessary: Countering violence, aggression, and hostility in our schools.* Alexandria, VA: Association for Supervision and Curriculum Development.

Curwin, R. L., & Mendler, A. N. (1999). Zero tolerance for zero tolerance. *Phi Delta Kappan, 81*, 119–120.

Curwin, R. L., & Mendler, A. N. (2000). Six strategies for helping youth move from rage to responsibility. *Reaching Today's Youth, 4*, 17–20.

Kohn, A. (1996). Beyond discipline: From compliance to community. Alexandria, VA: Association for Supervision and Curriculum Development.

Mendler, A. N. (1997). Beyond discipline survival: Reclaiming children and youth. *Journal of Emotional and Behavioral Problems, 6*, 41–44.

Mendler, A. N., & Curwin, R. L. (1983). *Taking charge in the classroom.* Reston, VA: Reston Publishing.

Chapter 8

Building Community

Objectives

Chapter 8 prepares preservice teachers to meet INTASC standards #4 (Instructional Strategies), #5 (Motivation and Management), #6 (Communication) and #9 (Reflective Practitioner) by helping them to:

- evaluate the use of external rewards as a way to control student behavior.
- learn to distinguish between productive praise and evaluative praise.
- evaluate the impact of teacher/student interactions on discipline.
- evaluate the impact of teaching style and strategies on discipline.
- learn to develop a sense of community within the classroom.
- involve students in resolving classroom problems.
- involve students in discussions of curriculum, procedures, and class problems.

Scenario

Preservice teacher Kelly Gaines had been hired to substitute teach for Daniel Herrera while he was on sick leave. She had spent some time with Mr. Herrera and had thought she was familiar with his classroom-management plan. She was surprised, however, when upon returning from lunch, a student asked if the class had earned a marble for the quiet way in which they had returned to class.

"I don't understand. What do you mean that you earned a marble?"

A student explained, "Mr. Herrera puts a marble in the jar if we walk back from the cafeteria quietly and in line. When the jar is full, we are given an afternoon with no work."

Confused, Ms. Gaines asked, "But aren't you *supposed* to walk quietly in the hall so that you don't disturb the other classes? Why should you earn a marble for doing what is right?"

The students looked to each other, confused at the question. Finally, Kevin tried to explain, "Well, we *always* get a reward for following the rules. *Why else* should we follow the rules?"

INTRODUCTION

Kelly Gaines is not the first person to question the use of classroom rewards and punishments. In the early 1970s, Haim Ginott questioned such behavioral approaches to classroom management and suggested that communication, not rewards and punishments, is the key to effective classroom discipline. Ginott (1972) stresses that teachers set the tone of the classroom through positive communication. He maintained that through caring, supportive interactions with students, a teacher builds a community of learners. Thirty years later, Alfie Kohn builds on Ginott's ideas and stresses that the ultimate goal of classroom management should not be on simple obedience but on having students behave appropriately, because they know it's the right thing to do, and because they can understand how their actions affect other people.

In 1991, Kohn proposed that the purpose of education is to produce not just good *learners* but good *people*. Such a goal, he stressed, cannot be achieved through behavioral techniques. Praise, privileges, and punishments can change student behavior, but they cannot change the student. Kohn contends that behavioral manipulation does not develop a commitment to being a caring and responsible person. Rewarding good behavior does not provide the motivation for continuing to behave appropriately when there is no longer any reward to be gained for doing so. In fact, Kohn maintains that the more teachers control their students through reward systems, the more difficult it is for students to become moral people who think for themselves and care about others (Kohn, 1991, 1996).

Therefore, Kohn stresses that the focus in classrooms must change from an emphasis on curbing negative behaviors to an emphasis on promoting positive ones. Ginott held a similar view and, as early as 1972, noted that ethical concepts such as responsibility, respect, loyalty, honesty, charity, and mercy cannot be taught directly but are taught through concrete life situations from people one respects. According to Kohn and Ginott, the only way to help students become ethical people, as opposed to people who merely do what they are told, is to have them construct moral meaning. Kohn (1991) suggests that if the goal is to have children take responsibility for their behaviors, teachers must allow students to make decisions about what is right and wrong.

Because Ginott and Kohn suggest that classroom management involves all classroom activities, their concepts are included as a system of classroom management. They stress that effective classroom management requires the building of communities, and that to do so, teachers must evaluate the manner in which they communicate with students, find alternatives to traditional punishments, and eliminate the focus on rewards and praise.

LOOKING AT STUDENT–TEACHER INTERACTIONS

Kohn (1996) proposes that central to effective classroom management are self-evaluations by teachers of what they consider important in the classroom, how they interact with students, and what they ask students to do. Too often, when problems develop, teachers automatically look at the students as the cause without evaluating their own roles in the problem. Kohn notes that teachers must always look first to their responsibility for creating situations and states, "Adults who blithely insist that children choose to misbehave are rather like politicians who declare that people have only themselves to blame for being poor" (p. 17).

Kohn (1996) proposed that what is needed is not another discipline plan but a whole new curriculum, because a huge proportion of unwelcome behaviors can be traced to a problem with what students are being asked to learn. In the past, teachers only focused on students who did not do as they were asked, rather than on what it was they were asked to do. When students are asked to spend their days completing endless worksheets, problems are going to develop and students will misbehave to make the time pass faster and to eliminate boredom.

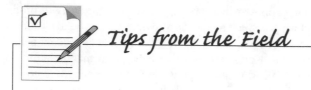

Tips from the Field

The most difficult classroom-management situation is when the entire class is unruly and it is hard to pinpoint who is creating the problem. In these situations, I think it is important to:

1. Look at yourself: Do you fully understand the material that you are teaching, and have you anticipated the problems that students may have? Are you presenting material that is too hard? Too easy? Are you connecting with your students? Do you have enough structure? Are you presenting yourself as a firm but caring teacher? Are you engaging in mannerisms that give away that you are insecure?
2. Are you allowing time to explain the new material? Or are you constantly going over homework for most of the period, barely having time to present the new lesson, assigning new homework at the last minute, thus creating a cycle where students are truly frustrated? Your timing may be off. Allow time to clearly present a lesson. Allow for practice in class.

Terri Husted
Middle School Math Teacher
Boynton Middle School
Ithaca, NY

As an elementary teacher in Israel, Ginott desired to discipline without humiliating, destroying self-worth, judging, or hurting his students. When he evaluated his own behaviors and interactions with students, he observed:

> I have come to a frightening conclusion. I am the decisive element in the classroom. It is my personal approach that creates the climate. It is my daily mood that makes the weather. As a teacher, I possess tremendous power to make a child's life miserable or joyous. I can be a tool of torture or an instrument of inspiration. I can humiliate or humor, hurt or heal. In all situations it is my response that decides whether a crisis will be escalated or de-escalated, and a child humanized or de-humanized (Ginott, 1972, p. 16).

ELIMINATING THE USE OF REWARDS AND PRAISE

Over thirty years ago, Ginott cautioned teachers and parents about the overuse of classroom praise and suggested that some children might actually get hooked on praise. Kohn (1993a, 1993b) also warned teachers about the overreliance on rewards and praise. In an interview with Brandt (1995), Kohn noted that at least 70 studies showed that extrinsic motivators such as grades, praise, and tangible rewards are not merely ineffective but are actually counterproductive to producing ethical, responsible individuals. Still, the use of praise and rewards has come to seem so natural to many teachers that even questioning the practice is surprising to them. After all, rewards and praise work. Countless teachers can attest that students will do tasks they dislike and find boring just to earn a sticker, piece of candy, or verbal praise.

Kohn (1991, 1993a, 1993b, 1995) objected to the use of praise for several reasons. First, rewards and praise work only for a short while and eventually lose their effectiveness. Unfortunately, the more rewards are used, the more they seem to be needed. Second, many students work for the reward but may never see the value of what they are learning. Learning becomes what one does to get a reward. Kohn identified two dozen studies that show that people expecting to receive a reward from completing a task simply do not perform as well as those who expect nothing. Third, and perhaps most importantly, Kohn (Brandt, 1995) suggested that much of the praise used by teachers is fundamentally fraudulent, in that the teacher is pretending to talk to the student but is actually using the student to make a point or to criticize the behavior of other students. For example, most teachers would be embarrassed and humiliated if the principal said, "I like the way you come to faculty meetings on time and are always prepared." Yet, such interactions happen in the classroom each day.

Unlike Kohn, Ginott (1972) did find some value in praise if the praise is appreciative rather than evaluative. When our statements describe a student's work, action, or accomplishments, the student's self-evaluation is positive and productive. **Appreciative praise** does not evaluate personality or judge character.

Students also make conclusions about themselves when they receive **evaluative praise**. Unfortunately, these conclusions are typically negative and destructive. Evaluative praise is often viewed as a threat and brings discomfort and fear. Ginott (1972) cautioned teachers to avoid praise that attaches adjectives to a student's character. Only praise that places no judgments on a student's character or personality makes the classroom a safe place in which students are free to try and to make mistakes. Table 8.1 outlines Ginott and Kohn's suggestions for using praise.

ALTERNATIVES TO PUNISHMENT

In 1972, Ginott stated that the essence of discipline is to find effective alternatives to punishment. He said,

> To punish a child is to enrage him and make him uneducable. He becomes a hostage of hostility, a captive of rancor, a prisoner of vengeance. Suffused with rage and absorbed in grudges, a child has no time or mind for studying. In discipline whatever generates hate must be avoided. Whatever creates self-esteem is to be fostered (p. 148).

Kohn (1996) also encourages teachers to find alternatives to punishment and to treat inappropriate behavior as a problem to be solved together in a supportive classroom community. In such an environment, disciplinary problems become opportunities for conveying values, providing insights, and strengthening self-esteem.

TABLE 8.1   *Characteristics of Effective Praise*

Do's and Don'ts of Effective Praise
Don't Praise Students, Only What Students Do
Make Praise as Specific as Possible
Avoid Phony Praise
Avoid Praise That Sets up Competition
Give Praise in Private
Avoid Praising a Student's Character
Avoid Praise That Compares or Condescends

Sources: Ginott, H. G. (1972). *Teacher and Child: A book for parents and teachers.* New York: Collier Books. Kohn, A. (1993). *Punished by rewards.* New York: Houghton Mifflin Company.

Therefore, Kohn (1996) is critical of traditional discipline programs that focus on punishment. He argues that such programs may temporarily change behavior but cannot help students become ethical adults. He further suggests that the goal of traditional discipline programs is to make children behave a certain way and to comply with adult demands rather than to support or facilitate children's social and moral growth (Brandt, 1995). Too often, in traditional programs, the lesson that is learned is that the price for displeasing adults is pain or embarrassment. Kohn suggests that corporal punishment is the worst example of the impact of traditional discipline, because it teaches children that aggression is acceptable.

More current discipline programs emphasize consequences and choices rather than merely focusing on punishment. However, in his interview with Brandt (1995), Kohn stated that the use of terms like *consequences* and *choices* are misleading. Kohn maintains that in most situations consequences are just "**punishment lite**," because the focus is still on controlling students. The creators of these discipline plans suggest that students choose their behavior, but Kohn fears that students actually have no choice, because they must decide between the lesser of two evils: choose to do what the teacher wants or choose to be punished. New disciplines, Kohn argues, are old disciplines with a new twist, designed to appeal to educators who are uncomfortable with the use of bribes and threats.

Kohn's primary problem with both traditional and more current discipline programs is that they fail to achieve what teachers desire and may actually interfere with what teachers are trying to accomplish in the classroom. Central to his argument is that punishment usually works only as long as the punisher is around. Kohn fears that traditional discipline warps the relationship between the punisher and the punished, with the result that the caring relationship between teacher and student is significantly compromised. Perhaps most disturbing is that when students are told to think of the consequences of their behavior, they only focus on the consequences to themselves, never to others. Kohn contends that traditional discipline fails to teach students to be compassionate or caring individuals. Consider the following examples of how traditional discipline fails to achieve what educators desire for their students:

Nathan has had a hard time concentrating during class. He had accidentally pushed a fellow student as they got on the bus and had been warned that he "would get it" when he got on the bus that afternoon. After observing that Nathan was distracted and had spent most of the morning staring out the window, Ms. Gamez warns, "Nathan, if you don't get back to work, I'm calling your mother and having you stay after school until you complete your work." Having suddenly found a way to avoid the trip home on the bus, Nathan continues to stare out the window.

As Justin and Kason return to the classroom, they noticed that the door to the storeroom has been left open. Peeking inside, they find boxes of candy that will be sold by the school baseball team for a fundraiser.

"Wow, look what's here. Grab some," Justin tells Kason as he stuffs a bar of candy in his coat pocket.

"We can't take this. We'll get in trouble."

"Not if we aren't caught. We'll just take one bar from each of the boxes. That way, no one will realize any is missing. It won't matter if no one catches us."

Laura O'Malley takes a deep breath and flops on to the couch in the faculty lounge. "You won't believe the morning I've had. I have got to find a new discipline plan."

Krystal Mathis turns from the soft-drink machine, "Why? What happened?"

"I have a list of consequences listed beside my rules, and the first time students break a rule, they are given a warning. Then if they break the rule again, they have to write in their behavior journals. Everyday, Carman breaks one of the rules. Today, I had had it and asked him why he continues to do the same thing day after day. You know what he said? He said, 'Well, I always get a warning before it counts, right?'"

Kohn and Ginott view discipline as more than punishment. They see classroom discipline as a means of helping students become caring, ethical individuals. Ginott (1972) stated that this does not happen through control but through a "series of little victories in which a teacher, through small decencies, reaches a child's heart" (p. 148).

BUILDING A CLASSROOM COMMUNITY

Many teachers fear that if traditional approaches to classroom management are removed as options for dealing with classroom problems, they will be powerless. Kohn (1996) stresses, however, that there isn't just one alternative to traditional discipline strategies but an unlimited number of options that are available to classroom teachers. These alternative approaches require more than a change in teacher behaviors. They require that teachers and students build a community of learners in which it is safe to try new ideas and even to fail. They require less emphasis on controlling students and more emphasis on having students grow into compassionate and responsible people. Therefore, according to Kohn (1996), the goal should be not finding another discipline plan but transforming our current educational structures.

Building a **classroom community** begins with students having a positive relationship with an adult who respects and cares about them. Kohn (1996) stresses that communities are built upon a foundation of cooperating throughout the day, with students continually being allowed to work together. Classrooms should have classwide activities in which

Cooperative learning is the key to building a classroom community.

students are provided an opportunity to work together toward a common goal. Students acquire a sense of significance from doing significant things, from being active participants in their own education. Finally, academic instruction can be used to build community. Community building should not be separate from what students are learning. Students should be provided explicit opportunities to practice **perspective taking**, through which they can imagine how the world looks from someone else's point of view (Kohn, 1997). Activities that promote an understanding of how others think and feel foster intellectual growth while helping students become more ethical and compassionate.

However, disturbances and disagreements are inevitable in a classroom of 20–30 students. Kohn (1996) states that how we view these disturbances is much more important than how we deal with them. Classroom conflict and disagreements should be viewed as an opportunity to help students solve problems and grow. They should be viewed as an opportunity to help students become active participants in their own social and ethical development. Kohn contends, however, that overall misbehavior will diminish when conflict is used as a time to help students think about the feelings of others and to focus on the needs of the entire classroom.

Most of the discussion of how to resolve classroom problems and how to build a community can take place in class meetings. Kohn (1996) states, "Apart from the invaluable social and ethical benefits of class meetings, they foster intellectual development as well, as students learn to reason their way through problems, analyzing possibilities and negotiating solutions" (p. 90). When students meet in a class meeting, they get the positive message that their voices count, they experience a feeling of community, they learn to problem-solve and make decisions, and they develop the ability to reason and analyze (Kohn, 1994).

Kohn (1996) is not an advocate of rule development, for several reasons. First, he finds that rules turn children into little lawyers who look for loopholes and ways around the wording. Second, rules turn teachers into police officers who emphasize enforcement rather than learning. Finally, when rules are broken, the typical reaction is to provide a consequence. Therefore, the emphasis is on punishing students rather than helping them grow into self-disciplined individuals.

Rather than creating rules, Kohn suggests that students engage in conversation about how they want the class to be. He argues that even very young children can begin with specific ideas of how they should treat one another. It is the wrestling with a dilemma and discussing conflicting perspectives that is important, not the rules that might be developed from the discussion. In creating rules, the process is the point. Rules in themselves are not valuable, but the conversation that gives rise to them is.

Kohn (1996) realizes that it will be impossible to eliminate all problems in the classroom. Even in the most nurturing environment, students will have problems with the teacher or with each other. Typically, the common response to conflict is to blame students and to look for a way to punish and control the students. Kohn suggests that a more valuable way to view these situations is to see them as an opportunity for students and teacher to work the problem out together.

The success of problem solving depends on many factors. It cannot occur unless there is a positive relationship between the student and the teacher. This relationship must be ongoing, so that when the teacher interacts with the student, the student trusts the teacher, and the student recognizes that the teacher has the student's best interest in mind.

Before working with the student, a teacher must analyze his or her own responsibility in creating the problem. He or she must question his or her own practices. Sometimes situations can be resolved with a change in teaching strategies or a change in unrealistic classroom requirements. The teacher must diagnose the situation by identifying the factors that caused the problem to occur. Finally, the teacher must determine the best time to work with students to solve the problem. In some cases, it is best to put off a conversation with a student until everyone is calm and ready to resolve the problem.

The process begins with asking the student, "What do you think we can do the resolve this problem?" The teacher should help the student consider the appropriate options and the possible results of each option. In some cases, the student may need to make restitution by restoring, repairing, cleaning up, or apologizing. Once the student has developed a plan, the teacher should check with the student to see whether the plan worked or whether new alternatives are necessary.

Problem solving requires skill and training on the part of both the teacher and the student. Therefore, skills involving how to listen, how to control anger, and how to see things from another's point of view must be learned and should be incorporated into classroom instruction.

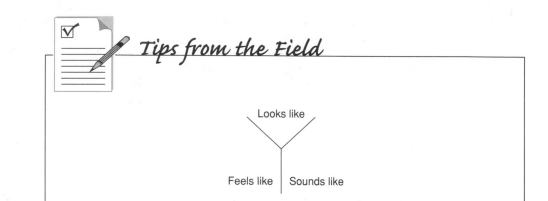

Tips from the Field

I use Y-charts as a tool to help the kids understand concepts, ideas, etc. I have found them especially beneficial for managing classroom behavior and understanding rules. Words like *respect* and *listen* are relatively abstract to 6-, 7-, and 8-year olds. I still use words like this but define what *respect* and *listen* mean and the set of behaviors they demand through the use of student-created charts. When I have a student who is struggling with a particular social skill or behavior, I Y-chart it with them. For example I had a student who was constantly giving put-downs to fellow students during group work. As I watched him, it was obvious that that was the only effective way he knew to get the attention of people in his group. He and I Y-charted positive ways of contributing to groups and positive ways of saying that he doesn't agree with what others have said. I did not invent Y-charts but have taken the ideas and played with, modified, and changed them to suit the needs of my students.

Penne Metcalf
Grade 3 Teacher
East Manjimup Primary School
Western Australia

Kohn (1996) fears that the current structure of most classrooms makes it difficult for a community of learners to be established. He notes that the time restraints of many classrooms, especially those of the middle school and high school, makes it difficult to establish the feeling of a community, in that a community cannot be built in 45-minute segments. Large classrooms with 20–30 students also limit the ability for students to get to know each individual student. However, the benefits of building a classroom community outweigh the obstacles in doing so.

BUILDING COMMUNITY IN THE CLASSROOM

Scenario

First-year teacher Patricia Sagasta had been determined to be different from the teachers she had had as a student. She wanted her students to understand why they should or shouldn't behave a certain way instead of only obeying rules to avoid punishment. So, at the beginning of the school year, she told her students that she wasn't going to establish a list of rules for them but that they would deal with situations as they arose. Things had gone remarkably well the first four weeks of school and for the most part, Patricia was very proud of how her students had behaved. That was until she had to have a substitute teacher in the room.

After a night of fighting a stomach virus, Patricia called her principal and requested a substitute teacher. She was horrified the next day to find a note from the substitute, Ms. Stewart, saying that Patricia's class was unruly and that she would never again agree to teach that class. Before the students arrived for the day, the principal came by to say that she had been called to Patricia's classroom when several of the students had thrown spitballs at Ms. Stewart. Patricia was surprised and wondered what would have caused such unusual behavior from her students and what she should do to see that the behavior was never repeated.

After roll had been taken and the required reports had been sent to the office, Patricia asked the students to form a circle around her so that they could have a class meeting. She began by saying, "I understand that there were problems yesterday when we had Ms. Stewart as a substitute. I want to read the note left me by Ms. Stewart."

After reading the note, Patricia looked out at a sea of dropped heads. "Now, I think we need to do two things. One, we need to determine why this behavior occurred, and we need to think about the consequences of yesterday's actions."

Immediately, Kortnee's hand went up. "Ms. Sagasta, I don't think it's fair that we all get punished. Some of us tried to do our work."

"Kortnee, I think you misunderstood me. I haven't said anything about punishment. But since you raised your hand, do you want to tell me why you think things got out of hand yesterday?"

"Well," Kortnee started as she twisted her hair around her finger, "Ms. Stewart wasn't nice like you. She started the day by yelling at us. She said she didn't know what we were supposed to be doing. She wouldn't let us go the centers, and then she gave us a bunch of worksheets to do. We tried to tell her what we did each day, but she wouldn't listen, and it just made her mad."

Embarrassed, Patricia realized that she had created part of the problem from the day before. Not expecting to have to miss the next day, she had taken her plan book with her, and there had been no instructions for Ms. Stewart. "Well, class, I have to take responsibility for Ms. Stewart not knowing what she was to do. I took my plan book home, and there were no written plans for her. That is my fault. I should always have plans here in case of an emergency. I think I need to apologize to Ms. Stewart for not doing my job, and I need to make sure I either leave my plan book or I need to have alternative plans for a substitute."

The students looked relieved to see that Ms. Sagasta was taking some of the blame. "However," Ms. Sagasta said, "do you think you should have acted as you did yesterday? Let's think of the consequences of your behavior yesterday. Can anyone think of the consequences?"

"Well, I guess we should miss recess today," offered Austin.

"Austin, I wasn't thinking about the consequences for you. I was thinking about the consequences for everyone. For example, how do you think Ms. Stewart felt last night? What do you think she thought about this class?"

Heads dropped. Because no one answered, Ms. Sagasta called on Kyah. "Kyah, if you had been Ms. Stewart, what would you have been thinking and feeling last night?"

"I guess I would have felt bad. I would have wondered if I should substitute teach. And I would think that this class is bad. I don't think I would have liked us very much."

"Is that how the class wants Ms. Stewart to feel?"

Together the class answered, "No."

"All right, we have discussed how Ms. Stewart feels. How do you think Ms. Anderson thinks or feels?"

Immediately, the class realized that the principal might now see the class differently. Payton raised his hand and said, "I don't want Ms. Anderson to think we are a bad class. We aren't a bad class. We are a good class."

"Payton, I agree. So we need to think how we can make sure Ms. Anderson sees you that way. All right, were there consequences for anyone other than Ms. Stewart or Ms. Anderson?"

Paige raised her hand, "Ms. Sagasta, do you feel bad about us? Do you not like us anymore?"

"Paige, I still like all of you, but I have to admit I was surprised by your actions. I'm not sure I trust you as much as I did. The class is going to have to win my trust back again."

"Ms. Sagasta, we are sorry. What if we write an apology to Ms. Stewart and to Ms. Anderson? Do you think that would fix things?"

"Well, Paige, I'm not sure everything can be fixed that easily, but I think it is a good first step. Why don't we divide into two groups; one group will write a note to Ms. Anderson, and the second group will write a note to Ms. Stewart."

"Ms. Sagasta, can we have three groups? I think one group should write a note to you."

Smiling, Ms. Sagasta said, "Yes, I think that is a fine idea. We will divide into three groups and when you finish, you can read your notes to the class. Then if everyone agrees, we will send them around the room so everyone can sign them."

STRENGTHS AND WEAKNESSES OF BUILDING COMMUNITY

Perhaps the greatest strength of Kohn and Ginott's ideas on classroom management is that they require teachers to consider their interactions with students. They emphasize the strong link between the way teachers talk to students and the way students behave in return. Morris (1996) considers the emphasis on creating a positive rapport between the student and teacher another important feature.

Although many agree philosophically with Kohn and Ginott, they question how realistic their ideas are in handling typical discipline problems. Neither Ginott nor Kohn has provided a synthesized model for classroom management. Many of their ideas focus on curriculum and teaching, not discipline. For many teachers, the strategies are too broad to use in addressing the daily problems they encounter. In addition, Manning and Bucher (2001) suggest that many of the ideas presented by Kohn and Ginott would be appropriate for middle and high school students but may be inappropriate for younger children.

Some teachers question how to make Kohn and Ginott's ideas work in classrooms in which children have become accustomed to traditional discipline methods. The transition from traditional classroom practice to one in which the focus is on self-responsibility and self-discipline may be very difficult for students and time-consuming for teachers.

SUMMARY

Alfie Kohn builds on Haim Ginott's ideas, written some 30 years earlier, that suggested that communication, not rewards and punishments, is the key to effective classroom discipline. Kohn and Ginott stress that the ultimate goal of classroom management should be on having students behave appropriately because they know it's the right thing to do and because they can understand how their actions affect other people. Therefore, Kohn stresses that the focus in classrooms must change from an emphasis on curbing negative behaviors to an emphasis on promoting positive ones. Ginott held a similar view and noted that ethical concepts such as responsibility, respect, loyalty, honesty, charity, and mercy cannot be taught directly but are taught through concrete life situations by people one respects. They stress that effective classroom management requires the building of communities, and to do so, teachers must evaluate the manner in which they communicate with students, find alternatives to traditional punishments, and eliminate the focus on rewards and praise.

KEY TERMINOLOGY

Definitions for these terms appear in the glossary:

Appreciative praise	Perspective taking
Classroom community	Punishment lite
Evaluative praise	

CHAPTER ACTIVITIES

Reflecting on the Theory

1. Robert Felts is a very angry, unreachable student. No matter what he is asked to do, he responds with a hostile comment. He calls his classmates names and seems to enjoy challenging and insulting his teachers. Most of his teachers have given up on him, because he always has the last word in any confrontation.

   How would Ginott and Kohn suggest that teachers work with Robert? Explain your reasoning.

2. In the opening scenario, Ms. Gaines questions why students should be rewarded for doing what is right. Does she have a legitimate concern? Do you agree that

there is too much emphasis on extrinsic reward in today's classroom? Image a classroom in which no rewards are given. Would such a classroom be possible? Why or why not?

3. Kohn suggests that corporal punishment teaches children that aggression is acceptable. Does corporal punishment still have a place in modern classrooms? Would you be comfortable using corporal punishment to discipline your students? Why or why not?

Developing Your Portfolio

1. Observe the interactions between a teacher and the teacher's students. Were the majority of the interactions positive? Were students praised? If so, what was the reaction to praise? What negative interactions did you observe? What positive interactions did you observe?

Developing Your Personal Philosophy of Classroom Management

1. Kohn suggests that "the ultimate goal of classroom management should not be on simple obedience but on having students behave appropriately because they know it's the right thing to do and because they can understand how their actions affect other people." Do you agree? How will you manage your classroom in such a way as to help students learn the "right" thing to do?
2. What strategies from "Building a Community" would you incorporate into your classroom-management plan?
3. One of the most famous quotes about teaching is the statement by Ginott that begins, "I have come to a frightening conclusion." Review the entire quote. Do you agree or disagree with Ginott's statement? Why?

RESOURCES FOR FURTHER STUDY

For further information about Alfie Kohn contact:
www.alfiekohn.org

CHAPTER REFERENCES

Brandt, R. (1995). Punished by rewards? A conversation with Alfie Kohn. *Educational Leadership, 53,* 13–16.

Ginott, H. G. (1972). *Teacher and child: A book for parents and teachers.* New York: Collier Books.

Kohn, A. (1991). Caring Kids: The role of the schools. *Phi Delta Kappan, 72,* 494–506.

Kohn, A. (1993a). *Punished by rewards.* Boston: Houghton Mifflin Company.

Kohn, A. (1993b). Rewards versus learning: A response to Paul Chance. *Phi Delta Kappan, 74*, 783–787.

Kohn, A. (1994). The truth about self-esteem. *Phi Delta Kappan, 76*, 272–282.

Kohn, A. (1995). *The risks of rewards*. ERIC Digests–ERIC Clearinghouse on Elementary and Early Childhood: Office of Educational Research and Improvement, Washington, DC. (ERIC Document Reproduction Service No. Ed 376990)

Kohn, A. (1996). *Beyond discipline: From compliance to community*. Alexandria, VA: Association for Supervision and Curriculum Development.

Kohn, A. (1997). How not to teach values? *Education Digest 62*, 12–17.

Manning, M. L., & Bucher, K. T. (2001). Revisiting Ginott's congruent communication after thirty years. *Clearing House, 74*, 215–219.

Morris, R. C. (1996). Contrasting disciplinary models in education. *Thresholds in Education, 22*, 7–13.

Chapter 9

Classroom Organization and Management Program (COMP)

Objectives

Chapter 9 prepares preservice teachers to meet INTASC standards #1 (Content Pedagogy), #3 (Diverse Learners), #4 (Instructional Strategies), #5 (Motivation and Management), #7 (Planning), #9 (Reflective Practitioner), and #10 (School and Community) by helping them to:

- understand the basic principles behind Classroom Organization and Management Program (COMP).
- recognize the importance of collaboration in supporting changes in teaching practices.
- determine appropriate instructional strategies to be used in teaching classroom rules and procedures.
- use the techniques presented in the six components of COMP.
- evaluate the research base on effective classroom management, which is the foundation for COMP.
- determine the characteristics and actions of effective classroom managers.
- recognize that management and instruction are integrally related.
- take into account the student differences in attention spans, learning modalities, and intelligences as they develop a personal classroom-management plan.
- evaluate how subject-area content impacts classroom-management strategies.

Scenario

First-year teachers Nick Napolitano and Monique Mathis had spent the weeks before school began preparing their lessons and their classrooms. After a long morning of work, Nick entered Monique's room with thoughts of lunch on his mind. "Do you want to get a pizza? Remember," he reminded Monique, "it won't be long before we can't go out for lunch."

"Sure, just give me five minutes to put this away," Monique said as she moved large poster boards to her desk.

Looking at one of the poster boards, Nick noticed that it was divided into four columns: Teacher Tasks, Student Tasks, Rules, and Procedures. Confused, he asked, "What is all this? What are you doing?"

"Well, I started to develop my classroom rules, and it occurred to me that I needed a set of different rules and procedures for each of the activities we will do. For example, the rules and procedures the students need when working on the computers are different from those they need when working independently. So, I've been thinking through each activity. See," she said, as she showed him a completed poster board, "these are the rules and procedures I've been working on for my computer center. I've thought through what I will have to do to make the center work well. I've listed the tasks the students will perform at the computer. Then I've developed rules for computer use, and I've developed the procedures I think we will need."

"This is way too much work. I think I'll wait and see what problems develop and deal with them then."

Grabbing her purse, Monique said, "Well, I keep remembering what I was told in my teacher–education program. My professor said that the returns of careful planning are 1000 percent. I'm hoping she was right. Now, let's get that pizza. I'm starving."

INTRODUCTION

Even though she is just beginning her first teaching assignment, Monique is already demonstrating the characteristics of an effective classroom manager. Monique is being proactive by planning ways to prevent student confusion and misbehavior, and she understands that management and instruction are interwoven. These same two elements are part of a classroom-management plan, **Classroom Organization and Management Program (COMP)**, created by Carolyn Evertson. COMP is the result of 30 years of research by Evertson and her colleagues that included over 5,000 hours of classroom observation. COMP was originally developed through a series of related studies funded by the National Institute of Education and conducted through the Research and Development Center for Teacher Education at the University of Texas in Austin and the Arkansas Department of General Education in Little Rock (Evertson & Harris, 1995). Since 1989, COMP has been implemented in more than 6,200 schools in the United States and the American territories.

COMP was developed from descriptive, correlational, and experimental research studies designed to discover successful key management practices and strategies. For over 30 years, Evertson and nationally recognized researchers such as Edmund T. Emmer, Julie P. Sanford, Barbara S. Clements, Linda M. Anderson, Catherine H. Randolph, Alene H. Harris, and Jere Brophy have examined successful classroom-management practices. Their research identified the following characteristics of successful classroom managers:

- Teachers whose students consistently gained in achievement organized classrooms in such a way that they ran smoothly, with a minimum of disruptions (Brophy & Evertson, 1976).
- Teachers whose classrooms were well managed analyzed classroom tasks in precise detail to determine the procedures and expectations required for students to be successful (Emmer, Evertson, & Anderson, 1980; Evertson & Anderson, 1979).
- Teachers in well-managed classrooms saw the classroom through the students' eyes. Therefore, they were able to analyze the students' needs for information (Emmer, Evertson, & Anderson, 1980; Evertson & Anderson, 1979).
- Teachers who were effective classroom managers monitored student behavior in order to quickly deal with disruptive behavior and potential threats to their system (Emmer, Evertson, & Anderson, 1980; Evertson & Anderson, 1979; Evertson & Emmer, 1982).
- Junior and senior high-level teachers who were effective classroom managers clearly communicated needed information, reduced complex tasks to essential steps, and had a good understanding of student skill levels (Evertson & Emmer, 1982; Sanford & Evertson, 1981).
- Teachers who were more effective classroom managers kept students engaged in academic work by organizing instruction (Evertson & Emmer, 1982; Sanford & Evertson, 1981).

- Teachers who were effective classroom managers not only created workable management systems but taught the systems to their students from the first day of the school year (Emmer, Evertson, & Anderson, 1980). The importance of this was verified by later research by Evertson, Emmer, Sanford, and Clements (1983) that found that after the beginning of the year, classroom patterns become established and mid-year changes require stronger, more intensive interventions.
- Teachers who were successful at blending academic and social skills had students who tended to stay on task, engage in appropriate behavior, and demonstrate higher achievement. These teachers recognized that they were teaching both academic and social skills, and that both academic and social behaviors are developmental (Evertson & Harris, 1996).

All of the variables identified as being significant in producing student achievement and reducing inappropriate and disruptive students are incorporated into COMP. Since Evertson began her research in the 1970s, classrooms have become more diverse, and a greater variety of academic activities are needed to meet students' needs. This increase in complexity demands even greater expertise in classroom management, and strategies for meeting the changing needs of classrooms are incorporated into COMP (Evertson & Harris, 1995).

The changing complexity of the classroom has also brought about a need for a definition of classroom management that more closely reflects the changing dynamics of today's classrooms. In an interview with Marchant and Newman (1996), Evertson said, "For a long time, classroom management has been and still is associated with control and discipline, and with questions about the best ways to get students to comply. We are simply saying that these notions of management are not compatible with building the kinds of learning communities we are trying to build where students have a stake in their own learning and their own community" (p. 31). (PIC)

Evertson and Harris (1999) suggest that a broader definition of classroom management is needed and that classroom management must be viewed as a holistic descriptor of teachers' actions in orchestrating all that teachers do to encourage learning in their classrooms. This includes creating predictable, orderly classrooms, establishing rules, gaining student cooperation in tasks, and coping with the procedural demands of the classroom. A holistic definition of classroom management is one that emphasizes a teacher's ongoing choices and actions rather than narrowly considering responses to misbehavior. Today's view of classroom management must be "all that teachers must do to encourage learning in their classrooms, including proactively setting up an environment that encourages learning and discourages wasting time, and orchestrating instruction in ways that promote and maintain student engagement" (p. 251).

When classroom management is viewed as orchestrating all that goes on in a classroom, a system of classroom management is needed. COMP was developed to provide such a system to teachers (Evertson & Harris, 1995). The central goal of COMP is to help teachers improve overall instructional and management skills through planning, implementing, and maintaining effective classroom practices. Additional goals are the improvement of student task engagement, the reduction of inappropriate and disruptive behaviors, the promotion of student responsibility for academic work and behavior, and the improvement

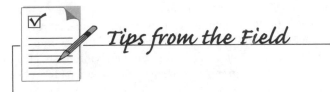

Tips from the Field

Don't try to reinvent the wheel. New teachers think they have to come up with some snappy original ideal for every concept they teach. Let me dispel the myth. I haven't had an original idea in twenty years. I've learned to sponge off others' ideas and weave them into my own to make magical lessons. However, it is important to give credit where credit is due. Use the Internet, professional magazines, and colleagues to gain great ideas. Go to professional meetings (a potpourri of great ideas) and absorb. Don't burn out. Bone up on what others can teach you.

Cynthia H. Lynch
Grade 4 Teacher
C.E. Hanna Elementary School
Oxford, AL

of student academic achievement. Evertson and Harris (1996, 1999) note the following key principles of COMP:

- Effective classroom management prevents problems rather than handling them after they occur.
- Management and instruction are integrally related.
- Students are active participants in the learning environment, and classroom management must take into account student differences in attention span, learning modalities, and intelligence.
- Professional collaboration supports changes in teaching practice.

COMP provides for the uniqueness of each classroom setting and seeks to promote thinking about classroom-management decisions, rather than simply presenting teachers with a "recipe" for effective management. COMP is comprised of six major components: Organizing the Classroom, Planning and Teaching Rules and Procedures, Managing Student Work, Maintaining Good Student Behavior, Planning and Organizing Instruction, and Conducting Instruction and Maintaining Momentum (Evertson & Harris, 1997). Few of these components are new to teachers. However, as Evertson (1985) states, the ordering of these components and the rationales for their use provide a conceptual framework from which teachers can make the critical decisions about their teaching on an everyday basis.

KEY ELEMENTS OF COMP

Just as the rationale for COMP developed from the research on effective classroom management, the six components of COMP are products of years of research into the characteristics of effective classroom managers. Table 9.1 provides the research base for these six components. The rationales and key elements for each of the six components follow.

TABLE 9.1 *Indicators of Effective Classroom-Management Practices*

	Number of Studies in Which Variable Was Measured*	Number of Studies in Which Variable Was Significant**	Percentage of Studies in Which Variable Was Significant
Teaching Practice Variables			
1. Readying the classroom			
Organizing classroom space and materials	10	8	80
2. Developing rules and procedures			
Efficient administrative routines	10	8	80
Appropriate general procedures	10	10	100
Efficient small-group procedures	6	5	83
3. Student accountability			
Checks for understanding	10	9	90
Routines for checking and giving feedback	10	10	100
Task oriented focus	10	10	100
4. Managing student behavior			
Reinforces good performance	10	9	90
Consistent management of student behavior	10	9	90
5. Monitoring			
Monitoring student behavior	10	10	100
Transitions between activities	10	8	80
6. Organizing instruction			
Attention spans	10	8	80
Good lesson pacing	10	8	80
Lessons related to student interests	6	8	75
7. Instructional clarity			
Describes objectives	10	8	80
Clear directions for academic work	10	6	60
Clear explanations and presentations	10	8	80
Student Behavior Variables			
High task engagement	8	7	88
Low amount of inappropriate behavior	10	8	80
Students use time constructively	7	5	71
Students take care of own needs	4	4	100
Students Outcome Variables			
Achievement gain in reading	3	3	100
Achievement gain in mathematics	3	3	100

Key variables from ten observational field experiments comparing teaching practices and student behavior in trained versus untrained teachers' classrooms.

*The number of studies in which the variable was measured.

**The number of studies in which the variable was measured in which it was statistically significant (or showed an effect size of ≥.40) in favor of the trained teachers.

Source: Herbert J. Walberg and Geneva Haertel: *Psychology and Educational Practice*, copyright 1997 by McCutchan Publishing Corporation, Richmond, California, 94806. Used by permission of the publisher.

☺ Organizing the Classroom

In many cases, the first impression about a teacher comes not from an interaction between the teacher and a student or a teacher and a parent but from the way the teacher has prepared the classroom. Everything in a classroom—the way the furniture is arranged, the types of materials displayed, the colors selected for the wall and bulletin boards, and the presence of or lack of clutter—sends unspoken messages about the teacher to students and their parents.

Teachers must be aware of the messages their classrooms convey and be sure that the messages are consistent with their values and goals. For example, Evertson and Harris (1997, 1999) state that classroom design sends a signal to students about how they are to interact and learn in the classroom. If desks touch or students sit together in groups at tables and chairs, the arrangement signals that collaboration and cooperation will be expected. If desks are arranged in traditional rows or are standing alone, the message is that their work will be done independently. Easily accessible learning centers and computer stations signal that they are there to be used by students. Comfortable chairs or pillows in a reading nook suggest that students will be expected to linger over a favorite book.

Problems develop when the message sent by the classroom arrangement does not match the teacher's style of instruction. If students are grouped together, they will talk to one another. If that is not the teacher's desire, traditional desks may be more appropriate. If materials are not to be used by students, teachers only invite problems when these materials are accessible to inquisitive hands. Teachers must analyze different arrangements for consistency with their instructional goals (Evertson & Harris, 1997).

Unfortunately, there are few ideal classrooms (Evertson, 1987). Few teachers have been fortunate enough to be able to design the space they will use as a classroom. Most teachers, especially new teachers, take the space assigned to them and strive to make it functional. However, regardless of the limitations of the space provided, teachers must consider three elements for effective organization of the classroom: visibility, accessibility, and distractibility.

Visibility.   Every student must be able to see teacher-led instruction, demonstrations, and presentations. Any instructional material that is presented via overhead, whiteboard, or monitor must be visible to every student without requiring them to move their chairs, turn their desk, or crane their necks (Evertson & Harris, 1997). Before the first day of class, teachers should sit in each student's desk to determine whether the student will be able to see and hear all teacher-led instruction.

It is equally important that the teacher can see all students, the student work areas, and learning centers. As Emmer, Evertson, and Worsham (2000) note, if students cannot be seen, it is difficult to determine whether they need assistance and to prevent off-task behavior.

Accessibility.   In order to provide the assistance needed and to maintain on-task behavior by proximity control, the teacher should be able to reach every student in the classroom quickly and without disturbing other students. High-traffic areas should be clear and separate. Careful attention must be paid to traffic patterns around pencil sharpeners, waste cans,

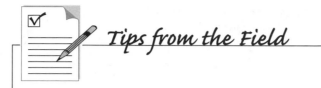

Tips from the Field

With more and more computers being used in the classroom, teachers need to limit the access to unauthorized sites by students. One way to avoid having students access inappropriate or unauthorized sites is to make sure that everything that appears on the computer monitor is accessible for view by the entire classroom.

   Knowing that the teacher or a classmate can easily see what is on the monitor, makes students less likely to access an inappropriate website. By having computer screens turned so the teacher can see them, teachers can work with groups or individual students while monitoring activity at the computer.

Anne Wall,
Grade 5 Teacher
Burt Elementary School
Clarksville, TN

and in-room water fountains. If areas for storing materials are poorly placed, distractions may occur when students get or return supplies. As Emmer, Evertson, and Worsham (2000) note, easy access to and efficient storage of instructional materials maintain lesson momentum and minimize wasted time. However, only teaching materials that students are allowed to touch should be left in places in which students gather.

Distractibility.   Before the first student arrives, the teacher should scan the room for distractions that might compete for the teacher's attention or encourage off-task behavior. Although teachers want classrooms that are attractive and inviting, they sometimes forget that excessive decoration can visually overstimulate some students. Other distractions include displays, toys, animal cages, and a myriad of other things that students may find more interesting than the material being presented. Remember that what might not be a distraction to the teacher or some students may distract others. Such distractions must be moved to another part of the classroom and away from the view of an individual student. Distractions that disrupt the entire classroom should be removed from the classroom.

   Evertson and Randolph (1999) stress that the way classroom space is used will have important implications for how students participate in class activities and how they interact with the teacher and each other. It is important to remember that how the classroom looks and feels will either hinder or support class activities. Consider how Nick, from the opening scenario, discovered that he had created a problem with the placement of his computer center.

   After his lunch with Monique, Nick decided that he needed specific rules and procedures for his computer center. He was pleased with the result and thought his

The creation of classroom procedures is a fundamental element of an effective classroom plan.

center was creative and very usable. However, he was disappointed the first day students used the center. Until students were working at the computers, he had not realized that students sharpening their pencils would have to lean over the students sitting at the computers to do so. After a day of quarreling and complaining by students either sharpening their pencils or working at the computers, Nick realized that he had to move the pencil sharpener or the computer center in order to resolve the problem.

ᴄ Planning and Teaching Rules and Procedures

Evertson and Randolph (1999) stress that rules and procedures are necessary to maintain lesson flow, continuity, and students' engagement in academic work. A carefully planned and systematically taught system of rules and procedures is necessary to communicate behavioral expectations to students and to ensure that the teacher's goals are met (Evertson & Harris, 1997). Efficient procedures and workable rules allow a variety of activities, or even several activities at a given time, to take place during a class with minimum confusion and wasted time.

TABLE 9.2   *Points to Consider in Rule Development*

- The rules should be stated so expectations are clear.
- Rationales for each rule should be provided.
- Rules should be selected that encourage a positive class climate.
- The list of rules should be kept as short as possible.
- Classroom rules should be consistent with school rules and policies.
- The students should be involved in rule development.
- Examples should be given to illustrate the rules.
- Rules should be taught in the same manner as other content.

Source: Evertson, C.M. (1987). Managing classrooms: A framework for teachers. In D. Berliner and B. Rosenshine (Eds.), *Talk to teachers*. New York: Random House.

Evertson and Harris (1997) state that rules are expected norms of general behavior. They make up the "constitution of the classroom" (p. 2.05e). They function to prevent or encourage certain behaviors. Unlike procedures, which change to meet classroom demands, rules do not change.

Evertson and Harris (1997) consider rule and procedure development the teacher's responsibility, and the teacher must make certain that the set of classroom rules and procedures is adequate and appropriate. However, many teachers include their students in the process of developing rules and procedures in order to promote ownership of rules and to encourage students to take responsibility for their behavior. The decision to involve students in rule making will depend on the maturity level of the students and the teacher's level of comfort in sharing responsibility with students.

Although it is important to keep the number of classroom rules short and manageable, the actual number of rules is not as critical as how rules are developed. Specific guidelines for rule development appear in Table 9.2.

Whereas rules lay out basic behavioral expectations, **procedures** are often the specific "how to's" that show students step by step how to successfully follow the rules (Evertson, 1987). Procedures function to make tasks routine, to communicate expectations for student behavior during a specific activity, and to aid in the transition from one activity to another. Unlike rules, they change according to needs that arise, and they have no prescribed number (Evertson & Harris, 1997).

Evertson and Harris (1999) note that both rules and procedures should be taught to students and that the teaching of rules and procedures is no different than teaching other content. Rules and procedures must be taught with an emphasis on developing rationale for the rules and procedures and on providing students with cues for self-monitoring. Teachers must remember that skills must be practiced, and a single presentation of a procedure is not adequate for student comprehension or continued use of the procedure. Consider how Monique teaches her classroom rules and procedures to her students:

> "Class, yesterday we looked at our second rule: 'We ask permission to use someone else's things.' Today we are going to discuss our third rule: 'We will use appropriate voices.' Who wants to tell me what this means?"

Several hands went up and Monique called on Murray. "I think it means that we should be quiet and not disturb others."

"Well, yes, there are times when we should be quiet, but does this mean we have to be quiet all the time? Are there times we can make lots of noise? Dana, when is it all right to make lots of noise?"

Hesitating, Dana said, "I guess it is all right to make lots of noise on the playground or in the gym."

"Dana, that is a great answer. Of course, you can make lots of noise on the playground. In fact," she says, as she moves to the tape recorder, "I made a tape of you when you were at recess yesterday. Let's hear how you sounded." As Monique played the tape of the children on the playground, several students laughed when they heard their own voices shouting or calling out to someone.

"Wow, you were making a lot of noise, but you weren't breaking a rule. That is how I *expect* you to sound when you are on the playground. Does everyone understand what I mean?" Monique looked around the room and noticed that all students appeared to understand. "Now, I want us to develop a procedure so you will know when you are and when you aren't making the correct amount of noise. I thought we might develop a number system. Let's create a system that goes from one to five. One will be the quietest you should be, and five will be the loudest you can be. So, when you can be really noisy, like on the playground, we would be at our highest level of noise. So, if I hold up five fingers, you know you can be as loud as you want. Let me write this on the board." Monique wrote a 5 on the board and then wrote beside it, "Loud shouting, yelling, laughing—appropriate for the playground or the gym."

"Now, let's think of the opposite of our number five. Can you demonstrate how you would sound if I held up one finger?" Monique watched as every student got still and became very quiet. "Wow, that is really quiet. When would we need to be that quiet?"

For the next hour, the students and Monique talked about the appropriate noise levels for their class. "OK, let's practice our procedure." Monique held up one finger and everyone got very quiet. When she held up two fingers, the students whispered to the person next to them. "Great job, now I think we will have to wait to practice level 5 until we are on the playground. Does everyone understand our procedure? Any questions?"

Managing Student Work and Improving Student Accountability

Evertson and Harris (1997, 1999) suggest that the ultimate goal of an effective classroom-management system is to teach student responsibility. Unfortunately, many students do not understand the connection between their effort and the results of their effort. Therefore, effective teachers not only hold students accountable for their academic work and their behavior but also teach them how to be accountable (Evertson & Randolph, 1999).

This is done by establishing a system of clearly communicated expectations for students and providing as much responsibility to students as possible. Evertson and Harris

(1997) note that effective student-accountability systems consist of two essential elements that must be designed and managed. One element establishes student responsibility by providing clear explanations about what students must do to be successful. The second element requires teachers to model responsible behavior by being consistent in their grading and feedback to students. For these two elements to be successful in developing independent learners, teachers must:

- *Provide clear and specific instructions for overall work requirements.* Evertson and Harris (1997) recommend that assignments and important instructions be put on a whiteboard, overhead projector, or flip chart and that assignments requiring detailed instructions should be provided both orally and in writing.
- *Communicate assignments and instructions, so that every child understands.* Teachers should go over instructions orally with the class, questioning students about their understanding of the directions and providing examples of the work expected. For large projects and assignments, substages should be developed with clear deadlines and goals for each of the substages.
- *Monitor students' work; keep track of what students are doing.* Evertson and Randolph (1999) stress that effective classroom managers monitor their classes and students for signs of student confusion. Monitoring indicates the importance and appropriateness of the assignment. Monitoring student progress helps identify students who are having difficulty and allows the teacher to encourage other students to keep working.
- *Establish routines for turning in work.* To enable teachers to keep accurate records about who completed their work, students should be told when and where assignments are to be placed.
- *Provide regular academic feedback to students; check their work.* Students' work should be checked in order to provide feedback and correctives, and rechecked to make certain students are learning concepts correctly (Evertson, 1987). Evertson and Harris (1997) suggest that teachers plan specifically and in advance how they will handle student work, how they will check the work, and what portion of students' grades will be based on tests, daily assignments, homework, and special projects.
- *Establish routines for handling makeup work.* Student accountability often fails when students are absent. Absent students miss instructions and directions for assignments. Establishing routines for handling makeup work is critical for effective teaching. Consider how Nick solved his makeup-work problem:

One morning Nick was waiting for Monique when she arrived at school. "Hey, Monique, come to my room. I want to show what I did over the weekend. You are going to be very impressed."

Laughing, Monique followed Nick into his room and to the computer on his desk. "All right. I'm waiting. Impress me."

"Look," Nick said as he pulled up the new web site he had developed for his class.

"Nick, I *am* impressed. How did you know how to do this?"

"Well, I knew some basics and just figured out the rest. But I want you to see the best part. When you click on homework, you not only see each day's homework, you can actually print out the assignment. Now, if a student is absent, the student or the student's parents can just come to the website and see what was missed. If students don't have a computer at home, they can go to the computer center and print out their assignments. I don't have to remember to tell the students what they missed, and students have no excuse for not keeping up with the homework. Now, let me show you what else you can do."

Maintaining Good Student Behavior

Unfortunately, even the most effective teachers will have students who challenge the classroom rules and procedures. In some cases, these challenges disrupt the classroom and interfere with other students or class activities (Evertson, 1989). In other cases, the challenge is not disruptive to others but results in off-task behavior. In either case, the teacher must intervene and redirect the student's behavior. However, as Evertson and Harris (1997) note, teaching, not punishment, is the goal.

Maintaining good student behavior requires a combination of consequences, intervention strategies, and communication. Having a reasonable set of positive, negative, and corrective consequences for rules and procedures, and consistently using them when appropriate, makes classroom expectations predictable to students and encourages them to be self-governing. It is important to have a range of consequences for two reasons. First, a range of consequences allows the teacher to deal appropriately with the level of misbehavior. Second, what might be punishment to one student might be rewarding to another. Having a pre-planned set of consequences and intervention strategies will increase the teachers' ability to manage the classroom (Evertson & Harris, 1999).

Positive consequences, in the form of extrinsic incentives or rewards, follow behavior and serve to increase or maintain behavior. Incentives and rewards can be emotional, psychological, or academic. The incentive and reward selected will depend on the age, interest, and maturity level of the student.

Corrective consequences are specific strategies for helping students manage their own behavior. In using a correcting consequence, the teacher has the student practice the desired behavior or procedure. In some cases, it is necessary to reteach the procedure to ensure that students understand what they are to do. The goal of corrective consequences is to help students consciously think about their actions. Evertson and Harris (1997) provide suggestions for two corrective consequences: self-recording and self-instruction. In self-recording, the students take responsibility by recording each time they exhibit a desired behavior. In self-instruction, students verbalize what they are to do.

Negative consequences are undesired consequences that follow a behavior and are used to decrease the unwanted behavior. However, Evertson and Harris (1992) note that punishment or negative consequences neither teach desirable behavior nor instill a desire to behave. They recommend that negative consequences and punishments be used only when it is necessary to respond to repeated misbehavior. Possible negative consequences include withholding a privilege or desired activity, isolating or removing students, assigning detention, or using a school-based consequence such as in-school suspension (Evertson, Emmer, & Worsham, 2000). Evertson and Harris (1997) remind teachers that "Your ultimate goal is to teach students appropriate behavior and to have them increase and/or maintain that behavior, not just stop behaviors that are disruptive or inappropriate" (p. 4.25E).

Intervention strategies redirect budding student misbehavior. Intervention strategies stop misbehavior, reinvolve students in the lesson, keep the climate of the classroom positive, and do not disrupt teaching. Selecting the best time to use intervention strategies depends on the teacher's belief about the cause of the problem. Possible intervention strategies include making eye contact, using proximity control, reminding students of the rule or procedure, and questioning students about their behavior.

When dealing with student misbehavior, it is always important to choose battles carefully. It is impossible to respond to each and every situation of off-task or inappropriate behavior. Some behaviors can be ignored, and others should never be ignored. In addition, the battles are different for different teachers. What one teacher considers important to control may not be important to another. For example, Monique and Nick found they disagree as to which behaviors to battle.

> When Monique joined Nick in the faculty lounge at lunch, she noticed that he was unusually quiet. "Hey, what's wrong? Have you had a rough morning?"
>
> "No, I guess not. Mr. Silkowski evaluated me this morning. He ranked me high on everything but classroom management. He said that often my students are too loud. I don't think they are too loud, do you?"
>
> Avoiding eye contact, Monique said "Well . . ."
>
> "Monique, do you agree with him? I realize I don't keep my students as quiet as your students, but the noise doesn't bother me. Why should it bother Mr. Silkowski?"
>
> "Nick, I realize that the noise doesn't bother you, but it might bother other teachers. I have to admit that sometimes my class can hear your students when they are playing a game or having a discussion. Then my students wonder why they have to be so quiet. And there is another problem."
>
> "What? What other problem?"
>
> "Well, have you considered what happens to your students when they leave you? I doubt that most teachers will be as tolerant as you are. Won't your students be confused about how much noise they are allowed to make?"
>
> Nick thought about what Monique had said, "Maybe. I will have to think about what you said. But, Monique, I don't want to have to use some 1–5 system like you do. That is just not me. I don't want to punish them for being excited about learning."
>
> "Then don't punish them. Reward them instead. Determine some reward you can give when students are talking at an appropriate level. Classroom management isn't only about punishing, you know."

Planning and Organizing Instruction

Too often, traditional classroom models overlook the critical relationship between instruction and management. Evertson and Randolph (1999) suggest that effective classroom management has typically been regarded as a precondition for instruction. However, in reality, the concept that management is isolated from content is faulty, because management carries messages about the value of content. How the classroom is being managed during particular learning activities must be considered with content as plans and activities are developed. Evertson and Randolph (1999) see good classroom-management practices as inseparable from good instructional practices. A critical element of COMP is planning for the interplay between management and instruction.

How teachers teach has changed as classrooms have moved from a teacher-centered focus to a student-centered focus. As Evertson and Randolph (1999) note, "Silent children seated in straight rows portray the history of American education, not its future" (p. 249). Teachers now present content using a full range of instructional strategies that include whole-group instruction, teacher-led groups, cooperative groups, student pairs, centers and stations, computerized and online instruction, and individualized instruction. Management demands in these classrooms are significantly different from those in teacher-centered classrooms (Randolph & Evertson, 1994).

For every classroom task, there are both academic and social dimensions (Evertson & Harris, 1997; Randolph & Evertson, 1994). In each situation, students not only have to determine what they are to learn but also how they are to participate in the learning process. Teacher-centered activities make different demands on both students and teachers than activities that are student centered. The more complex the instruction, the more important it is that teachers plan for both instruction and management. Regardless of the instructional method, it is the teacher's job to think through the learning process with a focus on the tasks of both the teacher and the students. Consider how Monique manages her class as she prepares her classwork using learning centers.

> After Monique's students completed their morning review, she asked them to gather around her on the reading rug. "Who noticed that the classroom looks different this morning?" Monique waited as every hand went up. "Well, today we are beginning a study of the Southeast. Now, around the room, I have created six learning centers. Each center focuses on one of the states we will be studying. Each center has activities you and your team members are to do at the center. You will spend two days at each center, and then you will move to the next center. You have worked in cooperative groups before, and our procedures for working in groups apply when you work in the centers. Katlin, will you tell us the procedures for working in groups?"
>
> When Katlin finished telling the procedures, Monique says, "Great job! Now, today I want to go over the rules and procedures for working in centers, and I want to go over what you will be expected to do at each center. Tomorrow, you will actually work in your centers. All right, our first center focuses on the state of Florida. Ginny, please read the written directions for this center."

❧ Conducting Instruction and Maintaining the Momentum

The first five elements of COMP are designed to establish a well-managed classroom from the beginning of the school year. The last element, Conducting Instruction and Maintaining the Momentum, provides consistency in maintaining the management system. Evertson and

Harris (1997, 1999) state that in order to reduce potential behavior problems and maintain student involvement in the instructional activities, teachers must:

- *provide clear instructions.* Communicating information and directions in a clear, comprehensible way is an important teaching skill. This begins with the teacher establishing appropriate objectives and helping students understand the relevance of what they are learning. Clarity includes providing clear procedural directions that enable students to know what to do and how to perform the task.
- *check for students' understanding of what they are to do.* Instructions for assignments must be given precisely, and the teacher must be able to respond to students' questions with understandable explanations. It also involves checking student understanding in other ways, such as questioning them, having students demonstrate the steps, or using other means of detecting potential problems with academic material.
- *monitor students' behavior.* Monitoring involves regularly surveying the class or groups to watch for signs of confusion. Teachers should make a practice of routinely checking students and attending to nonverbal cues in order to catch problems before errors are practiced and reinforced.
- *provide for smooth transitions.* It is during transitions that students most often waste time, get off task, or engage in inappropriate behavior. Teachers must plan for transitions as carefully as they plan for instruction.

At the end of a long day, Monique stopped by Nick's classroom to find him working on his lesson plans. "Trying to get ready for tomorrow?"

"No, I'm just making notes. Today was a disaster. The students were to start their social studies project today. I thought I was clear in my instructions, but no one seemed to understand what I wanted them to do. Then I tried to explain again, and things just got worse. So, I'm making notes. You know, if I teach this again next year, I don't want to make the same mistakes. Sometimes I find I spend more time thinking about what didn't work than I do making new plans."

"Well, don't stay too late. Hopefully things will go better tomorrow."

Returning to his plans, Nick says, "I'm working out all the details tonight, so that I make sure that tomorrow goes better than today did. Good night."

> (pic)

RESULTS OF RESEARCH OF PROGRAM

The effectiveness of COMP has been extensively researched since its implementation in 1989. The research on COMP was conducted in three phases—descriptive, correlational, and experimental. Program results have been measured with observational field studies, teacher's self-evaluation reports, and administration reports of observed classroom, teacher, and student change (Evertson & Harris, 1995, 1999). The three main findings from this research indicate that:

1. Students of teachers who had participated in COMP obtain greater gains in academic achievement, as measured by standardized tests, than do students of teachers who had not participated in the program.

2. Teachers who participated in COMP instituted classroom practices that resulted in classroom environments more conducive to students' learning.

3. Students of teachers trained to use COMP showed a significant decrease in inappropriate and disruptive behavior and a significant increase in academic achievement.

COMP in the Classroom

Scenario

By the end of their first year of teaching, Nick and Monique were proud of their accomplishments. They realized that part of their success had resulted from their friendship and collaboration. Throughout the year, they shared teaching ideas, discipline problems, and successes. Nick had become a better classroom manager because of Monique's influence. Nick helped Monique create a class website and taught her strategies for incorporating computer activities into her instruction. When Nick agreed to direct the Founder's Day pageant, Monique helped by designing and making the costumes. Recognizing what Nick and Monique had accomplished through their collaboration, Mr. Silkowski established a mentor program for all first-year teachers.

Strengths and Weaknesses of COMP

(Dic)

Perhaps the greatest strength of COMP comes from its research base. COMP was created from the research designed to identify the characteristics and actions of effective classroom managers, and since its creation, the success of the program has been extensively researched. This research provides credibility to the program.

Weinstein (1999) suggests that an additional strength of COMP is its emphasis on preventing inappropriate behavior rather than simply reacting to inappropriate behavior. COMP provides a body of knowledge and a set of practices that require thoughtful decision making by the teacher.

COMP provides a learner-centered approach to classroom management. Teaching self-management skills helps build a positive relationship between student and teacher.

However, some argue that for teachers dealing with violent or out-of-control students, COMP fails to provide guidance on how to deal with these difficult situations.

Summary

Classroom Organization and Management Program (COMP), created by Carolyn Evertson, is the result of 30 years of research. COMP was developed from descriptive, correlational, and experimental research studies designed to discover successful key management practices and strategies. A proactive approach, COMP is designed to help teachers improve overall instructional and management skills through planning, implementing, and maintaining effective practices. COMP provides a system of classroom management through proactive planning at the beginning of the school year and thoughtful decision making throughout the year. The system emphasizes the integration of management and instruction as a means of creating a positive learning environment.

KEY TERMINOLOGY

Definitions for these terms appear in the glossary:

Accessibility

Classroom Organization and Management
    Program (COMP)

Corrective consequences

Distractibility

Intervention strategies

Negative consequences

Positive consequences

Procedures

Visibility

CHAPTER ACTIVITIES

Reflecting on the Theory

1. Ms. Booker is reconsidering her teaching strategies. She had hoped to use collaborative learning as her primary teaching strategy. However, she is finding that she is uncomfortable with the noise level in the classroom. She finds she is constantly telling the students to lower their voices and everyone is miserable, especially Ms. Booker.

   How can Ms. Booker use the strategies presented in COMP to resolve her classroom problems?

2. One of the fundamental principles of COMP is that classroom management and instruction are integrally related. Do you agree? Why or why not?

3. Throughout the chapter, Nick and Monique worked together to improve their teaching and classroom management. What lessons did they learn from each other? Have you found that such cooperative collaboration occurs in most school settings? Explain your answer.

4. Evertson's research clearly shows a correlation between management and academic achievement. What might be some of the reasons for such a correlation?

Developing Your Portfolio

1. Consider one classroom procedure you will need in your classroom. Analyze this procedure and provide a listing of the behaviors expected of your students.

2. Evertson contends that the way a classroom looks and is designed sends messages to parents and students. Analyze a classroom in which you have observed to

determine what message the classroom is sending about:

- the teacher's instructional style
- the teacher's personal values
- the teacher's organizational skills
- the teacher's classroom management

3. Analyze the classroom in question 2 for accessibility, distractibility, and visibility.
4. Evertson contends that for every classroom task, there are both academic and social dimensions, because students must not only determine what they are to learn but also how they are to participate in the learning process. Consider the subject-area content you will teach. What are the social dimensions of learning your content? How must students participate in the learning process to learn your content? How will your subject-area content influence how you manage your classroom?

Developing Your Personal Philosophy of Classroom Management

1. Evertson and Randolph state, "Silent children seated in straight rows portray the history of American education, not its future." What is your reaction to this quote?
2. Would you be comfortable using COMP as your classroom-management plan in your classroom? Why or why not? Are there some strategies that you will definitely incorporate into your classroom-management plan?

RESOURCES FOR FURTHER STUDY

Further information about Classroom Organization and Management Program and resources for its use in the classroom can be found by contacting:

Dr. Carolyn Evertson
Dr. Alene H. Harris
Classroom Organization and Management Program
Vanderbilt University
Box 541
Peabody College
Nashville, TN 37203
(615) 322-8100

CHAPTER REFERENCES

Brophy, J. E., & Evertson, C. M. (1976). *Learning from teaching: A developmental perspective*. Boston: Allyn & Bacon.
Emmer, E., Evertson, C. M., & Anderson, L. (1980). Effective management at the beginning of the school year. *Elementary School Journal, 80*, 219–231.

Emmer, E. T., Evertson, C. M., & Worsham, M. E. (2000). *Classroom management for secondary teachers* (5th ed.). Needham Heights, MA: Allyn & Bacon.

Evertson, C. M. (1985). Training teachers in classroom management: An experimental study in secondary school classrooms. *Journal of Educational Research, 79,* 51–58.

Evertson, C. M. (1987). Managing classrooms: A framework for teachers. In D. Berliner and B. Rosenshine (Eds.), *Talk to teachers.* New York: Random House.

Evertson, C. M. (1989) Improving elementary classroom management: A school-based training program for beginning the year. *Journal of Educational Research, 93,* 82–90.

Evertson, C., & Anderson, L. (1979). Beginning school. *Educational Horizons, 57,* 164–168.

Evertson, C. M., & Emmer, E. (1982). Effective management at the beginning of the school year in junior high classes. *Journal of Educational Psychology, 74,* 485–498.

Evertson, C. M., Emmer, E. T., Sanford, J. P., & Clements, B. S. (1983). Improving classroom management: An experiment in elementary school classrooms. *The Elementary School Journal, 84,* 173–188.

Evertson, C. M., Emmer, E. T., & Worsham, M. E. (2000). *Classroom management for elementary teachers* (5th ed.). Needham Heights, MA: Allyn & Bacon.

Evertson, C. M., & Harris, A. H. (1992). What we know about managing classrooms. *Educational Leadership, 49,* 74–78.

Evertson, C. M., & Harris, A. H. (1995). *Classroom organization and management program: Revalidation submission to the program effectiveness panel, U. S. Department of Education.* Nashville, TN: Vanderbilt University. (ERIC Document Reproduction Service No. ED403247).

Evertson, C. M., & Harris, A. H. (1996). COMP: *Classroom organization and management program: An inservice program for effective proactive classroom management.* Washington, DC: National Diffusion Network.

Evertson, C. M., & Harris, A. H. (1997) COMP – *A workbook manual for elementary teachers* (5th ed.). Nashville, TN: Vanderbilt University.

Evertson, C. M., & Harris, A. H. (1999). Support for managing learning-center classrooms. In H. Jerome Freiberg (Ed.), *Beyond behaviorism: Changing the classroom management paradigm.* Boston. Allyn & Bacon.

Evertson, C. M., & Randolph, C. H. (1999). Perspectives on classroom management in learning-centered classrooms. In Hersholt C. Waxman and Herbert J. Walberg (Eds.), *New Directions for teaching practice and research.* Berkeley, CA: McCutchan.

Marchant, G. J., & Newman, I. (1996). Mentoring education: An interview with Carolyn M. Evertson. *Mid-Western Educational Researcher, 9,* 26–28.

Randolph, C. H., & Evertson, C. M. (1994). Images of management for learning-centered classrooms. *Action in Teacher Education, 16,* 55–63.

Weinstein, C. S. (1999). Reflections on best practices and promising programs: Beyond assertive classroom discipline. In H. Jerome Freiberg (Ed.), *Beyond behaviorism: Changing the classroom management paradigm.* Boston: Allyn & Bacon.

Part

III

Classroom Management as Instruction

Four models that have as their central focus the teaching of prosocial skills are presented in Part III: Classroom Management as Instruction. The first model presented in Chapter 10 is Barbara Coloroso's Inner Discipline. Chapter 11 provides a review of Ellen McGinnis and Arnold Goldstein's model, Skillstreaming. Several approaches to teaching Conflict Resolution and Peer Mediation are presented in Chapter 12. Finally, Forrest Gathercoal's model, Judicious Discipline, is the focus of Chapter 13. The models presented in Part III: Classroom Management as Instruction share the following characteristics:

- A key to effective classroom management is teaching appropriate behavior and social skills.
- Effective classroom management does not focus on behavior at a particular moment but on helping students develop positive interactions throughout their lifetime.
- Students must be taught to take responsibility for their behavior.
- The goal of classroom management is to establish habits of peacemaking.
- Teachers must help students to learn to make ethical judgments and decisions.
- Teachers must ensure that students' rights are honored and respected.
- Classroom management is a form of guidance.
- Discipline comes from the self, not from outside authorities.
- Students must share in classroom responsibilities.

Chapter 10

Inner Discipline

Objectives

Chapter 10 prepares preservice teachers to meet INTASC standards #2 (Student Development), #5 (Motivation and Management), #6 (Communication) and #9 (Reflective Practitioner) by helping them to:

- evaluate the philosophical tenets upon which Inner Discipline is based.
- understand the basic principles of Reconciliatory Justice.
- learn the importance of communicating six critical life messages to students.
- evaluate classrooms to determine whether they are a jellyfish classroom, brick-wall classroom, or a backbone classroom.
- learn techniques for applying Inner Discipline in the classroom.
- differentiate between punishment and discipline.

Scenario

Entering the biology classroom, eleventh-graders Gus Beebe and Brenton Hatch are cutting up. As Gus playfully punches Brenton in the arm, Brenton falls backward into the lab experiment that has been placed on the table. Before either boy knows what is happening, broken beakers and lab equipment cover the floor. The sound of breaking glass gets the attention of the other students and Ms. Schallenberger.

"Brenton, are you cut or hurt?" Ms. Schallenberger asks as she reaches the boys.

"No, I'm not hurt." Looking around at the destroyed lab equipment, Brenton says, "Gee, Ms. Schallenberger, we're sorry. We didn't mean for this to happen."

"I know you were just joking around, but now we have a big problem—a problem we need to solve quickly. Go to the storage room and get what you need to clean up this mess. While I start class, I want you to clean up this area. Then I want you to sit at the table in the back of the room and think about three things. First, how do you intend to replace the broken equipment? Second, given that your lab equipment is broken, how are you going to do your assignment? Finally, I want you to think of how you are going to keep this from happening again. I want the answer to these three issues when class is over." Turning from the boys, Ms. Schallenberger announces that it is time for class to begin.

INTRODUCTION

The first model presented as an example of Classroom Management as Instruction is Barbara Coloroso's theory, **Inner Discipline**. Like Ms. Schallenberger, Coloroso is more concerned with having students think about their behaviors and how their behaviors impact others than with providing punishments and consequences for inappropriate behavior. Coloroso (1994) sees the primary role of teachers as guiding students to make their own decisions and to take responsibility for their choices. The model is based on three key concepts:

1. Development of inner discipline is more important than traditional classroom control.
2. Problem solving is key to developing inner discipline.
3. Students must be taught *how* to think, not *what* to think.

TABLE 10.1 *Critical Life Messages*

Coloroso's Critical Life Messages for Students
• I believe in you.
• I trust you.
• I know you can handle this.
• You are listened to.
• You are cared for.
• You are very important to me.

Coloroso (1990) contends that through classroom instruction and positive teacher–student interactions, students are empowered to trust in themselves and to learn self-discipline. When students learn the supporting principles

- I like myself,
- I can think for myself, and
- there is no problem so great that it can't be solved,

they are buffered against life's evils such as drug abuse, sexual promiscuity, and suicide.

Coloroso (1994) stresses that empowering students begins with giving them a secure, safe, nurturing environment. Such an environment encourages creative, constructive, and responsible activity (Coloroso, 1997). In this environment, students are encouraged through the communication of one or more critical life messages. These critical messages, which appear in Table 10.1, can be communicated through the teacher's words or actions.

Coloroso suggests that these messages need no definition or explanation. If communicated in a caring, sincere manner, students will accept these messages and be empowered by them.

THREE TYPES OF CLASSROOMS

Coloroso (1990) observes that schools and individual classrooms in these schools follow one of three models. According to Coloroso, classrooms can be described as jellyfish classrooms, brick-wall classrooms, or backbone classrooms.

The **jellyfish classroom** has no structure. Like a jellyfish, the teacher's expectations are constantly shifting. In such classrooms, punishments are arbitrary and inconsistent. Therefore, students are never quite sure of how they are to act or respond. Students cannot predict whether they will or will not be punished for violations to classroom policy, because punishment is based on gender, ethnicity, or some other personal characteristic rather than on a fixed discipline plan. If there are rules, they are vague and contain phrases like "Be kind" or "Be thoughtful" without giving students a clear meaning of what is expected of them.

The **brick-wall classroom** is a dictatorship in which rules are rigid and unbending. Like a brick wall, teachers are unyielding in how they handle the classrooms. Individual

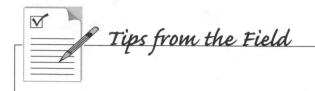

Tips from the Field

I want to build a relationship with my students. One way of doing this is through dialogue journals (5″ × 7″ spiral notebooks) where kids can write about anything they wish, and they put it in a basket on my desk. I take a few home each night and write personal notes to the kids, asking them about what they write or praising them for something in class. I also hold weekly class meetings where we discuss problems in class and work out solutions. I stress that we are a community.

Colleen King
Grade 1 Teacher
Parkview Elementary School
Carpentersville, IL

needs or motivations are not considered when giving consequences for inappropriate behavior. Rules are used to control or manipulate students, and all power is in the hands of the teacher. Often, the students are controlled by physical threats, humiliation, and bribes. In the brick-wall classroom, students are told *what* to think, not taught *how* to think.

The **backbone classroom** provides a consistent structure that is flexible and functional. Students are listened to and learn to respect themselves and others. Students learn to accept their own feelings and to act on these feelings in a reasonable way. In the backbone classroom, students are given second chances, because mistakes are viewed as opportunities to learn. The goal is to teach students how to problem solve and to think before they act (Coloroso, 1994). Teachers model the desired behaviors by:

- acknowledging their own feelings and labeling them.
- admitting that they are angry, hurt, or afraid, and by modeling appropriate ways to express these feelings.
- making assertive statements about themselves.
- acknowledging students' feelings as real and legitimate without passing judgment on those feelings.
- teaching students how to handle their own problems.

DISCIPLINE IN A BACKBONE CLASSROOM

The focus of teachers in backbone classrooms is on discipline rather than on punishment. Coloroso (1990, 1994, 2001) stresses that contrary to popular belief, discipline is not synonymous with punishment. To Coloroso, there is a clear distinction between punishment and discipline. Coloroso describes punishment as punitive actions that:

- are adult-oriented,
- require judgment,
- impose power from without,
- arouse anger and resentment, and
- invite more conflict.

Such actions include physical isolation, embarrassment and humiliation, shaming, emotional isolation, grounding, and brute force. Under the guise of discipline, physical and emotional violence toward children is allowed and legitimized. However, Coloroso stresses that teachers should never rely on such actions to promote the positive behaviors teachers desire in their students.

According to Coloroso (1994), discipline differs from punishment because discipline involves real-world consequences or interventions or a combination of both. Discipline deals with the reality of the situation, not with the power and control of the teacher. Discipline gives life to a student's learning in a way that punishment cannot because it:

- shows children what they have done wrong.
- gives them ownership of the problem.
- gives them ways to solve the problems they created.
- leaves their dignity intact (Coloroso 1997, 2001).

Discipline allows students to make legitimate choices and to face the consequences of these choices. **Real-world consequences**, according to Coloroso (1994), either happen naturally or are reasonable consequences that are intrinsically related to a student's actions. Although natural consequences are often the greatest learning tool, if the natural consequences are life threatening, morally threatening, or unhealthy, the teacher must intervene and provide real-world consequences that are safe and appropriate.

With real-world consequences, actions and consequences match. Coloroso suggests that teachers use the acronym RSVP to determine whether a consequence is appropriate:

R Is the consequence *reasonable*? For example, it is reasonable to expect students who leave their lunch table dirty to return to the cafeteria and clean up their mess. It is *not* reasonable to require them to clean the entire cafeteria. The first consequence requires students to be responsible for their own behavior, whereas the second punishes them rather than teaches a life lesson.

S Is it *simple*? Many times, when consequences are given, other people are inconvenienced by the consequences. For example, requiring students to miss recess while they complete homework is a simple consequence. Requiring students to come to school on Saturday morning requires coordination between the teacher, the parents, and other school personnel. Although such a consequence might be reasonable, it is not simple.

V Is it *valuable* as a learning tool? Any time a consequence is given, the teacher must analyze the lesson to be learned. In the first two examples, students are taught that they must be responsible for their behaviors. If in the first example, however, the teacher had required the students to write "I will not leave the lunch table dirty" a hundred times on the blackboard or in their notebooks, the students would have learned little.

P Is it *practical*? Does the consequence take time away from the goal of the class? Often, consequences prevent students from being involved in the classroom and learning the required material. For example, Coloroso (1990) points out that students who are tardy are often required to leave the classroom to retrieve a tardy note. The result is that they are even later to class and have missed even more of the required material. Such a consequence is not practical, because it is counter to the goal of the classroom.

Regardless of how reasonable the consequences of inappropriate behavior are, students will try to get teachers to back down or give in on punishments they hand out. They use what Coloroso calls the three cons—begging, bribing, weeping, wailing, and teeth gnashing; showing anger and aggression; and sulking—to get teachers to change the consequences. However, if the consequences meet the four conditions outlined above, such tactics on the part of student should be ignored.

RULE SETTING IN THE BACKBONE CLASSROOM

Although Coloroso is less concerned with rule development than with helping students to become productive classroom citizens, she recognizes that rules are necessary in all areas of society. Coloroso (1997, 2001) proposes that rules should be simple, clearly stated, and related to life's expectations. She suggests that such expectations, whether at a job or as a student, fall into four categories:

- Show up on time.
- Be prepared.
- Do assignments.
- Respect your own and others' life space.

When students choose to break or ignore these rules, they must learn that choices have consequences. However, these consequences should be designed to teach rather than to punish.

PROBLEM SOLVING IN A BACKBONE CLASSROOM

Coloroso (1994) considers problem solving a key to helping develop inner discipline. Therefore, it is the teacher's responsibility to help students develop problem-solving skills. The age of the students will determine the teacher's involvement in the process of problem solving. If the student is in middle or high school, the teacher may simply be a "sounding board" for the student who is reviewing several options for solving the problem. If the student is in elementary school, the teacher may need to suggest solutions or actively intervene if the student is not mentally, emotionally, or physically capable of solving the

Coloroso stresses that teachers must help students learn problem-solving skills in order for students to develop inner discipline.

problem. The goal for all students is to develop problem-solving skills that will serve them for their entire lifetime.

Coloroso stresses that before beginning the process of solving a problem, it is critical to know who "owns" the problem. Who is involved in the problem will also determine the amount of involvement by the teacher. If the problem is between a student and the teacher, the teacher must be involved in the solution. If the problem is between a student and another student, the teacher may act as facilitator who helps the students develop a plan for solving the problem. This empowers students by sending them a message which says, "You have a problem; I know you can solve it" (Coloroso, 1990 [film]).

Coloroso (1994) provides six steps to teaching problem solving:

1. *Identify and define the problem.* Part of defining the problem is allowing students to discuss their feelings. Students need to realize that everyone has the right to be happy, concerned, joyful, sad, angry, or frustrated. The critical issue, therefore, is not what students are feeling but how they *handle* those feelings. Students must learn that although they cannot always control situations, they can control their *reactions* to situations.

In defining the problem, it is important to help students get to the root problem. Often the focus is on the result of a problem rather than the actual problem itself. For example, if Eric goes to sleep in each class, having Eric move around the classroom or get a drink of water may temporarily solve the problem. However, it does not solve the fact that Eric is not getting enough sleep at night. The solution may need to involve parents, other students, other faculty members, and administrators. Students alone cannot solve some problems.

2. *List possible solutions*. Encourage students to consider every possible solution and to brainstorm without passing judgment. Allow students time to think about possible solutions.

3. *Evaluate the options*. Students should first list the options and then consider the consequences of these options. The teacher is there to guide, to support, to encourage, and to help students think through each solution carefully. If the option creates a bigger problem, nothing has been resolved. As students evaluate the options, they must be conscious of the effect of the solution on others and ask:

> Is it unkind?
> Is it hurtful?
> Is it unfair?
> Is it dishonest?

4. *Choose one option*. Although there may be several ways to solve a problem, students must decide on the plan of action they will follow. In some cases, multiple steps may be needed to resolve the issue. Teachers should help students prioritize the steps that must be taken. It is helpful to start with a goal that is achievable in a relatively short period of time to provide for reinforcement of the effort.

5. *Make a plan*. If the plan involves several steps, it is important to have students act on one step and report the result. It may then be necessary to revise the plan if the original solution is not working.

6. *Reevaluate the problem and the student*. Coloroso (1994) stresses that this is an important missed step in problem solving, but that it is important in the learning process. This review should include a discussion of the causes of the problem and how to avoid them in the future.

Coloroso (2001) states that the six-step problem-solving model allows for **Reconciliatory Justice**—Restitution, Resolution, and Reconciliation. Restitution involves fixing the damage that has been done to another person's property. Resolution requires identifying and correcting the deeper issues causing the situation. Reconciliation is the process of helping those hurt by the situation to heal. Through this process, students are taught to fix problems they create, to prevent situations from happening again, and to heal with people they have harmed.

CLASS MEETINGS IN THE BACKBONE CLASSROOM

Many classroom problems can be solved through the six-step problem-solving model. If the problem is more complex or affects several people, a class meeting may be needed to find a solution. Coloroso (1990) notes that much stress and tension can build in an average

Tips from the Field

I learned a wonderful technique for solving classroom problems from my cooperating teacher during my student teaching. She used a method called "Having a Bone to Pick." My cooperating teacher made copies of skeleton bones and placed each child's name on a bone. Her name also appeared on a bone. These were placed on a bulletin board. Whenever a student had a problem with another child or with the teacher, they went to the board and "picked a bone." At the end of the day, she allowed fifteen minutes for resolving issues. If a student had picked the bone of another student, they went to a quiet location to work out their differences. If a student had picked the teacher's bone, he or she came to the teacher's desk to discuss the issue. This discipline plan teaches children to resolve their problem in a diplomatic way and prevents small issues from escalating.

> Candida Phelps
> Special Education Teacher
> Rivermont Elementary School
> Hixen, TN

school day and, if unresolved, can cause students to be tired, irritable, and unable to concentrate. The class meeting is an excellent way to reduce this stress and tension.

Class meetings are wonderful vehicles for teaching democracy. Coloroso (1997) stresses that students learn democracy through experiences. To learn democracy, students must participate in activities that allow them to resolve conflicts in a nonaggressive manner.

Coloroso (1994) states that there are three basic requirements for class meetings:

1. The problem must be important and relevant to the entire class.
2. The teacher must be willing to provide nonjudgmental leadership.
3. The meeting must be handled in such a way that all feel willing to share, and students feel it is safe to express their feelings.

INNER DISCIPLINE IN THE CLASSROOM

Scenario

As sixth-grade social studies teacher Elizabeth Shepherd begins class, she notices that Saki is standing at her desk with tears streaming down her face. Moving to her, she asks, "Saki, what is wrong?"

"I can't find my homework. I did my homework last night and put it in my backpack, but now I can't find it." Going through her things again, she says through her tears, "I have to find it. I worked hard on my homework." Then noticing that her best friend, Jana, is laughing, she turns, "Jana, did you take my homework? This isn't funny."

Jana stops laughing, "I don't have it. I swear, I didn't take it."

"Well, you were laughing because I lost it. What kind of friend does that? You aren't my friend. I hate you." Then, realizing what she has said, Saki runs from the room.

Calmly, Ms. Shepherd says, "Students, your daily review is on the overhead. I want you to start on it immediately while I check on Saki. Ms. Champion is here if you have questions."

After a brief search, Ms. Shepherd finds Saki in the girls' restroom. Putting her arm around Saki, she says, "Saki, wash your face and then let's go somewhere we can talk."

When Saki becomes calmer, Ms. Shepherd questions her, "I've never seen you act this way before. Now tell me what's wrong."

"I'm trying to make an A in this class. I made a B last six weeks, and my parents put me on restriction. I'm not allowed to use the telephone for six weeks. Now, I've lost my homework, and I'll lose those points. And I said those awful things to Jana, and she won't be my friend anymore. I can't do anything right." She started to sob again. "I mess everything up."

"Well, let's think how you can fix this. I think you have an A in my class with or without your homework. The homework only counts for five points, so it isn't a big concern. But if you did the homework, I would like to give you the grade. Is there any way to get your homework to me today?"

"I could call my Mom. Would you take it if she brought it to you after school today?"

"Yes, I would. In fact, maybe your mother and I need to talk about your grades. I think you are doing very well in my class. I would like to talk to her about that. Do you want to call her, or do you want me to?"

"No, I will call her. But, what am I going to do about Jana? I told her I hate her. I shouldn't have done that."

"Well, let's think for a minute. If Jana had said that to you, what would you want her to do?"

"I would want her to apologize and tell me she didn't mean what she said." Saki's face brightened, "I need to tell Jana that. I know we have class now, but could I talk to Jana for just a minute and then call my mother?"

"Yes, I will send Jana to talk to you. I'm going back to class. After you talk to Jana, go to the office and call your mother. Then you need to come back to class. We will talk at the end of the class about what your mother said."

STRENGTHS AND WEAKNESSES OF INNER DISCIPLINE

There is no research data to verify the effectiveness of Inner Discipline, but many accept its validity. This is because they agree with the philosophical tenets on which Inner Discipline is based:

- Students are worth the effort it takes to make them responsible, resourceful, and caring individuals.
- Teachers shouldn't treat children in ways they wouldn't want to be treated.
- Intervention techniques must not only work but must leave a student's dignity intact (Coloroso, 2001).

For teachers who share these tenets, Inner Discipline is an effective classroom-management model.

However, some wonder whether the consequences Coloroso proposes are actually punishments presented in a different format. Others argue that the process of dealing with each student individually and taking the time to help him or her discover the solutions to problems is a time-consuming one. Many teachers argue that this process takes valuable time away from the main responsibility of the teacher—classroom instruction. Others see this process as necessary to developing self-discipline and personal responsibility.

SUMMARY

Barbara Coloroso's classroom-management model, **Inner Discipline**, is based on three key concepts: (1) developing inner discipline in students is more important than maintaining traditional classroom control, (2) problem solving is key to developing inner discipline, and (3) students must be taught *how* to think, not *what* to think. Coloroso describes classrooms as either jellyfish classrooms, brick wall classrooms, or backbone classrooms, and stresses that it is only in the backbone classroom that students learn to accept their own feelings and act on these feelings in a reasonable way. The focus of teachers in backbone classrooms is on helping students make legitimate choices and to face the real-world consequences of these choices.

KEY TERMINOLOGY

Definitions for these terms appear in the glossary:

Backbone classroom   Jellyfish classroom
Brick-wall classroom   Real-world consequences
Inner Discipline   Reconciliatory justice

CHAPTER ACTIVITIES

Reflecting on the Theory

1. When Ms. Fowler's fourth-period class returned from lunch, two of the students discovered that money had been taken from their backpacks. Deciding to watch the room more carefully when the students were at lunch, Ms. Fowler returned to the room early to discover Brad searching through a student's purse.

   How can Ms. Fowler use Reconciliatory Justice to resolve the problem with Brad? Would you be comfortable using Reconciliatory Justice to resolve this problem? Why or why not?

2. Coloroso shares many ideas with several other theorists presented in this text. Which of Coloroso's ideas have been presented in other theories? What appear to be the major differences in Coloroso's theory and others you have studied?

3. Consider how Ms. Schallenberger handled the situation with Brenton and Gus in the beginning scenario. Do you think the situation was handled appropriately? Should Brenton and Gus be punished for their behavior?

4. How are the consequences described in Coloroso's model different than traditional punishment? Are "real-world consequences" just punishments with a different name? Explain your answer.

Developing Your Portfolio

1. Analyze the interactions between a teacher and students which you have observed. Would you describe that classroom as a jellyfish classroom, a brick-wall classroom, or a backbone classroom? What factors led to your conclusion?

Developing Your Personal Philosophy of Classroom Management

1. Review the philosophical tenets of Inner Discipline. Which of these match your personal philosophy of classroom management? Which do you disagree with? Why?

2. Coloroso introduces the concept of Reconciliatory Justice in the classroom. What value do you see in Reconciliatory Justice? How could you use Reconciliatory Justice in your classroom?

RESOURCES FOR FURTHER STUDY

For more information about Inner Discipline, contact:

Barbara Coloroso
Kids are Worth It, Inc.
P.O. Box 621108
Littleton, CO 80162

CHAPTER REFERENCES

Coloroso, B. (1990). *Winning at teaching—without beating your kids.* Video. Littleton, CO: Kids are Worth It.

Coloroso, B. (1994). *Kids are worth it!: Giving your child the gift of inner discipline.* New York: William Morrow.

Coloroso, B. (1997). Discipline that makes the grade. *Learning, 25,* 44, 46.

Coloroso, B. (2001). *Parenting and teaching with wit and wisdom.* Littleton, CO: Kids are Worth It.

Skillstreaming

Objectives

Chapter 11 prepares preservice teachers to meet INTASC standards #1 (Content Pedagogy), #3 (Diverse Learners), #4 (Instructional Strategies), #5 (Motivation and Management), #7 (Planning), and #9 (Reflective Practitioner) by helping them to:

- use knowledge about human behavior drawn from education and psychology to develop strategies for teaching prosocial skills to students.
- understand the basic principles behind Skillstreaming.
- learn the four-step process of teaching social skills to students.
- evaluate the curriculum of Skillstreaming.
- determine appropriate instructional strategies to be used in social skills.

Scenario

First-year teacher Theresa Sagasta is very disappointed in the progress of her third-grade students. Academically, the students are doing well, but socially there are daily struggles in the classroom. She is concerned that some students seem unaware of socially acceptable behavior and are physically and verbally abusive to their classmates. By the end of the first semester, she has tried several discipline plans but has come to the conclusion that punishment is not the answer. Expressing her concerns to her principal, Theresa explains, "Sometimes I feel like I'm asking the students to perform tasks they have never learned. Many of my students simply don't know how to respond to their classmates. They are treating their classmates the way they have been treated by parents, siblings, and friends. I have decided I must teach them how to interact with each other, not just expect them to know what to say and do. My students need to learn prosocial skills as much as they need to learn reading, math, and science."

INTRODUCTION

Ellen McGinnis and Arnold Goldstein (1997) agree that many students exhibit inappropriate behaviors not because they are willful or lack self-control but because they have never been taught appropriate social skills. They suggest that expecting students to act in nonaggressive, socially acceptable ways without teaching the required prosocial skills is similar to asking students to work long-division problems without first teaching them how to divide.

In the early 1970s, McGinnis and Goldstein developed **Skillstreaming,** a prosocial instructional program. McGinnis and Goldstein recognized that the majority of discipline programs in the early 1970s relied on behavioral techniques, such as punishment and negative and positive reinforcement, to manage student behavior problems. Although positive reinforcement has proved to be effective in increasing positive behaviors, it is only effective if students have demonstrated the desired behavior. Conversely, many students displaying inappropriate behaviors never receive positive reinforcement from their teachers. These students constantly face consequences for acting inappropriately without having been taught the skills to change their behavior.

McGinnis and Goldstein (1997) suggest, therefore, that rather than focusing on rewards and punishments, educators must teach prosocial skills in the same planned and systematic way that academic skills are taught. They contend that the time spent trying to deal with these behavior problems is better spent teaching students how to prevent conflicts or to deal with conflicts in an effective, socially acceptable manner.

McGinnis, Goldstein, Sprafkin, and Gershaw (1984) stress that prosocial instruction is critical, because the lack of social skills will impact students throughout their lifetimes. Their research suggests that prosocial skill deficits in students are related to school maladjustment, delinquency, peer rejection, academic problems, personal unhappiness, interpersonal difficulty, and adjustment problems in adolescence and early adulthood.

Advocates of Skillstreaming also stress that the lack of prosocial skills is rarely the fault of the students. McGinnis et al. (1984) give the following reasons for students' failure to respond appropriately in social situations:

- They are unaware of the appropriate behavior. For example, if students have only witnessed aggression as a response to anger, they will know of no other response than aggression when they feel angry or threatened. They simply have no other options from which to choose.
- They may have been told how to respond but never had the opportunity to practice the skill. In many cases, students can verbalize the appropriate actions when questioned but may be unsure when to use them. Educators understand the importance of practice and regularly have students practice the correct responses to drills for fire, weather, or intruders in the building, but they rarely require students to practice responding appropriately to social situations. Without practice, students will never display the desired behaviors as a natural part of their lives.
- They may be emotionally immature or unstable and therefore unable to act in a way they know is socially acceptable. Emotions such as anxiety, fear, or anger may prevent students from thinking and responding effectively.
- They may not understand the appropriate time and place to display particular behaviors. This lack of behavioral flexibility prevents students from adjusting their behaviors to a variety of situations, people, and settings.

Many students don't choose to behave inappropriately; they simply don't know how to respond appropriately. In these cases, the students need direct and planned teaching, not punishments (McGinnis et al., 1984).

To meet the needs of these skill-deficient students, discipline programs must be instructional in nature. McGinnis et al. (1984) stress that it is not enough to merely tell a student that an action is not acceptable; additional measures must be taken to teach appropriate behavior. Skillstreaming provides a method for systematically teaching students the behaviors necessary for effective and satisfying social interactions.

When it was first introduced in the early 1970s, Skillstreaming was one of the first social-skills training approaches for adults and adolescents. Skillstreaming is now used in hundreds of schools. Skillstreaming was first used with small groups and in individual classrooms. Now it is used in general education on a schoolwide or districtwide basis. McGinnis and Goldstein (1997) contend that Skillstreaming is most effective when it is a systemwide effort, with instruction held during the school year in every school and continually reviewed, refined, retaught as needed, and reinforced in subsequent years.

Through Skillstreaming, students are taught to solve problems that occur in their daily lives, to be assertive in handling situations that cause them stress or unhappiness, and to increase the chance that they will have satisfying relationships with others (McGinnis & Goldstein, 1997). Therefore, teachers like Theresa should never be concerned that they are neglecting instruction in major content areas when they incorporate Skillstreaming as part of their curriculum. Instead, they should be confident they are teaching their students some of life's most important lessons.

ELEMENTS OF SKILLSTREAMING

Skillstreaming has its roots in both psychology and education. McGinnis and Goldstein (1997) describe it as a psychoeducational skill-training approach that was first termed Structured Learning and later renamed Skillstreaming. Central to Skillstreaming is a focus on four direct-instruction principles: modeling, role playing, feedback, and transfer. Cognitive-behavioral interventions, such as problem solving, anger control, and verbal mediation, are embedded in the instructional format.

McGinnis et al. (1984) stress that the goal is to arrive at a teaching prescription tailored to the individual skill assets and deficits of each student. Although Skillstreaming provides remediation for students who are significantly deficient in prosocial skills, it is also intended for the regular-education population whose behavior is not significantly problematic but who will benefit from learning and improving upon prosocial skills.

Skillstreaming presents a change in focus and philosophy from many classroom-management plans, in that it makes the assumption that misbehavior occurs because students lack needed prosocial skills. When misbehavior is viewed as a skills deficit rather than as defiance on the part of the student, the teacher sees misbehavior as a lack of knowledge and something within the teacher's ability to control. By using Skillstreaming, teachers can focus on proactive instruction rather than on reacting to misbehavior.

Each skill to be taught is first broken down into its specific steps and taught through a four-step process: modeling, role playing, feedback, and transfer. Because research verifies that behaviors can be learned, strengthened, weakened, or facilitated through modeling, the first step in teaching each skill is **modeling**. The process begins by the teacher or Skillstreaming trainer talking about the skill to be taught. The discussion includes why the skill is needed and when it should be used. The teacher, a classmate, or the Skillstreaming trainer then models the skill for students. The modeling display presented to the students should demonstrate the behavioral steps that make up a given skill in a manner that can be understood by the students, based on their age and maturity (Goldstein & McGinnis, 1997; McGinnis et al., 1984).

It is important that two examples of the skill to be learned are modeled. McGinnis et al. (1984) cite research that indicates that modeling will be more effective if the skill is modeled in a clear and detailed manner, presented in an order from least difficult to most difficult, and repeated until the entire group understands the process. Consider how one teacher helps students learn the behavioral skill of apologizing:

Each week, fourth-grade teacher Elizabeth Peacher and guidance counselor Cayce Stevens work with Ms. Peacher's class on a prosocial skill. This week the

I use songs to get the attention of my first graders. For example, to the tune of "Are You Sleeping?" I sing, "Are you ready? Please sit down. Time to quiet down now. Time to quiet down now. Hands on desk. Hands on desk."

Marta E. Galindo
Grade 1 Teacher
Rubin Chavira Elementary School
Del Rio, TX

skill is on how to apologize. "All right, class, who can tell me a time when you needed to apologize or when someone needed to apologize to you?" Seeing Kyle's hand, Ms. Peacher asks, "Yes, Kyle, can you give me an example?"

"Well, if someone tripped me on the playground, I would want them to apologize."

"That's a great example. Can anyone give me another?"

Angela raised her hand. "If I said something that hurt someone's feelings, I would need to apologize for that."

"Those are two great examples. Ms. Stevens and I will demonstrate a situation very similar to the one that Kyle mentioned. I want you to watch, and then we will talk about what happens."

For the next few minutes, the students watch as Ms. Peacher pretends to round a corner and run into Ms. Stevens. When she does so, Ms. Stevens drops her books. "Ms. Stevens, I'm so sorry. I didn't mean to run into you. Are you hurt?"

"No, I'm not hurt. I was just a little startled."

"Well, let me help you with your books. And I will try to slow down when I round corners in the future."

Ms. Peacher turns to the class, "All right class. What did you think? Did I need to apologize to Ms. Stevens?"

Lora was the first to answer, "Yes, and you needed to help her with her books. I thought you did the right thing."

For the next few minutes, the students talk about the situation that had been modeled and then watch as classmates Kristen and Lindsey model a situation in which a toy is broken.

McGinnis et al. (1984) point out that modeling alone is not sufficient to change behaviors, because the positive effects are often short lived. For students to adopt the skill and to use the skill daily, they must have the opportunity to practice and rehearse the behaviors performed by the model. It is not enough that students watch others model appropriate behaviors; each student should have a chance to demonstrate their understanding through **role playing**.

An important element for teaching new skills is giving students an opportunity to role play the skills they are learning.

McGinnis et al. (1984) note that behavior or attitude change through role playing will be more likely to occur if certain conditions are met:

- Students verbalize the steps for completing the behavior before beginning the role play.
- Students choose whether to participate or not.
- Students understand the importance of the skill learned.
- Students are allowed to improvise in enacting the role-play behaviors.
- Students are rewarded through approval or reinforcement for enacting the behaviors.

Ms. Peacher continued, "Now that each of you has had a chance to watch Ms. Stevens and me, and Lindsey and Kristen model the skill of apologizing, we are going to allow each of you to participate in a role-playing exercise. We are going to divide you into groups of four. Each group will get an envelope, and inside the envelope are situations in which apologizing might be appropriate. You are to draw a slip of paper from the envelope to determine whether you will be the one apologizing or the one receiving the apology. While you act out your situations, Ms. Stevens and I will go from group to group to watch and help if needed."

McGinnis et al. (1984) note that neither modeling nor role playing alone is enough to change behavior. However, they are important, because through modeling and role playing, the student discovers what to do and how to do it.

Providing students **feedback** on how they did during their role play is critical. Emphasis should be placed on how well the student displayed the appropriate behavioral steps. In the beginning, performances will appear stiff and unnatural to the student, so it is important to encourage students to continue and to reinforce them for their efforts.

McGinnis et al. (1984) note that the following types of reinforcement can be provided:

- Material reinforcement, such as food or money.
- Social reinforcement, such as praise or approval from others.
- Self-reinforcement, in which students evaluate their individual behavior.

Effective performance feedback should include all three types of reinforcement. Because research on learning has consistently shown that behavior change occurs most effectively when the reinforcement immediately follows the desired behavior, it is important that students be evaluated during and immediately following their role play. Once the desired behaviors are established, reinforcement can occur on an intermittent schedule. However, because behaviors that are not rewarded occur less often, it is important that teachers reward students throughout the year, whenever they see the desired behavior exhibited. One way of doing this is by giving citizenship tokens that can be traded in for a reward at the end of a period of time.

As the groups role played the situation they were given, Ms. Stevens and Ms. Peacher moved from group to group giving praise and encouragement. When all groups finished, Ms. Peacher said, "All of you did a wonderful job. I think you heard the laughter coming from Ryan's group. I think Ryan and Dylan may have a future in the theatre. Ryan, would you and Dylan like to do your role play for the entire class?"

Reinforcement is important in instituting desired behaviors that last throughout the student's lifetime. However, the behaviors to be reinforced must occur with sufficient correctness and sufficient frequency for reinforcement to have its intended effect (McGinnis et al., 1984).

The ultimate goal of Skillstreaming is that students **transfer** the skills learned to their daily lives. As McGinnis et al. (1984) note, "The main interest of any teaching program, and where most teaching programs fail, is not in students' performance during training activity, but, instead, in how well they perform in their real lives" (p. 19). To facilitate this transfer, it is critical that students be given opportunities to use the behaviors they have role played. Some of these must occur during the school day, so the classroom should be structured to allow students to interact with one another—to talk, work, and play together.

> After Dylan and Ryan performed their role play and the class rewarded them with thunderous applause, Ms. Peacher assigned the students homework for the week. Passing out the written directions, she explained, "Throughout this week, I want you to practice the skill of apologizing. Each time you apologize, I want you to write a description of the event. I want you to tell how you felt after apologizing and what you would do differently in the future. I hope you can describe situations that occur here at school, with your friends, and at home."
>
> "Ms. Peacher, what if I don't need to apologize to anyone? How can I do the assignment?"
>
> "Well, this assignment may help you think of situations in which you should apologize but haven't in the past. However, if you haven't had the need to apologize at least once by the end of the week, talk with me and we will see if I need to extend the assignment. Any questions before we go to gym?"

SKILLSTREAMING PROCEDURES

Although Skillstreaming was originally designed to be used with groups of students who had skill deficits, it is equally effective when used with an entire class. Skillstreaming can easily be integrated into subject areas that deal with health, personal development, or interpersonal development. McGinnis et al. (1984) note that classroom teachers may decide to instruct their entire class in prosocial skills for a variety of reasons. The teacher's goal may be preventive, with the aim of improving the class climate and preventing problems from developing. In some cases, Skillstreaming provides a way for socially competent peers to serve as models for those students who have social-skills deficits. Many teachers see Skillstreaming as a mechanism for providing instruction for successful and happy lives.

In some cases, small groups of students with specific needs may be pulled from classrooms to work with social workers, psychologists, or counselors in Skillstreaming sessions. McGinnis et al. (1984) recommend that groups have no more than five to eight students who share deficiencies in specific skills or skill areas.

Tips from the Field

I teach my students about the "productive hum" level of sound in the room. I get the students in small groups to demonstrate what it sounds like. I tell the students that this is the sound level you'd find in most offices. People aren't silent. They're inter-acting, but they're respectful of each other's need to keep the noise level down so people can think and work.

> James F. Linsell
> Grade 6 Social Studies Teacher
> 2002 Michigan Teacher of the Year
> Eastern Elementary School
> Traverse City, MI

Whether Skillstreaming sessions take place in a regular classroom or with small groups, research by Goldstein, Sprafkin, Gershaw, and Klein (1980) shows that sessions work best with two trained adults leading the group. The leaders can be classroom teachers, guidance counselors, or parents who have had Skillstreaming training. These leaders need to possess these specific skills:

- Excellent oral communication and listening skills
- Excellent teaching ability
- Flexibility and capacity for resourcefulness
- Enthusiasm
- Ability to work under pressure
- Interpersonal sensitivity
- Knowledge of human behaviors and adolescent development
- Ability to manage behavior problems that may occur during the session

It is critical that trainers are sensitive to the cultural diversity of their students. As Cartledge and Milburn (1996) note, "Social skills trainers must differentiate between social skills deficits that need to be changed and the cultural differences that either need to be respected in their current form or simply need to be switched according to specific social conditions" (p. 1).

Skillstreaming sessions should be held three to five times per week. They should be frequent enough for a substantial number of skills to be taught over the course of a school year, so that students have opportunities to practice the skills in real-life situations (McGinnis et al., 1984). For first- and second-graders, the recommended length of sessions is twenty minutes. Fifth- and sixth-graders can benefit from sessions that are 30–40 minutes long.

Parental involvement should be an integral part of the Skillstreaming program. Parents should be informed during an orientation meeting about Skillstreaming and its benefits for their children. Volunteer parents can provide additional help in the Skillstreaming sessions.

SKILLSTREAMING COMPONENTS

The skills presented in Skillstreaming sessions come from two sources. Individual teachers may identify a list of skills needed by their students. McGinnis et al. (1984) suggest that students identify skills they feel they need. Alternatively, sometimes during instruction in a selected prosocial skill, the teacher may identify the need for training in a different skill.

Most teachers and schools using Skillstreaming, however, use the developed list of skills provided by McGinnis and Goldstein (1990, 1997). These skills have been derived from 30 years of research and correlate with "best practice" research. The skills presented are those identified through research to be related to peer acceptance, academic achievement, personal adjustment, and positive self-concepts.

Prosocial skills have been developed to meet the needs of specific age and maturity levels. For students who are preschool through grade 1, McGinnis and Goldstein (1990) have developed six groups of skills, which include 40 specific skills. The six major categories of skills for this age group include: (1) Beginning Social Skills, (2) School-Related Skills, (3) Friendship-Making Skills, (4) Dealing with Feelings, (5) Alternatives to Aggression, and (6) Dealing with Stress.

McGinnis et al. (1984) suggest that it is necessary to simplify the behavioral skill steps for very young students. Pictorial cues that illustrate these steps will help such younger children and other nonreaders understand the concepts.

At the elementary school level (grades 2–5), 60 prosocial skills have been divided into five skill groups: (1) Classroom Survival Skills, (2) Friendship-Making Skills, (3) Dealing with Feelings, (4) Alternatives to Aggression, (5) Dealing with Stress. The first groups of skills, Classroom Survival Skills and Friendship-Making Skills, are the best skills to use for introducing students to the Skillstreaming process (McGinnis et al., 1984).

Skillstreaming skills for adolescents (grades 6–12) have been divided into six groups of 50 specific skills. The six groups are (1) Beginning Social Skills, (2) Advanced Social Skills, (3) Dealing with Feelings, (4) Alternatives to Aggression, (5) Dealing with Stress, and (6) Planning Skills (Goldstein et al., 1980; Goldstein & McGinnis, 1997). Table 11.1 provides a list of the major categories of skills for all age levels.

McGinnis et al. (1984) stress that many of the skills, specifically those dealing with alternatives to aggression, provide students with impulse-control training. This is critical for students who display aggression or violent tendencies. Goldstein et al. (1980) describe the skill-deficient adolescent as aggressive, withdrawn, and immature. These students often feel inferior, self-conscious, shy, anxious, hypersenstive, and timid. Goldstein et al. (1980) note that while skill-deficient adolescents may be proficient in their ability to fight and disrupt, they are lacking the skills needed to maintain self-control, negotiate or problem solve, or deal with their or another's anger.

The good news is that research about the causes of violence in our society and schools shows aggression and violence to be primarily learned behaviors. Often the only response students have learned to threat or aggression is violence. When taught alternative responses, students react in more productive ways. Therefore it is critical that schools provide alternatives and help students learn that nonviolent choices exist (McGinnis & Goldstein, 1997).

TABLE 11.1 *Components of Skillstreaming*

Components of Skillstreaming		
Preschool to Grade 1 Skills	**Elementary (Grade 2–5) Skills**	**Adolescent (Grade 6–12) Skills**
(1) Beginning Social Skills	(1) Classroom Survival Skills	(1) Beginning Social Skills
(2) School-Related Skills	(2) Friendship-Making Skills	(2) Advanced Social Skills
(3) Friendship-Making Skills	(3) Dealing with Feelings	(3) Dealing with Feelings
(4) Dealing with Feelings	(4) Alternatives to Aggression	(4) Alternatives to Aggression
(5) Alternatives to Aggression	(5) Dealing with Stress	(5) Dealing with Stress
(6) Dealing with Stress		(6) Planning Skills

Source: McGinnis and Goldstein, Skillstreaming in Early Childhood.
Source: McGinnis and Goldstein, Skillstreaming in the Elementary School Child.
Source: Goldstein, Sprafkin, Gershaw, and Klein, Skillstreaming the Adolescent.

SKILLSTREAMING IN THE CLASSROOM

Scenario

When Hugh Sowada moved from his position as assistant principal at an elementary school to principal of Primrose Hill Middle School, he wanted to incorporate Skillstreaming into the curriculum. He had seen significant positive behavior changes in the elementary students through the Skillstreaming sessions and felt that the middle-school population would benefit as well. Drawing teachers from each of the school's three grade levels and from each team, he formed a committee to investigate the advantages of using Skillstreaming at the middle-school level and to determine how it could work at Primrose Hill. Skeptical at first, the committee became convinced that the program was worthwhile after reviewing the literature. Knowing that further training was necessary, three teachers attended a summer workshop on Skillstreaming and brought back manuals and videos to help in training the entire faculty.

The committee also gave careful consideration to how the skills would be taught. Because each class had an advisory period of thirty minutes at the beginning of the day, it was determined that three days a week a skill from the list of skills provided in the training manuals would be emphasized in the sixth and seventh grades. The eighth-grade teachers agreed to focus on skills not covered in the list and to address issues that arose throughout the year.

During the first week of school each student took home a letter informing parents about Skillstreaming and inviting them to a meeting to learn more. Parents were also solicited to aid in the Skillstreaming sessions. One mother agreed to create a weekly bulletin board to reinforce the skill being taught in the sixth and seventh grades.

By the end of the first year, the entire faculty had become believers in the effectiveness of Skillstreaming. In addition to the Skillstreaming sessions, they had developed a peer-mediation program with the hopes that all students at Primrose Hill would learn to solve problems in a peaceful, mature manner.

STRENGTHS AND WEAKNESSES OF SKILLSTREAMING

Perhaps the greatest strength of McGinnis and Goldstein's Skillstreaming program is the emphasis placed on teaching students the skills needed to live successfully in society. Although these theorists conducted considerable research to determine the skills needed at various grade levels, they also gave consideration to how students learn and the most effective ways of teaching these skills.

The teaching methods and specific skills used in Skillstreaming have been validated by research conducted over a 20-year period. In addition, the amount of research on the impact of Skillstreaming is extensive. McGinnis and Goldstein (1997) provide a bibliography of over 120 research articles and reports on the effectiveness of Skillstreaming.

Skillstreaming is a cost-effective approach to classroom management, in that it is not an expensive program to implement. Although support material exists, the most important requirements for implementing a Skillstreaming program are caring, trained leaders.

The criticism of Skillstreaming focuses mainly on the time and energy required of the classroom teachers. Many teachers are already overwhelmed by the amount of material they are required to present and by other noninstructional duties they are asked to perform. Some consider the teaching of prosocial skills the responsibility of guidance counselors or school social workers rather than that of overly taxed classroom teachers.

SUMMARY

Ellen McGinnis and Arnold Goldstein (1997) suggest that many students exhibit inappropriate behaviors not because they are willful or lack self-control but because they have never been taught appropriate social skills. In the early 1970s, they developed **Skillstreaming,** a prosocial instructional program designed to teach students the behaviors necessary for effective and satisfying social interactions. Through Skillstreaming, students are taught to solve problems that occur in their daily lives, to be assertive in handling situations that cause them stress or unhappiness, and to increase the likelihood of their having satisfying relationships with others. Each skill to be taught is first broken down into its specific steps and taught through a four-step process: modeling, role playing, feedback, and transfer.

KEY TERMINOLOGY

Definitions for these terms appear in the glossary:

Feedback   Skillstreaming
Modeling   Transfer
Role playing

CHAPTER ACTIVITIES

Reflecting on the Theory

1. In Ms. Resnik's sixth-grade class, students frequently get into arguments. Most of these altercations begin when one student calls another student a derogatory name. When she intervenes, Ms. Resnik usually hears, "I was only kidding." Regardless of the intent, the result is loss of class time, hurt feelings, and adversarial feelings between students.

   How can Ms. Resnik use Skillstreaming to change the behavior of her sixth-grade students?

2. McGinnis and Goldstein suggest that the majority of misbehavior is a result of skill deficiencies rather than defiance on the part of students. Do you agree? Why or why not?

3. In the classrooms you have observed, what were the prevalent social skills that appeared to be lacking by students?

Developing Your Portfolio

1. Determine which social skills you consider important for your students to understand and use. Using the four-step process of Skillstreaming, prepare a lesson plan to teach this skill.

Developing Your Personal Philosophy of Classroom Management

1. Skillstreaming is based on the assumption that it is the responsibility of the classroom teacher to provide instruction in the social skills required for a productive life. Others would argue that the teaching of these "life" skills is the responsibility of the family and community. What is your stand on this issue? Explain your reasoning.

2. Would you be comfortable using Skillstreaming in your classroom? Why or why not? Are there some strategies that you will definitely incorporate into your classroom-management plan? Why?

RESOURCES FOR FURTHER STUDY

Further information about Skillstreaming and resources for its use in the classroom can be found by contacting:

Dr. Arnold P. Goldstein and Dr. Ellen McGinnis
Research Press
Dept. 22W
P.O. Box 9177
Champaign, IL 61826
217-352-3273

CHAPTER REFERENCES

Cartledge, G., & Milburn, J. F. (1996). *Cultural diversity and social skills instruction.* Champaign, IL: Research Press.

Goldstein, A. P., & McGinnis, E. (1997). *Skillstreaming the adolescent—Student manual.* Champaign, IL: Research Press.

Goldstein, A. P., Sprafkin, R. P., Gershaw, N. J., & Klein, P. (1980). *Skillstreaming the adolescent.* Champaign, IL: Research Press.

McGinnis, E., Goldstein, A., Sprafkin, R. P., and Gershaw, N. J. (1984). *Skillstreaming the elementary school student: A guide for teaching prosocial skills.* Champaign, IL: Research Press.

McGinnis, E., & Goldstein, A. (1990). *Skillstreaming in early studenthood: Teaching prosocial skills to the preschool and kindergarten student.* Champaign, IL: Research Press.

McGinnis, E., & Goldstein, A. (1997). *Skillstreaming the elementary school student* (Revised Ed.) Champaign, IL: Research Press.

Chapter 12

Conflict Resolution and Peer Mediation

Objectives

Chapter 12 prepares preservice teachers to meet INTASC standards #3 (Diverse Learners), #5 (Motivation and Management), and #9 (Reflective Practitioner) by helping them to:

- understand the basic principles behind conflict resolution and peer mediation.
- evaluate approaches to conflict resolution.
- learn how conflict resolution and peer mediation can be used to reduce conflict based on differences in gender, sexual orientation, class, ethnicity and physical and mental abilities.
- learn how to apply strategies from conflict resolution and peer mediation in the classroom.
- understand the basic reasons for conflict within a classroom.
- evaluate the appropriateness of using a conflict resolution approach in their classrooms.

Scenario

Third-grade teacher Jennifer Cunningham was helping Allison with her math when she heard a loud crash at the computer center. When she reached the computer center, she found the chair overturned, Jamil on the floor, and Sean standing over Jamil. Helping Jamil to his feet, she asked, "Do you guys want to tell me what is going on here?"

Obviously upset, Sean quickly explained, "It was my time to use the computer, but Jamil wouldn't move. I pushed him to get him out of the chair, and the chair turned over. I wasn't trying to hurt him."

Jamil turned to Sean, "I'm not hurt, but you had no business pushing me. I was going to let you use the computer as soon as I finished my game."

Ms. Cunningham stopped the argument. "Okay, let's talk about this. Sean, which of our rules did you break?"

"Not to touch anyone without permission."

"And what is the consequence for breaking this rule?"

"I have to get detention after school."

Turning to Jamil, Ms. Cunningham asked, "And Jamil, you weren't following our procedures for computer use, were you? What is the consequence for not following our procedures?"

"I lose my next turn at the computer, but Ms. Cunningham, I only needed a few more minutes. Sean should have waited. He shouldn't have pushed me."

Not wanting to be the only one at fault for the situation, Sean quickly said, "You always hog the computer. It's not fair. You're selfish."

"All right, boys, that's enough. I'm more concerned about your relationship with each other than who is at fault or who should be punished. Now, I want to give you a chance to work this out between you. Are you willing to go to the Peace Corner and resolve this problem?"

In unison, the boys said, "Yes, Ms. Cunningham."

"Good. When you have finished, come see me and tell me how you plan to keep this from happening in the future."

INTRODUCTION

In the past few years, resolving classroom problems through conflict resolution and peer mediation has become an accepted part of many schools' discipline plans. Peterson (1997) found that by 1995 there were 5,000 such programs in U.S. schools, and the number rises each year. In some cases, conflict resolution and peer mediation is used by an individual teacher, such as Ms. Cunningham, as a means of teaching social skills and resolving classroom conflicts. In other cases, it is a schoolwide approach, in which participation, support, and resources extend beyond a single classroom.

Donna Crawford and Richard Bodine developed one of the earliest and best-known approaches to conflict resolution. They consider conflict as an inevitable part of life and suggest that learning how to respond to it constructively is essential for peaceful schools and successful lives. As Bodine, Crawford, and Schrumpf (1994) note: "Conflict is a natural, vital part of life. When conflict is understood, it can become an opportunity to learn and create. The challenges for students in conflict are to apply the principles of creative cooperation in their human relationship" (p. 51).

Crawford and Bodine (1996, 2001) view conflict resolution as a viable alternative to traditional classroom-management programs, because they found that much of classroom misbehavior is actually unresolved conflict. They suggest that, too often, teachers managed the issues arising from conflicts without dealing with the problems that created the misbehaviors in the first place. Students who have had their behavior controlled by traditional management methods of punishments—time–out, detention, suspensions, and expulsion—learn little about alternative ways of dealing with their misbehavior. Students and teachers should approach conflicts as an opportunity for growth and conflict resolution as a means for learning effective alternatives to aggression and violence (Crawford & Bodine, 2001).

CAUSES OF CLASSROOM CONFLICT

As Bodine, Crawford, and Schrumpf (1994) stress, conflict is a part of life, and without conflict there would be no personal growth or social change. It is important that students learn effective ways of dealing with the types of conflict they will encounter throughout their lives. Kreidler (1984) suggests that the causes of classroom conflicts reflect those of society and typically revolve around issues of needs, values, and resources. In addition, conflicts arise from the classroom environment and from interactions between students or between students and the teacher.

Many of the conflicts in the classroom center on the desire to meet basic needs, including the need for power, friendship and affiliation, and self-esteem and achievement. Bodine, Crawford, and Schrumpf (1994) note that conflict resolution is extremely difficult when students perceive that others are threatening their psychological needs. It is important for teachers to understand that conflicts over unmet psychological needs are often played out against the backdrop of limited resources. Students appear to be in conflict over physical things when in reality, the need may be much deeper and more fundamental. If psychological issues are left unresolved, the conflict will appear again and again.

Conflicts may arise over limited resources (time, money, property) and are typically the easiest to resolve. The goal is to teach students that cooperating rather than competing for scarce resources is in their best interests.

Conflicts involving different values (beliefs, priorities, principles) tend to be more difficult to resolve than those about resources. When students' values are challenged, they feel threatened. Conflicts over values involve the use of words such as *honest, equal, right*, and *fair*. Through effective conflict resolution, however, students can learn that resolving a values conflict does not mean that they have to change or realign their values. Often, agreeing that each person views the situation differently is the first step toward resolution. If students can learn to accept each other's differences in beliefs, they will be able to deal with the issue in conflict rather than focusing on their differences.

The diversity of today's classrooms provides an arena for conflict as students learn and play with students from backgrounds different from their own (Crawford & Bodine, 1996). This diversity may lead to misunderstandings or misperceptions of the intentions, feelings, needs, or actions of others. Reactions to differences often take the form of prejudice, discrimination, harassment, and hate crimes. Conflict-resolution education programs provide a framework for addressing these problems by promoting respect and acceptance through new ways of communicating and understanding. Although complex, these conflicts can be resolved by increased awareness, understanding, and respect.

Kreidler (1984) suggests that sometimes the classroom teacher is the source of conflict in the classroom. Teachers who create a highly competitive atmosphere will have classrooms full of conflict. When teachers favor one student or group of students, tension and jealousy are created. Too often, teachers place irrational or impossible expectations on students. Students often feel that rules are inflexible or that consequences are not applied equally. All of these teacher-created situations create an atmosphere of fear and mistrust.

RESPONSES TO CONFLICT

According to Bodine, Crawford, and Schrumpf (1994), responses to conflict can be categorized into three basic groups: soft responses, hard responses, and principled responses. In both soft and hard responses, students negotiate from these positions, either trying to avoid or win a contest of will.

Soft responses usually come from students who are friends or students who want to keep peace in the classroom, school, or neighborhood. In many cases, the students want to agree, and they negotiate softly to do so. Avoidance is a common response, and is achieved by withdrawing from the situation, ignoring the conflict, and denying emotions. Accommodation is another response that offers protection from aggression by other students. With both avoidance and accommodation, resentment grows and eventually feelings of disillusionment, self-doubt, fear, and anxiety about the future develop. For example, consider a typical middle-school situation in which avoidance is the chosen response:

When Callie Davis transferred to Chapman Middle School, she was pleased when Shauna, one of the more popular girls in the eighth grade, wanted to be her friend. Now, Callie fears that Shauna just likes her so that she can borrow Callie's

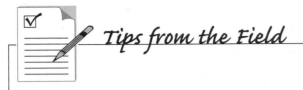

Tips from the Field

Most research indicates that lecturing in the classroom is the least effective method of instruction. On the other hand, hands-on, teacher-guided, student-centered learning and exploration prove to be the most effective practices. Furthermore, when people are busy, they tend to stay focused on the tasks at hand. Therefore, when students are actively engaged in an activity that they enjoy and that employs a variety of learning styles, the chances of students disengaging from learning significantly decreases, and classroom management problems virtually disappear.

> David McKay
> 2002 Washington State
> Teacher of the Year
> Grades 9–12 English Teacher
> Aberdeen High School
> Aberdeen, WA

clothes. Every time Shauna comes to Callie's house, she asks if she can borrow a blouse or pair of jeans. Callie's wardrobe is slowly being emptied, but she is afraid that if she confronts Shauna, Shauna will not only stop being her friend, but she will lose the circle of friends she has made through Shauna.

In contrast to soft responses are **hard responses** to conflict, in which adversaries war until one is victorious. Hard responses to conflict are characterized by confrontations that involve threats, aggression, and anger (Bodine, Crawford, & Schrumpf, 1994; Kreidler, 1984). In hard responses, pressure is applied as those in conflict try to have their own way. Hard responses typically result in one of two outcomes. One outcome is that the more aggressive student wins, and the other loses. The second outcome involves a lose/lose situation in which the desire to hurt or get even with the other student provokes vindictive actions. Consider how a hard response results in a lose/lose situation for Demario and Ryan:

> Demario Wamble dreads riding the school bus, because he has become the target of bullying by Ryan Poole. On the first day of school, Ryan made Demario move so Ryan could sit closer to his friends. Now, making Demario move each morning has become a game for Ryan. No matter where Demario sits, Ryan decides he wants to sit where Demario is sitting and threatens Demario until he relinquishes his seat.
>
> After weeks of such treatment, Demario is plotting revenge. On the ride to Ryan's stop, Demario hides thumbtacks in the seat. Carefully avoiding the sharp points, Demario can't wait until Ryan once again threatens him and makes him relinquish his seat.

Principled responses to conflict are proactive rather than reactive. Students who use principled responses have developed communication and conflict-resolution skills (Bodine, Crawford, & Schrumpf, 1994). Principled responses to conflict are characterized by each student seeking to understand the other while trying to be understood. Principled negotiators are skilled, active, empathetic listeners. Principled negotiators focus on the interests of both sides and strive to create situations in which each person wins. The following example shows how Jade and Leigh use a principled approach to resolve their differences:

> For the last few days, tension has been mounting in Mr. Merriwether's class. Best friends Jade and Leigh are no longer speaking to each other, and the other students have begun to take sides in the dispute. Taking the girls aside, Mr. Merriwether learns that Jade has accused Leigh of telling a secret that Jade shared with Leigh. Realizing that the girls want to remain friends, he suggests that they participate in peer mediation. After one session with the peer mediator, the girls put aside their disagreement and become friends once again. Mr. Merriwether is pleased when peace returns to his classroom.

The three types of responses to conflict produce different outcomes. The actions students choose when they are involved in a conflict will either worsen or lessen the problem. Soft positional bargaining is considered a lose/lose approach to conflict. Students do not deal with the root of the problem, and eventually both students lose. In hard positional bargaining, a win-lose situation is created that can be self-destructive as well as destructive to the opponent. Only through a principled approach, such as conflict resolution or peer mediation, can issues be resolved in a peaceful, productive manner.

PRINCIPLES OF CONFLICT RESOLUTION

Crawford and Bodine (2001) propose that conflict resolution offers an alternative approach to classroom management that brings the disputing parties together, provides them with the skills to resolve the dispute, and expects them to do so. Because there are different approaches to conflict resolution, Kreidler (1984) recommends that teachers consider the following when choosing a conflict-resolution technique:

- *The age and maturity level of the students involved.* Younger students may need adult intervention to help in the resolution of the problem. If one of the students is angry and poses a danger to others, the teacher's presence is needed to ensure the safety of all involved.
- *The time and place appropriate for intervention.* Conflict resolution requires time for those in conflict to express feelings and to consider solutions. Such negotiations cannot take place quickly or in a public forum. In some cases, students may need a cooling-off period before beginning negotiations.
- *The type of conflict.* Whole-class problems may require a group meeting, whereas issues between individual students may be resolved by the students or through the use of a mediator.

Tips from the Field

Use humor to diffuse difficult situations. Children are less defensive and become willing to go along with virtually any teacher expectation when their teacher approaches a situation with a smile instead of a growl. (This works well when dealing with administrators, too!)

Tracy Callard
Intermediate Teacher
2002 Kansas Teacher of the Year
Horace Mann Elementary School
Wichita, KS

The type of intervention used must meet the specific needs of those involved. There are three basic types of conflict resolution available for use by students and teachers: mediation, negotiations, and consensus decision making (Crawford & Bodine, 1996, 2001).

The most commonly used and best-known method is **mediation**. Mediation is a problem-solving process in which conflicting students meet face to face to work together to resolve the dispute assisted by a neutral third party (Bodine, Crawford, & Schrumpf, 1994). Mediation can take place within the classroom setting or in the context of a schoolwide program available to all students.

Essential to the success of the mediation process is the mediator who orchestrates the prescribed step-by-step procedure, asking questions and ensuring that those in conflict hear each other. Although the role of mediator can be filled by the teacher, the principal, or another adult, it is best filled by a fellow student or students who have been trained to be peer mediators. Peer mediation has the advantage of demonstrating to students that they have the ability, by communicating and cooperating, to resolve their differences without adult intervention. When peer mediators are used, they should be selected from groups that represent the general student population in terms of race, gender, achievement, and behavior. Bodine, Crawford, and Schrumpf (1994) stress that students as young as third grade have the ability and sophistication to serve as co-mediators in such a program.

In **negotiations**, conflicting students work together, unassisted, to solve their dispute. Negotiation can be a powerful tool, especially within a classroom in which all of the students have been trained in conflict resolution. Bodine et al. (1994) suggest that classrooms have a negotiation center or "peace corner" where students in conflict sit face-to-face to conduct the negotiation while other classroom activities proceed concurrently.

The final option available to teachers is **consensus decision making**. This is a group problem-solving strategy in which all parties affected by the conflict collaborate to create a plan of action that all parties can and will support. Crawford and Bodine (2001) suggest

TABLE 12.1   *Steps in the Conflict-Resolution Process*

Six Critical Steps for Resolving Conflicts
Step 1: Set the stage
Step 2: Gather perspectives
Step 3: Identify interests
Step 4: Create options
Step 5: Evaluate options
Step 6: Generate agreement

this strategy of group problem solving when conflict affects the entire class. The vehicle for group problem solving is the class meeting.

The purpose of such class meetings is to solve a problem rather than to determine who is to blame or who should be punished. Through the process, an agreement is reached that is acceptable to the group. This may mean that the decision will be the best resolution of the conflict for the group as a whole but may not be the best solution for individual students.

Classroom teachers facilitate group problem solving through class meetings. To begin, teachers review the process and list key issues to be resolved. The focus is on the *process*, and the teacher is there only to ensure that all the steps in the process are completed rather than to lobby for a particular outcome. Teachers can provide their points of view by asking questions. Teachers restate agreements as they occur and help the class develop a plan for solving the problem.

THE CONFLICT-RESOLUTION PROCESS

Crawford and Bodine (2001) propose that the steps in conflict resolution should be taught to all students, not just those with disruptive behaviors. The problem-solving process incorporates the following steps (see Table 12.1):

Step 1: Set the stage

Whether the method of conflict resolution is mediation, negotiation, or group problem solving, all participants must agree to participate and cooperate to solve the problem. If at any point the participants indicate a lack of desire to cooperate, the process ends. Without cooperation, the process is futile.

In conflict resolution, it is important that ground rules be set. Doing so begins with a review of the steps involved in conflict resolution. It is important to determine whether there is a need for confidentiality. With elementary-age students, strict confidentiality may not be required. However, confidentiality may become increasingly important as the age of those in conflict increases and the issues in dispute become more personal and sensitive.

All parties must agree that there will be no name calling or put-downs. All must view themselves as partners in trying solve the problem. When all agree to the ground rules, the process can begin.

Step 2: Gather perspectives

During conflict resolution, all students have an opportunity to express their opinions and to be heard. If one student has requested mediation, that student should be the first to describe the problem. The mediator alternates between those in conflict, asking for clarification and summarizing each person's point of view, until all issues have been heard. It is important that the mediator use open-ended questions rather than questions that can be answered with "yes" or "no."

In this step, mediators must help participants deal with problems of perceptions and emotions. When dealing with problems of perception, it is important to remember that conflict is not necessarily based on reality but in how students *perceive* the situation (Bodine et al., 1994). It is ultimately each student's perception that defines the problem. Understanding each other's perceptions opens the way to resolution.

Emotionally-charged students may be more ready to fight than to work together cooperatively to solve the problem. Fear can be played out through a show of anger. Having students identify both their own emotions and those of the other side opens the way to understanding.

Bodine et al. (1994) suggest that as mediators work with the students they should be careful to:

- **Attend** to the nonverbal behaviors so that all can fully understand what everyone is thinking and feeling.
- **Summarize** or restate facts by repeating the most important points, organizing interests, and discarding extraneous information. In summarizing, the mediator acknowledges emotions by stating the feelings each person is experiencing.
- **Clarify** by using open-ended questions and statements to obtain more information and ensure understanding.

Step 3: Identify interests

The mediator asks participants to explain what they want from the process. Critical to the success of the process is the determination of shared interests. Shared and compatible interests are the building blocks for resolving the conflict.

The goal is to separate the students from the problem by focusing on interests rather than on positions (Bodine et al., 1994). Understanding the difference between positions and interests is crucial, because interests, not positions, define problems. Students should come to see themselves as working side by side and attacking the problem rather than each other.

Step 4: Create options

Creating options involves a brainstorming process. Because evaluation hinders creativity, the process of *generating* options is separate from the process of *evaluating* options and from creating an agreement. This step allows students the opportunity to design potential

It may be necessary for the teacher to act as the mediator as students learn to resolve conflicts.

solutions without the pressure of deciding which is the best decision. Brainstorming is used to separate inventing from deciding.

Step 5: Evaluate options

Using group problem solving, evaluation options are divided into two parts. The first part establishes criteria for evaluating options. The second part is the actual evaluation of options. The following must be considered as the participants evaluate the option:

> Does the option help everyone involved?
> Is the option fair?
> Can the option solve the problem?
> Can the group do it?
> Does the option violate school rules or policies?

Step 6: Generate agreement

After those in conflict have discussed the available options, the mediator asks students to make a plan of action describing what they will do.

ADDITIONAL APPROACHES TO CONFLICT-RESOLUTION EDUCATION

Crawford and Bodine (2001) identify three additional approaches to conflict-resolution education. The first is the **curriculum approach**. Using this approach, students receive instruction in a separate course, distinct curriculum, or daily or weekly lesson plan. Instruction is provided in listening skills, critical thinking, and problem solving, which not only resolves classroom problems, but also enhances all learning.

The **peaceable classroom** is the second approach to conflict-resolution education. It is possible to develop a peaceable classroom in any school (Bodine et al., 1994). The peaceable classroom is a warm and caring community in which five qualities are present:

1. Cooperation: Students learn to work together and trust, help, and share with each other.
2. Communication: Students learn to observe nonverbal clues, communicate accurately, and listen actively.
3. Tolerance: Students learn to respect and appreciate other students' differences and to understand how prejudice impacts the classroom.
4. Positive emotional expression: Students learn self-control and to express feelings of anger and frustration in ways that are not aggressive or destructive.
5. Conflict resolution: Students learn the skills for responding creatively to conflict in the context of a supportive, caring community.

Peaceable classrooms are the building blocks of the **peaceable school**, the last approach to conflict-resolution education. Crawford and Bodine (2001) describe the peaceable school approach as a whole school methodology that builds on the peaceable classroom approach by using conflict resolution as a system of operation for managing the entire school. Using this approach, the adults and students involved learn and use conflict-resolution principles and processes. In the peaceable school, students learn about peacemaking in the social context of the classroom and the school. In the peaceable school, interactions between students, between students and adults, and between adults are designed to value human dignity and build self-esteem.

CONFLICT RESOLUTION IN THE CLASSROOM

Scenario

When Karen Aquino's sixth-grade class won Stapleton Middle School's Accelerated Reader contest, she never dreamed that winning would cause a major conflict in the classroom. As part of their prize, the class had been given a field trip to a location of their choosing. Where the class would spend their free day had become the issue of daily battles between the boys and the girls.

The boys wanted to go a professional ballgame. The girls wanted to go to a mall and to a movie. Because they couldn't agree, a class meeting was called to resolve the issue. After the students had gathered in a circle and Ms. Aquino had reviewed the ground rules, she asked, "Who wants to start?"

Benjamin raised his hand and said, "We think we should go to a professional baseball game. There are more boys than girls, so the majority should win."

"So, you are suggesting that the majority should win and that the minority, the girls in this case, should just go along, whether they are happy or not?"

Several of the girls raised their hands, and Ms. Aquino called on Kayla. "All the boys ever want to do is play ball. Whenever we have free time, they start a ball game, and they don't want the girls to play. We are tired of being left out. Beside, the girls read more books, and that is why we won. We wouldn't have this prize if it weren't for the girls, so we should be ones to decide where we go."

Daniel was recognized, "I guess I can see the girls' point of view, but none of the boys want to go to a mall. Is there anything the girls would like that is outside?"

Several of the girls wanted to speak, but Ms. Aquino called on Lindsey, "Well, I would like to go to a park or to the zoo. Then the girls could picnic and the boys could play ball. I like the idea of being outside. We are inside all the time at school. On our free day, we should do something different."

"Could we do both?" Kimree asked. "I know that the zoo has a picnic area and a playground. I like the idea of going to the zoo. I would vote for that."

"I think we are making progress," Ms. Aquino noted. "Let's see if we have any consensus. How many of you think the idea of going to the zoo and having a picnic at the park is a good idea?" Several students hesitated, looking around the group to see how their friends would vote. Slowly hands went up, and in seconds every hand was up. "Wonderful: I think we have reached an agreement that will please everyone. I'm proud of your willingness to work through this problem."

STRENGTHS AND WEAKNESSES OF CONFLICT RESOLUTION

With students exposed to a daily diet of talk shows on which the participants yell and scream at each other rather than actively work to resolve conflicts, it is critical that students learn that there is another way to resolve conflicts. Crawford and Bodine's conflict-resolution model is an important alternative, because it invites participation and expects those who choose to participate to plan for more effective behavior.

An additional strength in Crawford and Bodine's model is that faculty and students work and learn together while supporting one another. Conflict resolution and peer mediation promote academic and social growth, in that they increase skills in listening, critical thinking, and problem solving—skills basic to all learning.

School-based conflict-resolution programs reach every child in the school. They are critical in changing the total school environment and creating a safe community that promotes nonviolence. When youth experience success with negotiation, mediation, or consensus decision making in school, they are more likely to use these conflict-resolution processes elsewhere in their lives.

Unfortunately, conflict-resolution programs, whether classroom or schoolwide, require additional time and planning on the part of teachers and administrators. Many teachers contend that they simply don't have the extra time needed to implement the plan.

Others note that conflict resolution works only if all participants are willing to cooperate and be actively involved in reaching a solution. If one of the parties in the conflict refuses to participate, then the process fails, and more traditional discipline methods have to be implemented.

SUMMARY

Conflict resolution and peer mediation are accepted parts of many schools' discipline plans. Donna Crawford and Richard Bodine propose that conflict resolution offers an alternative approach to classroom management that brings the parties of a dispute together, provides them with the skills to resolve the dispute, and then requires them to use these skills to resolve the problem. There are three basic types of conflict resolution available for use by students and teachers: mediation, negotiations, and consensus decision making.

KEY TERMINOLOGY

Definitions for these terms appear in the glossary:

Conflict Resolution	Negotiations
Consensus decision making	Peaceable classroom
Curriculum approach	Peaceable school
Hard responses	Principled responses
Mediation	Soft responses

CHAPTER ACTIVITIES

Reflecting on the Theory

1. A committee of faculty, administrators, and parents at Liberty High School are reviewing the school's zero-tolerance policy. They incorporated the policy two years earlier as a response to an increase in the number of fights they were seeing between students. However, in most cases the fights were the result of misunderstandings and could have easily been resolved before punches were thrown. They fear that a reversal in the zero-tolerance policy will send a message that violence is tolerated, but they also realize that the policy creates more problems than it resolves.

    How could the establishment of a conflict-resolution program at Liberty High School provide an alternative to their zero-tolerance policy?

2. This chapter presents three approaches to conflict resolution. Do you consider all three equally effective, or is there one you would be more comfortable implementing? Why?
3. In the first scenario, Jamil and Sean agreed to negotiate. Should they still face the consequences for their behavior at the computer center? Why or why not?

Developing Your Portfolio

1. Consider conflicts you have observed between students. What were the causes of these conflicts? What could the teacher have done to prevent these conflicts? Could these conflicts have been successfully resolved through conflict resolution and peer mediation?

Developing Your Personal Philosophy of Classroom Management

1. One of the criticisms of conflict resolution is that it requires a great deal of time and planning by the classroom teacher. Do you think the benefits of conflict resolution are sufficient to offset the time commitment by the teacher? Is this an approach you will use in your classroom? Why or why not?
2. Do you feel that conflict resolution is a solution to all conflicts that occur in schools? Are there types of students or students of certain grade levels who might not respond to conflict resolution? Are there types of conflict that must be dealt with by teachers and administrators rather than by students? Explain your answer.

RESOURCES FOR FURTHER STUDY

Further information about conflict resolution and resources for its use in the classroom can be found by contacting:

Donna Crawford
National Center for Conflict Resolution Education
Executive Director
110 West Main Street
Urbana, IL 61801
(217) 384-4118

CHAPTER REFERENCES

Bodine, R. J., Crawford, D. K., & Schrumpf, F. (1994). *Creating the peaceable school: A comprehensive program for teaching conflict resolution. Program Guide.* Champaign, IL: Research Press.

Crawford, D. K., & Bodine, R. J. (1996). *Conflict resolution education: A guide to implementing programs in schools, youth-serving organizations, and community and juvenile justice settings.* Washington, DC: U.S. Department of Justice, Office of Juvenile Justice and Delinquency Prevention, and U.S. Department of Education, Office of Elementary and Secondary Education, Safe and Drug-Free Schools Program.

Crawford, D. K., & Bodine, R. J. (2001). Conflict resolution education: Preparing youth for the future. *Juvenile Justice, 8,* 21–29.

Kreidler, W. J. (1984). *Creative conflict resolution.* Glenville, IL: Scott, Foresman.

Peterson, G. J. (1997). Looking at the big picture: School administrators and violence reduction. *Journal of School Leadership, 7,* 456–479.

Chapter 13

Judicious Discipline

Objectives

Chapter 13 prepares preservice teachers to meet INTASC standards #3 (Diverse Learners), #5 (Motivation and Management), and #9 (Reflective Practitioner) by helping them to:

- understand the basic principles behind Judicious Discipline.
- understand how Judicious Discipline helps all students, regardless of backgrounds, abilities, and behaviors, to feel that they are a part of the school community.
- evaluate the rights of students guaranteed by the United States Constitution.
- establish class rules based on three core amendments: the First, Fourth, and Fourteenth Amendments.
- learn that all classroom management strategies must protect students' due process.
- evaluate the balance between individual rights and responsibilities.
- learn the appropriate application of Judicious Discipline in the classroom.

Scenario

The student council at John F. Kennedy Middle School is struggling to develop a new dress code. The members of the council agree that the way many of their classmates dress is offensive, but they are hesitant to place too many restrictions on the student body. Frustrated, Aaron says, "I still think we have no right putting restraints on what someone wears. How about our right to free speech? Isn't the way we dress one of the ways we express ourselves? Doesn't the Constitution protect our personal rights even if we are students?"

Mr. Reedy, the student council sponsor, tries to explain. Remembering a line he learned from one of his education classes, he says, "Aaron, students don't leave their personal rights at the schoolhouse door. Of course you have your rights, but the rights of an individual student can't interfere with the rights of others. Therefore, we have to carefully balance our decisions to ensure that the rights of an individual student don't interfere with the rights of all the other students to learn or to participate."

Shaking her head in confusion, Kennisha says, "I don't think this group is smart enough to figure this out. How does a school ever manage to balance the rights of a thousand individuals with the needs and interests of the entire student body?"

INTRODUCTION

Kennisha's question is a good one, and one that administrators, teachers, and school boards struggle with on a daily basis as they strive to establish and maintain a learning environment that ensures justice and equality. Forrest Gathercoal (2001) addresses these issues through his classroom-management model, **Judicious Discipline**. Noting that one of the most important jobs of educators is the teaching of citizenship, Gathercoal proposes that

Judicious Discipline teaches citizenship by requiring educators and administrators to acknowledge and respect students as citizens. Gathercoal suggests that citizenship is best learned when educators teach students about their individual rights and allow students to exercise their rights within the school and its classrooms.

Judicious Discipline is both a philosophy and a framework for classroom management and school discipline. Forrest Gathercoal (2001) describes Judicious Discipline as "a management style based on the synthesis of professional ethics, good educational practice, and students' constitutional rights and responsibilities" (p. 15). Judicious Discipline allows teachers to move beyond punishments and rewards to the development of personal responsibility and moral behavior.

F. Gathercoal (2001) stresses that a classroom-management model such as Judicious Discipline is needed for two reasons. One is the increasing diversity in our classrooms. The constitutional framework of Judicious Discipline ensures equality that cuts across cultural, ethnic, and religious lines. F. Gathercoal (2001) contends that Judicious Discipline helps all students, regardless of backgrounds, abilities, and behaviors, realize that they have a valued place in the school community. Through Judicious Discipline, intolerance and prejudices can be replaced with concern for others, feelings of self-worth and confidence, a sense of belonging, and a cooperative attitude.

The second reason for the need for a classroom model with an emphasis on student rights is the shift from "in loco parentis" to the realization that students "no longer shed their constitutional rights at the schoolhouse gate" (F. Gathercoal, 2001, p. 51). Until 1969, court decisions historically supported the concept of "**in loco parentis**," which granted to educators the same legal authority over students as that of parents. Early courts' decisions applied the same "abuse tests" used for parents to educators, and unless abuse was evident, courts rarely interceded. Today, the situation is much different. "In loco parentis" has been replaced by language that addressees the constitutional rights and responsibilities of students. F. Gathercoal (2001) notes that today "our public schools and classrooms have become, in fact, microcosms of the United States of America" (p. 51).

Judicious Discipline is an approach to classroom management that provides educators with a foundation for teaching citizenship. This is primarily done through daily student–teacher interactions. Educators using Judicious Discipline become role models who practice the values of a democratic society through the professional and ethical relationships they establish with all members of their learning community (McEwan, P. Gathercoal, & Nimmo, 1999).

Judicious Discipline is unique, because the constitutional language that is used promotes reasoned decision making and a peaceful school climate. P. Gathercoal & Nimmo (2001) describe Judicious Discipline as a citizenship approach, based on the U.S. Bill of Rights, that teaches students about their rights and responsibilities for living and learning in a democratic society.

THE BILL OF RIGHTS

The foundation of Judicious Discipline is the U.S. Bill of Rights. The Bill of Rights, the first ten amendments to the U.S. Constitution, were written to protect three basic human

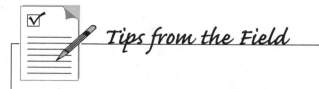

Tips from the Field

My most effective classroom management "trick" is always to have fast-paced lessons and to keep students focused on the task at all times. I must know my lesson so well that I can constantly run and work the class while being aware of potential issues and problems before they appear. If students are actively engaged in their own education, they will not have time to stray from the purpose of the class. I have found, in many classes I observe, that time is wasted by the teacher preparing class material during instructional time. Thus students know that their time is being wasted, and they act out. To prevent this, teachers must be prepared with all materials ready when instruction begins.

David Neves
Music Teacher and Band Director
2002 RI Teacher of the Year
Scituate High School-Middle School
Scituate, RI

values: freedom, justice, and equality. F. Gathercoal (2001) notes that it is important that students understand that in our nation's constitutional democracy, individual human rights are as important as the needs and interests of the majority. Three of those amendments—the First, Fourth, and Fourteenth—specifically apply to schools. Teachers who practice Judicious Discipline teach students the concepts of these three amendments and how they apply in the school environment.

The First Amendment

Congress shall make no law respecting an establishment of religion or prohibiting the free exercise thereof; or abridging the freedom of speech or of the press; or of the people peaceably to assemble, and to petition the government for a redress of grievances.

According to F. Gathercoal (2001), the First Amendment protects freedom of speech, freedom of expression, freedom of press, freedom of religion, and the right to assemble peacefully. Until the late 1960s, the courts rarely applied the First Amendment to students. However, during the years following the Vietnam War, numerous judicial decisions related to matters concerning free speech were litigated. In addition, issues concerning student rights to publish and distribute material on school premises have been raised in the court. However, it has been matters related to church-state and school relationships that have been most troublesome for courts to resolve.

The constitutional framework of Judicious Discipline ensures equality that cuts across cultural, ethnic, and religious lines.

The Fourth Amendment

The right of the people to be secure in their persons, houses, papers, and effects against unreasonable searches and seizures, shall not be violated, and no warrants shall issue but upon probable cause, supported by oath or affirmation, and particularly describing the place to be searched, and the persons or things to be seized.

This amendment addresses situations in which it is necessary for teachers and administrators to take property from students. Effective school management requires school personnel to adhere to guidelines similar to those law-enforcement officers have to follow when taking property from students. The Fourth Amendment protects students' property at school and requires teachers and administrators to have reasonable cause to search lockers or desks (F. Gathercoal, 2001).

The Fourteenth Amendment

All persons born or naturalized in the United States, and subject to the jurisdiction thereof, are citizens of the United States and of the state wherein they reside. No state shall make or enforce any law which shall abridge the privileges or immunities of citizens of the United States; nor shall any state deprive any person of life, liberty, or property, without due process of law; nor deny to any person the equal protection of the laws.

F. Gathercoal (2001) notes that two phrases of the Fourteenth Amendment have had a significant impact on public education. The first, known as the "due-process clause," provides the legal basis for reasonable rules and a fair process for balancing student rights. Educators who understand and are able to apply the concepts of due process to student conflicts are viewed as just and fair. In order to have the right to appeal, courts require that there be a state action. Therefore, only students in public schools enjoy due process. Administrators and teachers must understand that every rule or decision made in a public institution is subject to review by another person, board, or court and that all rules and decisions made in public schools are appealable.

The last cause, known as the "equal-protection clause," serves as the constitutional foundation for prohibiting all forms of discrimination. The Fourteenth Amendment provides equal protection under the law and protects against discrimination based on sex, race, national origin, disabilities, age, or religion.

COMPELLING STATE INTERESTS

Providing a balance to the individual rights held by students are four time-tested public-interest arguments crafted in the courts for the precise purpose of limiting constitutionally protected freedoms (F. Gathercoal, 2001). These arguments are well grounded in legal principles and history and are the line of reasoning that allows for individual rights. Authority for denying people their civil rights comes from Article I, Section 8 of the Constitution, which reads, in part, "The Congress shall have power to provide for the common Defense and General Welfare of the United States." This general-welfare clause acts as the legal foundation for legislative bodies representing the needs and interests of the majority.

This legal concept is commonly referred to as "compelling state interests," and simply means that in some cases the welfare and interests of the majority are more compelling than the rights of an individual. These compelling interests give educators all the legal authority they need to create and carry out fair and equitable school rules (F. Gathercoal, 2001; Larson, 1998).

The following four **compelling state interests** assure that the needs and interests of the majority are balanced with the rights and needs of individuals:

1. **Property Loss and Damage:** an interest that acts as steward for the care and appropriate use of individually and state-owned property.
2. **Threat to Health and Safety:** an interest that serves a fundamental purpose of government to protect the health and safety of students who attend public schools.
3. **Legitimate Educational Purpose:** an interest that legitimizes administrators', teachers', and the educational institution's license to make arbitrary decisions that are based on sound educational practice and the mission of the school.
4. **Serious Disruption of the Educational Process:** an interest empowering schools with the professional responsibility to deny student rights that seriously disrupt student activities (P. Gathercoal & Nimmo, 2001).

TABLE 13.1   *Principles of Judicious Discipline*

Student Rights of Freedom, Justice, and Equality Provided through the First, Fourth, and Fourteenth Amendments	Student Responsibility Expressed in Four Compelling State Interests:
	    Property Loss and Damage
	    Threat to Health and Safety
	    Legitimate Educational Purpose
	    Serious Disruption of
	    the Educational Process

Exercise of Rights and Responsibilities in the Appropriate Time, Place, and Manner	

School rules and policies based upon these four compelling state interests are upheld in court. Educators not only have a legal *authority* to deny student constitutional rights, but it is their professional *responsibility* to prohibit student behaviors if those behaviors are deterimental to the welfare of the school (P. Gathercoal & Nimmo, 2001).

TIME, PLACE, AND MANNER

When students are taught about the need for balancing their rights with the rights and interests of society, they come to understand that there is always an appropriate time, place, and manner for exercising their individual rights. McEwan et al. (1999) note that Judicious Discipline teaches students to examine their actions critically by looking at their behaviors in light of the "appropriate time, place, or manner" criteria.

Judicious Discipline is composed of ten basic principles. The principles of individual freedom, justice, and equality provided by the First, Fourth, and Fourteenth Amendments are balanced with the four compelling state interests—property loss and damage, legitimate educational purpose, health and safety, and serious disruption. Providing the bridge between individual rights and the needs of the majority are the questions of reasonable time, place, and manner. Table 13.1 shows the balance between these principles.

IMPLEMENTATION

Because the concepts presented in Judicious Discipline are counter to the typical behavior-management approaches presented in schools, it is critical for teachers to provide classroom instruction about the concepts of Judicious Discipline (McEwan et al., 1999). F. Gathercoal (2001) stresses that such activities should begin on the first day of school, in order to communicate trust in students' abilities to reason and to act appropriately.

Teachers incorporating Judicious Discipline into their classroom structures begin by introducing students to the rights encompassed in the concepts of freedom, justice, and equality (McEwan et al., 1999). Students are taught that they have the freedom to express themselves in their speech, their clothing, their writing, and in other aspects of their lives. However, it is also made clear to students that a free society only functions successfully when all citizens understand and abide by the limits to those freedoms. Students then develop classroom and school expectations by rewording the four compelling state interests into positive behavioral statements and language they understand.

P. Gathercoal and Nimmo (2001) suggest that the teacher define each positive behavioral statement by conducting a democratic class meeting. From the first day of class through the rest of the school year, class meetings can serve as the lifeblood of a democratic community. Class meetings are important, in that they create a sense of enfranchisement for students. Paul Gathercoal (2000) stresses that democratic class meetings provide students with a sense of value and belonging, and are therefore an essential part of the effective operation of all Judicious Discipline classrooms. Class meetings can give students a feeling of significance and eliminate most of the reasons students resort to "power struggles." Landau and P. Gathercoal (2000) stress the following key elements of democratic class meetings:

- Teachers and students determine who can call a class meeting and when meetings should be held.
- All students and the teacher should be seated so that everyone can see the faces of the others in the class meetings.
- The teacher sets the ground rule that individual names will not be used during the class meetings. The purpose is to discuss issues rather than individuals.
- The teacher reminds students of the expectation that they will stay on the topic and avoid sharing personal information during the class meetings.
- Students should never be coerced to participate in the class meeting.
- Each student and teacher should be encouraged to have a class-meeting journal. Immediately following each meeting, both teachers and students should take a few minutes to record their thoughts about what took place.
- Students and the teachers should write down the goals they set for themselves after or during the class meetings.

McEwan (1991) stresses that Judicious Discipline is not designed to supplant other discipline models or to be used alone. She feels that Judicious Discipline is most successful when used with other student-centered discipline approaches. Judicious discipline is designed to be integrated into these other approaches by specifically framing the decision-making process of management in the language of human rights and responsibilities. Dreikurs's model, Logical Consequences, is often used as a complimentary piece to Judicious Discipline.

DEVELOPING RULES AND CONSEQUENCES

After a classroom discussion of the rights and responsibilities of students, classroom rules are developed together. However, F. Gathercoal (2001) notes that it is not the rules that keep students in school and behaving appropriately but rather the philosophy and attitude with which educators approach rules that convince students that they belong. The philosophy

When visiting a school in Scotland, I learned about a program to prevent bullying in schools. Friends against Bullying (FAB) is designed to reduce the amount of bullying among students by dealing with bullying behavior and teaching students ways of dealing with bullying by other students. From kindergarten to eighth grade, students are encouraged to report incidences of bullying. Students who bully meet with the principal, counselor, and parents in order to discuss needed changes in behavior. Students who are bullied participate in counseling sessions to learn to be assertive in order to stop future bullying. When all members of the school—students, teachers, administrators, staff, and parents—treat bullying as a serious problem that must be stopped, the incidences of bullying are greatly reduced.

Deborah Newman
Grade 7 English/Reading Teacher
Wassom Middle School
Fort Campbell, KY

upon which all rules and decisions are based is critical to whether school will be an inviting and safe place for students.

The four compelling state interests are the basis for classroom rules (McEwan, 2000). Educators should work to develop rules that emphasize the behavior desired and empower students to think for themselves. Rules should be written clearly for the educational level of those affected. It is imperative that students fully understand the meaning of rules in order to meet the adequate-notice requirement of the Fourteenth Amendment. Consider how the students in Ms. Stafenau's fifth-grade class develop rules from the four compelling state interests:

"Class, now that we have discussed the four compelling state interests, we are going to use these interests to develop our class rules. I want to divide you into groups and have each group suggest rules that we might want for our class that relate to the compelling state interests you are assigned."

After the groups discussed possible rules for their classroom, Ms. Stafenau asked each group to report. "Wade, your group had the compelling state interest of Health and Safety. What rules did you develop?"

As Wade listed each rule, he also wrote the rule on the whiteboard. "We developed the following four rules:

Be careful with your words.
Walk when inside the school or classroom.
Keep hands and feet to yourself.
Use classroom equipment safely."

"Your group did an excellent job. I noticed that you expressed the rules in positive terms. We may want to consider this for all our rules. Nina, your group had the compelling state interest of Property Loss and Damage. What rules did your group develop?"

Nina came to the front of the classroom. "Our group had one rule similar to the first group: 'Be careful with classroom equipment.' We could only think of two other rules. They are:

> Ask permission before using someone else's things.
> Treat school property with respect."

"Very good. Seth, your group had Serious Disruption of the Educational Process. What rules did you group develop?"

"Well, we said ours as don'ts," Seth explained as he came to the front of the room, "but they can be changed if you want. Here are our rules:

> Don't touch anyone without permission.
> Don't make noise while others are working.
> Don't use bad language.
> Don't talk when someone else is talking."

As Seth returned to his desk, Ms. Stafenau explained, "Well if we decide to write our rules in positive terms rather than negative, I think we can easily change what you wrote. All right, our last group is Karlisa's. What rules did you develop for Legitimate Educational Purpose?"

"We developed three rules. They are:

> Come to school prepared to learn.
> Bring needed materials to class.
> Work quietly and on time."

Reviewing the students' work, Ms. Stafenau said, "All of you did a great job. Now let's decide if we will keep all the rules or select the ones we think will best serve our class."

Judicious rules necessitate judicious consequences (Larson, 1998). One important concept of the Judicious Discipline model is that it focuses on teaching appropriate behavior, not punishing inappropriate behavior. When students misbehave, teachers act as mentors, viewing students' problems as an educational opportunity. When a problem does occur or a rule is broken, Judicious Discipline advocates approaching the situation as a teachable moment.

Teachers begin by asking questions. Behavior questions should be approached by asking general questions of inquiry and concern in an effort to encourage students to talk about their perceptions of the event. It means approaching the problem from the perspective of the student with the intent of getting to the heart of the problem and understanding the student's point of view. F. Gathercoal (2001) stresses that questions have a way of "softening the blow" to those who might be in the wrong and allowing them to save face and recover. By asking leading questions and listening carefully, the underlying issues begin to emerge. The students then have the opportunity to tell about the situation, recalling what happened, explaining perceptions of the situation, making predictions about what is likely to happen, and suggesting possible choices based on recollections and predictions. The question/reflecting process is important, because, as F. Gathercoal (2001) states, "Good communication lies not in the words we use, but in the spaces between the words. The longer the spaces, the more we are sharing power with our students" (p. 120).

Consequences should flow logically from the student's misbehavior and not be designed to punish students. When rules are broken, the discussion needs to center around two important questions: What needs to be done now? What can we learn from this? Consider the questions Mr. Davis asks a student who has vandalized the school:

When Springlake High School principal Paul Davis saw the graffiti written on the back wall of the gym, he feared he knew who had written "Coach Greene is unfair. Coach Greene sucks." The day before, basketball coach Joel Greene had cut tenth-grader Bastian Borowik from the team. A review of the campus video-surveillance tapes confirmed that sometime during the night, Bastian had used spray paint to express his anger on the back wall of the school.

Within minutes of the opening of school, Bastian sat in the principal's office. After showing Bastian the incriminating evidence, Mr. Davis asked, "Bastian, do you want to tell me why you did this?"

Defensively, Bastian responded, "You are always talking about our rights. Well, don't I have the right to say what I want? What happened to free speech?"

"You absolutely have the right to free speech, and there were several ways you could have expressed your anger over being cut from the team. If you had written a letter to the school paper or come to talk to me, those would have been appropriate actions. If you wanted to walk with a sign around school stating that you think the coach is unfair, you would have had my permission. But you didn't consider two other things when considering your rights. First, one of our compelling state interests is protection of school property. Now, the back wall of the gym will have to be repainted. Second, remember that there is an appropriate time, place, and manner in which to do everything. You went about this in the wrong manner. We have a game tonight. Your classmates aren't going to be happy to have what you wrote on the wall of the gym displayed during our game. So, we need to think what you need to do next. What do you think? How do we fix this? What do we do now?"

Bastian dropped his head. Embarrassed by his own behavior, he thought of what he could do to make up for the problems he had created. Finally, he said, "First I need to apologize. I need to apologize to Coach Greene, and I need to apologize to the school. I think I should apologize to Coach Greene in private, but I will apologize to the school when you make the morning announcements, if that is all right."

"I think that is a good way to start. What are we going to do about the wall?"

"I'll repaint the wall. If I start this morning, do you think it will be done by tonight? I guess we need to call my parents and tell them what I've done. I may need their help in buying the paint I need."

"I think you are developing a good plan. I'm going to leave you alone so you can call your parents. We will talk again after you get off the phone."

There are two important aspects in determining consequences for each student's misbehavior. The first is understanding the real nature of the problem, and the second is taking into account individual differences among students (McEwan, 2001). By definition, judicious consequences are designed to take into account individual differences among students in order to meet the emotional and learning needs of each person involved. Because consequences are educational by nature, students who misbehave simply may have different ways of learning from their mistakes. As a result, different consequences are necessary. Age and the mental, emotional, and physical condition of the students being punished are factors that must be considered when determining reasonable consequences.

Judicious consequences are never malicious, cruel, or excessive. Table 13.2 provides a listing of discipline methods that should be avoided when using Judicious Discipline.

Conferences, community service, apology, and restitution are along the many appropriate options available. It is most important for educators using Judicious Discipline to be flexible about consequences, because what is most appropriate for one situation may not be for another. F. Gathercoal (2001) notes that this flexibility helps to avoid the mistake of being locked into predetermined responses that fail to meet the needs of the individual student or the student body as whole.

TABLE 13.2   *Discipline Practices to Avoid*

Demeaning students

Judging or lecturing students on their behaviors

Comparing students

Criticizing students

Demanding respect

Refusing to apologize

Accusing students of not trying

Asking students why they misbehave

Getting into a power struggle

Becoming defensive

Losing control

Intimidating students

Punishing the class for one student's misbehavior

Acting too quickly without information

Believing that all students should be treated equally

Source: Forrest Gathercoal, 2001.

JUDICIOUS DISCIPLINE IN THE CLASSROOM

Scenario

Realizing that many of the sixth-grade students entering Westover Middle School had never been taught using a classroom-management plan like Judicious Discipline, the sixth-grade teachers spend much of the first week of classes discussing student rights and responsibilities. After spending time the first day providing an overview of Judicious Discipline, Ms. Umayam spent the second day discussing the issues related to the First Amendment.

Reading the First Amendment to the class, Ms. Umayam asked, "All right, what rights does this amendment give to you as individuals?"

Heather raised her hand and said, "Well, as a citizen I have freedom of speech. But does this mean I can say anything I want to anyone, including a teacher?"

"Well, having personal rights doesn't give us total freedom to do anything we want. Remember what we talked about yesterday. If your rights interfere with those of the majority and are in conflict with one of the compelling state interests, then your rights might be limited. Can anyone think of an example?"

Brittney answered, "Well, if I stood in the middle of the hall and yelled, 'Run! Run!' I might cause chaos. That might be a threat to health and safety."

"Exactly! In addition to considering the compelling state interests, we have to consider the proper time, place, and manner for our actions. So yelling 'run' in a crowded hallway might never be appropriate, or it might be the right thing to do if there was some immediate danger in the hall. So we have to always remember that our personal freedoms have to be balanced with the compelling state interests and with whether it is the appropriate time, place, and manner for our actions."

STRENGTHS AND WEAKNESSES OF JUDICIOUS DISCIPLINE

Judicious Discipline is the only model for school and classroom management that is based on principles of democracy and operates at the principled level of moral development. Since its introduction in the 1980s, those using it have found that Judicious Discipline:

- empowers students to be strong in character.
- encourages higher-order thinking skills through real social situations as students are invited to describe, explain, predict, and make reasoned choices.
- minimizes classroom stress and anxiety for both students and teachers because of the environmental emphasis on human rights and individual dignity.
- serves as a real-life model for the same system of rules and responsibilities under which students will live when they leave school.
- teaches students accountability, self-efficacy, tolerance, cooperation, and mutual respect.
- promotes fairness and consistency by balancing individual freedom, justice, and equality with the needs and interests of society.

- contributes to a decrease in dropout rates, in acts of violence in and around schools, and in referrals to the office, while also resulting in an increase in any levels of daily attendance (F. Gathercoal, 2001; P. Gathercoal & Nimmo, 2001).

Most importantly, Judicious Discipline does not wait for problems to occur. Teachers who use this constitutional framework for classroom rules and decisions teach students to resolve classroom conflicts peacefully in a democratic forum.

However, not everyone will find Judicious Discipline as a workable model for their classrooms. If teachers do not believe that students have the ability to think and behave responsibility, a democratic model will not work for them. F. Gathercoal (2001) notes that much of the success of Judicious Discipline comes from the teacher's ability to trust their students, teaching them the concepts of rights and responsibilities, and acting in ways consistent with civil responsibility. To teach one thing and do another is abuse of power and is disrespectful to the human rights of the students.

It is time consuming to use an approach such as Judicious Discipline. P. Gathercoal and Nimmo (2001) found that teachers need time to make Judicious Discipline work. Converting to a democratic school community takes time, because students and teachers are not accustomed to reacting in this manner. It takes time to process new perceptions and expectations.

Finally, there are students who may not be cognitively or emotionally able to respond to an approach like Judicious Discipline (Larson, 1998). Students who are emotionally unstable or who suffer from physiological disorders may not respond to the principles of Judicious Discipline. For Judicious Discipline to be effective, students must have reached a level of moral development that allows them to understand socially agreed-upon standards of individual rights. This will lessen its effectiveness with very young children and those who are not cognitively able to process these ideas.

SUMMARY

Administrators, teachers, and school boards struggle daily to establish and maintain a learning environment that ensures justice and equality for all students. Forrest Gathercoal addresses these needs through his classroom-management model, ***Judicious Discipline***. Judicious Discipline is both a philosophy and a framework for classroom management and school discipline, and is composed of ten basic principles. The principles of individual freedom, justice, and equality provided by the First, Fourth, and Fourteenth Amendments are balanced with the four compelling state interests—property loss and damage, legitimate educational purpose, health and safety, and serious disruption. Providing the bridge between individual rights and the needs of the majority are the questions of reasonable time, place, and manner.

KEY TERMINOLOGY

Definitions for these terms appear in the glossary:

Compelling state interests   Judicious Discipline
In loco parentis

CHAPTER ACTIVITIES

Reflecting on the Theory

1. In the middle of Mr. Lee's discussion of noun/verb agreement, Deidre England exclaimed, "Yuk, there's chewing gum stuck to the bottom of this desk." After class, Mr. Lee was disappointed to find chewed gum stuck to several of the desks. He thought he had been fair to all students when he allowed students to chew gum in his class. Now, he is considering disallowing all gum chewing.

   How could Mr. Lee use the principles of Judicious Discipline to resolve this problem?

2. There are those who suggest that Judicious Discipline can work only when it is a schoolwide plan and will not be effective for an individual classroom. Do you agree? What problems could develop if Judicious Discipline were used only in an individual classroom rather than by an entire school?

3. Give an example of when the rights of an individual student should come before the rights of the student body as a whole.

Developing Your Portfolio

1. What rules could you develop for your class based on the four compelling state interests?

2. Judicious Discipline teaches students to examine their actions critically by teaching them to examine their behaviors in light of the "appropriate time, place, or manner" criterion. Develop an activity to help students understand this concept.

Developing Your Personal Philosophy of Classroom Management

1. Judicious Discipline requires a great deal of time and planning by the classroom teacher. Do you consider the benefits of Judicious Discipline sufficient to offset the time commitment by the teacher? Why or why not?

2. Consider the age and maturity level of the students you will be teaching. Would Judicious Discipline be an effective classroom-management tool to use with these students? Why or why not?

RESOURCES FOR FURTHER STUDY

Further information about Judicious Discipline and resources for its use in the classroom can be found by contacting:

Forrest Gathercoal
Caddo Gap Press
3145 Geary Boulevard
Suite 275
San Francisco, CA 94118
Telephone 415/392-1911
Fax 415/956-3702

CHAPTER REFERENCES

Gathercoal, F. (2001). *Judicious discipline*. San Francisco: Caddo Gap Press.

Gathercoal, P. (2000). *Conducting democratic class meetings: School violence and conflict*. New Orleans, LA: Annual Meeting of the American Educational Research Association. (ERIC Document Reproduction Service No. ED442736)

Gathercoal, P., & Nimmo, V. (2001). *Judicious (character education) discipline programs.* Seattle, WA: Annual Meeting of the American Educational Research Association. (ERIC Document Reproduction Service No. ED453124)

Landau, B. M., & Gathercoal, P. (2000). Creating peaceful classrooms. *Phi Delta Kappa, 81*, 450–455.

Larson, C. (1998). *Judicious discipline*. Beijing, China: Annual China–U.S. Conference on Education. (ERIC Document Reproduction Service No. ED427395)

McEwan, B. (1991). *Practicing Judicious Discipline: An educator's guide to a democratic classroom*. Davis, CA: Caddo Gap Press.

McEwan, B. (2000). *The art of classroom management: Effective practices for building equitable learning communities*. Upper Saddle River, NJ: Merrill/Prentice Hall.

McEwan, B., Gathercoal, P., & Nimmo, V. (1999). Application of Judicious Discipline: A common language for classroom management. In H. Jerome Freiberg (Ed.), *Beyond behaviorism: Changing the classroom management paradigm*. Boston: Allyn & Bacon.

Part
IV

Developing a Personal System

The last two chapters of this text provide information to assist teachers in designing a personal system of classroom management. Chapter 14 provides information for creating a safe learning environment for all students and explores issues related to multi-cultural and socioeconomic factors, physical and mental disabilities, and at-risk behaviors. Chapter 15 helps the individual teacher put together all elements of classroom management into a comprehensive program.

Chapter 14

Creating Safe and Welcoming Classrooms for All Students

Objectives

Chapter 14 prepares preservice teachers to meet INTASC standards #2 (Student Development), #3 (Diverse Learners), #5 (Motivation and Management), #6 (Communication), #7 (Planning), #8 (Assessment), #9 (Reflective Practitioner), and #10 (School and Community) by helping them to:

- learn strategies for creating a classroom environment that respects individual differences.
- recognize the importance of collaboration in supporting the diverse needs of students.
- access appropriate services and resources to meet exceptional learning and social needs.
- use knowledge of different cultural contexts (socioeconomic, ethnic, cultural) in managing student behavior.
- take into account student differences as they develop a personal classroom-management plan.
- appreciate the cultural dimensions of communication to foster culturally sensitive communication by and among all students in the classroom.
- understand how factors in students' environments outside of school influence their lives and learning.
- become cognizant of the various laws that protect the rights of students.
- identify students who have a tendency toward violent or abusive behavior.

Scenario

In preparation for student teaching, preservice teacher Rebecca Choi is spending time in the classroom of her cooperating teacher David Libertore. During the first hours of observing, Rebecca is amazed to watch as one student routinely moves in a circle around his desk. Watching more carefully, Rebecca notices that a circle has been drawn on the floor surrounding the desk. Several times throughout the morning, the student paces around the circle, always careful not to cross the painted line.

Curious about the student's strange behavior and the purpose of the painted line, Rebecca asks Mr. Libertore about him.

"Oh, you mean Travis. Travis is ADD, and even with medication, we have found that Travis simply can't stay in his seat. I spent the first six weeks of this year constantly telling Travis to sit down. We finally devised a plan that allows Travis to stand up and move around. As long as he doesn't move beyond the line on the floor, I leave him alone."

"Doesn't his constant movement bother the other students?"

"I think they have gotten used to him. For the most part, they ignore him. I assure you, we are getting a lot more done now than we were when I was constantly stopping instruction to tell Travis to sit down."

Pondering this solution, Rebecca asks, "But is this fair? The other students aren't allowed to walk around whenever *they* wish to."

Trying to explain, Mr. Libertore asks, "Rebecca, have you noticed the microphone I wear? Allen has a hearing impairment. I wear a microphone, and he wears earphones so he can hear me. Now the other students aren't allowed to wear earphones. Is that fair?"

"But Allen has a disability. You are required to accommodate for his disability."

"So does Travis. I accommodate Allen by wearing a microphone, and I accommodate Travis by drawing a line around his desk and giving him space to move around." Seeing that Rebecca was still struggling with the concept, Mr. Libertore said, "To be an effective teacher, you must find ways to meet the needs of all your students. Sometimes that means you have to think outside the box and do things a little differently. I think the solution we have found for Travis meets his needs, allows me to do my job, and is fair to the other students. Accomplishing all three of these goals isn't always easy, but it is worth the effort to try in every case."

INTRODUCTION

Mr. Libertore's classroom is typical of classrooms across the United States, because today's classrooms are more diverse than at any other period in history. This diversity requires a departure from the one-size-fits-all approach to classroom management used in the past. To be effective classroom managers, teachers must be aware of the cultural and social issues that impact student behavior. Socioeconomic levels, religion, family structures, home backgrounds, culture, race, and gender influence student behavior (Evertson, Emmer, & Worsham, 2000). If teachers do not understand these factors that contribute to student behavior, they may use inappropriate techniques to stop misbehaviors, show a lack of understanding or care for students, misinterpret student behavior, and, too often, create situations that cause students to retreat further from the classroom environment.

Weinstein and Mignano (1997) stress that teachers are also required to deal with the small percentage of students who act out, who are violent, and who pose a threat to themselves, the teacher, or the other students in the classroom. Today's classrooms contain a greater number of children who are at risk for academic failure because of conditions associated with poverty, maternal prenatal exposure to alcohol and drugs, low birth weight, lead poisoning, neglect, violence, or malnutrition. Students with learning, behavior, or physical disabilities bring additional challenges to the classroom. The increasing number of students who are at risk, along with increasing diversity, makes managing classrooms more challenging now than during any other period of history.

Contributing to the complexity of these issues is the fact that the training and experiences of many classroom teachers have done little to prepare them for the decisions required in classrooms of the twenty-first century. Many of the classroom-management techniques used today were developed when classrooms were less diverse. The result is that teachers lack the skills to deal with the daily situations they encounter. Grossman (1995) stresses that teachers must be aware of the unique needs of each student, the strategies that will work best with particular groups, and the legal ramifications of the diversity issues that may arise from their instructional and management decisions.

CLASSROOM MANAGEMENT AND CULTURALLY DIVERSE STUDENTS

Frequently cited statistics reveal that, within the next 30–40 years, 40 percent of the public-school population will be composed of ethnic or racial minorities (Cartledge & Milburn, 1996). Many of these students will be first- or second-generation Americans, have English as their second language, endure poor socioeconomic conditions, and have unstable family situations. Cultural misunderstandings are inevitable and can have a negative impact on students and teachers.

No teacher wants to discriminate, but as Grossman (1995) notes, a teacher does not have to be prejudiced to use biased classroom-management techniques with students. Well-meaning teachers who lack cultural sensitivity can misperceive and misunderstand students' behaviors when they interpret those behaviors based on their own lifestyles, values, and perspectives. Using their own experiences as the benchmarks for appropriate behaviors, teachers may perceive behavior problems that do not exist, not notice problems that do exist, misunderstand the causes of students' behaviors, and use inappropriate techniques in dealing with students' misbehaviors.

It is critical, therefore, that teachers are able to differentiate between behaviors that need to be changed and cultural differences that either need to be respected in their current form or simply need to be redirected to meet specific social conditions. Cartledge and Milburn (1996) remind teachers that culture is not something that students invent. Instead, students have been socialized to behave according to traditions established over generations. Conflict can occur when the culture of the school is not in harmony with the culture each student brings to school.

When students are required to adjust to a culture that is significantly different from their own, they may become confused, anxious, and frustrated, because they don't know what is expected of them (Grossman, 1995). They may lack the means to interact appropriately and may develop interpersonal problems, because they may not understand the behavior of fellow students. They can also feel anxious and fearful about not being able to function adequately in the new culture or sad and depressed over the loss of their familiar way of life. Grossman (1995) calls this disorientation and confusion **culture shock.**

IMMIGRANTS

Recent increases in immigration, particularly from Latin America and Southeast Asia, have led to classes in which students come from a wide range of cultural and linguistic backgrounds (Weinstein & Mignano, 1997). When students immigrate to the United States, they may have trouble adapting to the new environment, causing them to become angry, anxious, sad, or depressed. Grossman (1995) stresses that imposing the school's culture on students without regard to the culture they bring with them can add to the stress of adjusting to a new environment.

Sensitive to their differences, students who are immigrants are likely to carve out for themselves patterns of behavior that are oppositional, incompatible with school success,

Tips from the Field

Time management in my classroom has always been important. During my 36 years of teaching, I have developed several techniques to save time and to keep students on task. I always begin the year by observing my students and then I put them in a seating arrangement. This helps me learn their names very quickly. When I check roll, I just look for vacant seats and, in a matter of seconds, mark those students who are absent. The seating arrangement also enables me to pass out graded papers quickly to my students. Each day I write the order of the day's classwork, activities, and homework on the board before class begins. It is the students' responsibility to write the homework for the night on their calendar when they enter the classroom. By following the order of class activities, the students and I stay on task without losing time.

Martha Barnes
Grade 8 Language Arts Teacher
Coopertown School
Springfield, TN

and self-destructive (Cartledge & Milburn, 1996). Grossman (1995) notes that students who are alienated, hostile, or suspicious of a dominant group often show this hostility at school. They may withdraw from their teachers and fellow students and act aggressively toward them. They may disbelieve and reject much of what they are taught in class.

When possible, Grossman (1995) suggests that teachers accept behavior caused by culture shock. Teachers need to be aware of and sensitive to situations that put students in conflict with their own customs and culture. If an activity is not appropriate or acceptable to students, then teachers, students, and parents should work together to find an alternative.

Teachers can make the classroom a safe haven for refugees who had to leave their homelands and sometimes even their families. Many of these students have been traumatized by their experiences and may be frightened by physical aggression, threats, or verbal confrontations among students. When confronted with topics such as war, starvation, and crime, they may become anxious and should be allowed to engage in another activity or leave the class until the discussion is terminated (Grossman, 1995).

MINORITY GROUPS

The population of the United States is rapidly becoming less European American with the fastest-growing student groups in American schools being African Americans, Latinos, and Asian Americans. Schools are now realizing that disparities in instruction, expectations, and discipline based on race can prevent the educational success of an entire category of young people (Schwartz, 2001). This change in school demographics requires all teachers to evaluate their interactions with students from minority groups.

AFRICAN AMERICANS

Grossman (1995) states, "African-American students are especially prone to have difficulty in school because of incompatibilities between the way many of them are encouraged to behave in their communities and the expectations of their teachers" (p. 143). Many African-American students are more expressive and intense in their interactions than their classmates. This causes many European-American teachers to fear that African-American students are being more aggressive and assertive than those students may intend to be. Attributing to them a level of anger that does not exist, teachers incorrectly react and intervene when no intervention is necessary (Cartledge & Milburn, 1996). Grossman (1995) notes that often teachers use different classroom-management techniques with African-American students as they spend more time anticipating possible misbehavior by African-American students. Teachers must develop an understanding of the nonverbal and verbal communication styles of African-American students in order to demonstrate that they value and respect all students.

LATINOS

Latino students also struggle to meet the expectations of their teachers and fit into the culture of their European-American classmates. Teachers must understand that when Latino students are made to compete against their will, criticized in front of their peers, recognized for their achievements, or coerced into other behaviors that are culturally at odds with theirs, they may feel rejected, abused, or picked on by their teachers. They may become insecure and anxious, rebel against such treatment, or withdraw from all attempts to succeed in school or to have relationships with their teachers. Because Latinos are less likely to state their unwillingness to do what others ask or expect from them, teachers can misperceive situational, emotional, and behavioral problems as personality problems (Grossman, 1995). It is important that educators take into consideration the vast array of nonverbal communications that some Latino students use to express their feelings.

ASIAN AMERICANS

Teachers also treat Asian-American students differently from European-American students. As they do with African-American and Latino students, teachers often have misperceptions about Asian Americans. As Cartledge and Milburn (1996) note, Asian Americans are unique among minorities in that their prevailing image is that of superachievers. However, many Asian-American students find the struggle to live up to behavioral stereotypes of academic and social superiority as unfair as those students who bear the burden of prejudicial inferiority.

Many strive daily to establish their competence and worth. If unable to meet the expectations of teachers, they may react in self-destructive means by acting out or withdrawing. When teachers equate "quiet" with "good," students who need help may be overlooked and experience school failure and other social problems as a result. Teachers must also be aware that Asian Americans represent a diverse group with different cultural and linguistic backgrounds.

APPROACHES FOR DEALING WITH DIVERSITY ISSUES

There is considerable disagreement among teachers about how to handle conflicts that occur when the culture of the school is incompatible with the culture of the student's family and community. Grossman (1995) describes four different approaches to resolving such conflicts: accommodation, assimilation, bicultural accommodation, and empowerment.

Accommodation

Many educators believe that, in order to be successful classroom managers, teachers must understand and treat their students as individuals. The **accommodation** approach requires teachers to adapt their management techniques to students' ethnicity, socioeconomic status, context, gender, and other individual characteristics (Grossman, 1995). Advocates of the accommodation approach caution that when students are exposed to unfamiliar and inappropriate classroom-management techniques, they are more likely to reject their teachers' management approaches and less likely to change their behavior. An example of the accommodation approach for dealing with culture conflict is demonstrated by the plan the faculty and administration at Cunningham Elementary School developed to accommodate Muslim students during Ramadan:

> At the request of community leaders, teachers and administrators at Cunningham Elementary School met with a group of parents and community leaders to discuss the needs of Muslim children during Ramadan. Parents explained that during Ramadan, many of their children would be fasting during daylight hours. Therefore, it would be very uncomfortable for their children to sit in the cafeteria with the other children during lunch. Understanding their concerns, school administrators agreed that parents could request that their Muslim children be provided an alternate lunchtime location when the other students typically go to the cafeteria. When teachers expressed concern about students participating in rigorous physical exercise while abstaining from food and liquids, it was agreed that these students would be excused from activities such as running or aerobic exercise during the time they were fasting. At the end of the meeting, the parents felt that their concerns had been heard and that the school leaders were truly concerned for their children.

The accommodation approach is not without its critics. Some suggest that the diverse nature of our schools makes it impossible to accommodate educational approaches for all ethnic groups found in any particular school. Grossman (1995) notes that many fear that cultural descriptions can lead to misleading overgeneralizations. Others argue that treating some students differently than others is discriminatory.

Assimilation

A great many educators believe that the best way to deal with cultural incompatibilities is for students to adopt the school's culture. Advocates for the **assimilation** approach argue that non-European-American students and their families should adapt to the mainstream culture in the schools, because everyone in America should speak the same language, follow the same laws, and share the same morality (Grossman, 1995).

Others suggest that assimilation can have disastrous affects. Such was the case of Rose Fiorella's grandfather:

> When Rose Fiorella completed her degree in elementary education, she was sad that her grandfather had not lived to see her graduate, because it had been the story of her grandfather's first year in America that had inspired Rose to teach. When Rose's grandfather Francisco Fiorella entered second grade, he spoke no English. Hearing him speak Italian, his teacher had rapped his knuckles with a ruler and yelled, "No Italian! We speak only English here." Because eight-year-old Frankie knew no English, he became mute. In fact, he remained mute the entire year. He spoke only at home and at church. Because Frankie refused to speak, his teacher decided he was incapable of learning and insisted that he be placed in a special school. Only the intervention of his father's boss had prevented this from happening.
>
> It had always made Rose sad to hear of the mistreatment of her bright, articulate grandfather. When he had heard that she wanted to be a teacher, he told her to always look for the best in every child. It was a promise Rose planned to keep when she entered the classroom.

Bicultural Approach

The **bicultural approach** teaches that students should adapt their behaviors to the requirements of the situation. The bicultural approach allows students to fit into the dominant culture of the school and also into their culture at home. Proponents of mutual accommodation believe that students are enriched by the ability to mix two cultures and function in a multicultural world (Grossman, 1995).

Critics maintain that bicultural approaches can place students in conflict situations. If students' parents and friends do not approve of the cultural perspective of the school, conflict will increase. Others suggest that students may experience identity confusion if they experience conflicting pressures from home and school. Consider how Ms. Dix explains a bicultural approach to one of her students:

> Harris High School assistant principal Shawana Dix was surprised when Dasan complained about his treatment in the cafeteria. "This school wants all of us to act white," he complained. "Some of us were cutting up in the cafeteria and got in trouble. They told want us to sit down, be quiet, and act white. We think you should do something about it."

Concerned, Ms. Dix asks, "Did someone actually tell you to sit down and 'act white'?"

"Well, no, but that's what they meant. Don't you get tired of acting white around here?"

"Dasan, I don't think of how I act here as 'acting white.' I think of how I act as being a professional. You see, you have to act in certain ways in certain places. It may have nothing to do with race. For example, do you talk to your mother the way you talk to your friends? Do you talk to your pastor the way you talk to your friends?"

"No."

"So, you have already figured out that there are different ways to act in different places. That's part of being mature. I act one way here at work, one way at home, and another when I'm out with my friends. In none of those cases do I think of what I do as 'acting white.' Instead, I think of it as acting like an adult."

Empowerment

The last approach for resolving cultural conflict is to empower students to resolve their own cultural conflicts. This approach teaches students that there are various ways to deal with conflict, educating them with the possible advantages and disadvantages of each, and helping them to select solutions that meet their needs. Grossman (1995) found that those critical of the **empowerment approach** fear that many students will not have the ability or maturity to make reasonable choices. However, even second-graders can be taught to resolve cultural differences:

> When second-grader Christopher Adkins used a racial slur when teasing his friend Jerome, his teacher pondered how to best handle the situation. The two boys had been best friends, and she didn't want to see the incident damage their friendship. Rather than punishing Christopher, she pulled the two boys together and asked Jerome to tell Christopher how he felt when Christopher called him the name. When Jerome told Christopher how his feelings had been hurt and that he thought Christopher didn't like him, Christopher started to cry. "I'm sorry, Jerome. I shouldn't have said what I did. Please forgive me." The meeting ended with the two boys shaking hands and going off to play together.

CLASSROOM MANAGEMENT AND STUDENTS WITH DISABILITIES

For today's teachers, the question is not *if* they will accommodate students with disabilities but *how* they will accommodate these students. **PL 94-142**, which later came to be known as IDEA—the **Individuals with Disabilities Education Act** (See Table 14.1 for a review of this legislation), clearly indicates that students with disabilities should be placed in the **least-restrictive environment**. This means that students with disabilities will be spending part or all of the day in the regular classroom. Many teachers see the inclusion of special-needs students in their classroom as a blessing, providing an opportunity for everyone to

TABLE 14.1   *Chronology of IDEA (Individuals with Disabilities Education Act)*

1975	PL 94-142 Education for All Handicapped Children Act (EHA): Established the principle of free, appropriate education in the least restrictive environment for all children with disabilities. Guaranteed parents' rights, the right to due process, appropriate assessment and fair hearing and appeal. Required each child with a disability to have an Individualized Education Program (IEP).
1983	PL 98-199 Amendments to EHA: Emphasized planning for the transition of secondary students and provided incentives for services for children from birth to age 3, including parent training and information centers.
1986	PL 99-457 Amendments to EHA: Created new incentives for early intervention, including programs for infants and toddlers and their families. Required an Individualized Family Service Plan (IFSP) for each child/family served.
1988	PL 100-297 Amendments to EHA: Included the Jacob K. Javits Gifted and Talented Students Education Act of 1988, which reestablished federal involvement in programs for the gifted with demonstration grants, a national research center, and various national leadership activities.
1990	PL 101-476 Individuals with Disabilities Education Act (IDEA): An amendment to EHA. Replaced the term *handicapped* with *disabilities* in EHA and earlier EHA amendments. Reaffirmed EHA's requirement of a free, appropriate education. Designated assistive technology as a related service in IEPs. Required a transition plan at least by age 16 in the IEP. Strengthened the commitment to inclusion in community school. Retained the requirements of a full continuum of placements.
1991	PL 102-199 Amendments to Individuals with Disabilities Act: Extended authorization of appropriations and revised the early intervention program of services for infants and toddlers with disabilities.
1997	PL 105-17 Amendments to Individuals with Disabilities Act: Focused on improving teaching and learning. Emphasized the Individualized Education Program (IEP) as the primary tool for enhancing children's involvement and progress in the general curriculum. Gave schools new flexibility to discipline students with disabilities who bring weapons or illegal drugs to school.

learn tolerance and acceptance. Others see inclusion as a burden. How teachers view the inclusion of special-needs students into their classroom has an impact on the success of these students and the classroom environment as a whole.

As Weinstein and Mignano (1997) note, truly inclusive classrooms are those in which students learn and work together, in which diversity is not just tolerated but valued and respected. It is not enough for children with special needs to be included physically; they must be included socially.

The inclusion of students with special needs into the mainstream of education and regular classrooms presents specific challenges. The successful integration of special-needs students requires teachers to understand the nature of each student's disability, to use effective teaching and classroom-management strategies, and to collaborate with other teachers, professionals, parents, and community agencies. Each student identified as having a disability should have an **individual education program (IEP)** that outlines specific needs, required accommodations, and expected outcomes. Teachers must familiarize themselves with each student's IEP and understand the accommodations needed. Burns and Allen (1998) stress that for all students to achieve appropriate learning results, accommodations must be implemented in both the curriculum and in classroom-management strategies.

Schulz, Carpenter, and Turnbull (1991) note that managing the behavior of special-needs students is one of the primary factors in determining successful mainstreamed placements. To do so, two factors must be considered. First, are there behaviors that would typically be considered inappropriate but that are beyond the control of the student? Second, are there behaviors that can and should be curtailed in order for the student to deal more effectively with the instruction presented and with classmates?

Behaviors that cannot be changed because they are a manifestation of the student's disability will require careful monitoring by the teacher to ensure that interventions do not violate the legal protections provided by IDEA or the student's IEP. As Osborne and DiMattia (1998) note, this is especially true when disciplinary sanctions result in a change in placement for a student with a disability.

For less-serious behavior problems, a change in expectations by the teacher and fellow students is needed, and it will be necessary to explain the student's behavior to classmates. If behavior is a serious issue, Evertson et al. (2000) suggest that it is advisable to overlook minor inappropriate behavior, reinforce acceptable behavior, and reduce known stressors. A positive, supportive, structured, and predictable environment is key to helping the special-needs student feel safe and accepted.

Schulz et al. (1991) stresses that inappropriate behavior that can be changed should be replaced by acceptable behavior, and this change alone can make a tremendous difference in the degree to which students are accepted by teachers and peers. The teacher must determine whether the student has the prerequisite skills to make such changes. An assessment of the student's current level of performance may reveal skill deficiencies requiring intervention and individual instruction as a strategy for improving behavior.

To effectively work with students with disabilities and their parents, Weinstein and Mignano (1997) and Evertson et al. (2000) suggest that teachers use the following strategies:

- Be informed about the various special services that are available and know how to obtain access to those services.
- Examine the classroom arrangement to determine whether there are factors that may create problems for students with disabilities. This includes analyzing the physical arrangement of desks and other classroom materials and eliminating distractions.
- Use cooperative learning to minimize the problem of children with special needs being isolated and rejected socially.
- Enlist the assistance of other students and teachers. Students can serve as tutors on academic tasks, buddies who assist with difficult activities, or advocates who watch out for the welfare of children who have special needs.
- Use a variety of instructional strategies to meet the learning styles and special needs of all students.
- Develop communication skills that will allow the teacher to work more effectively with troubled or disaffected students. Learn to listen and to talk to students in ways that allow them to explain their needs.
- Defuse situations before they get out of hand. Teachers must recognize when stress levels are rising and be aware of situations that might provoke "acting out" behaviors.

CLASSROOM MANAGEMENT AND CHILDREN AT RISK FOR ACADEMIC FAILURE AND SOCIAL ISOLATION

Children who are frightened, homeless, hungry, or abused don't leave these problems at the classroom door. Therefore, classroom teachers must be aware of the impact these issues have on the classroom. Behaviors that appear to be misbehavior may actually be a result of the lifestyles of these children. Children who are hungry may appear unmotivated or uninterested. Children who steal may be doing the only thing they know how to do to acquire what they need. Children who sleep in class may not have safe places to sleep when away from school. Children who act aggressively or act out sexually may be victims of physical or sexual abuse. Teachers who view misbehavior as disobedience often attempt to control students with punishments and autocratic classroom management without trying to understand the underlying motivations behind behaviors. Table 14.2 provides a list of the legislation to protect the rights of at-risk students.

TABLE 14.2   *Benchmark Legislation for the Protection of Exceptional Students*

Elementary and Secondary Education Act of 1965

Authorized grants for elementary and secondary school programs for children from low-income families. This law was the beginning of Head Start.

Bilingual Education Act of 1968

Provided federal funding to encourage local school districts to try approaches incorporating native-language instruction.

Drug Abuse Education Act of 1970

Provided for development, demonstration, and evaluation of curriculum on the problems of drug abuse.

Comprehensive Bilingual Education Act of 1973

Extended funding to the training of bilingual teachers.

Child Abuse Prevention and Treatment Act of 1974

Provided financial support to states that implemented programs for identification, prevention, and treatment of child abuse and neglect.

McKinney-Vento Homeless Assistance Act of 1987

Designed to ensure that homelessness does not cause homeless children to be left behind in school. Provided grants to state agencies to ensure that homeless children, including preschoolers and youth have equal access to free and appropriate public education.

No Child Left Behind Act of 2001

Designed to close the gap between disadvantaged and minority students and their peers by providing stronger accountability for results, expanding flexibility and local control, expanding options for parents, and emphasizing teaching methods that have been proven to work.

☑ ✒ *Tips from the Field*

I try to create an atmosphere of "family" among my students. I teach a "Behavioral Adjustment" class in which I have eleven boys, all identified as "seriously emotionally disturbed." I began the school year by calling each student two days before school began and communicating to them how "our" class was going to be great because they were in it. I'd tell them a little about myself and ended on a positive note. Throughout the year, anytime I would refer to our class or to a situation, I would use the term "our." I found this created a feeling of ownership. I would always say, "our computer," "our class library," "our friend John." The principal was amazed at the complete turn around of these students.

Michele Reyle
Special Education Teacher
Kenwood Elementary School
Clarksville, TN

POVERTY AND HOMELESSNESS

In 2000, 16.1 percent of U.S. children under the age of eighteen lived in poverty. Poverty rates among African-American and Latino children were much higher than those among white children. Grossman (1995) found that between 1979 and 1989, the numbers of Latinos, European-American, and African-American children living in poverty increased by 29 percent, 25 percent, and 6 percent, respectively, leading to an overall rise of 19 percent. These children often come to school poorly fed, clothed, and without the school materials needed to be successful.

In 1999, the National Coalition for the Homeless reported that families with children constitute approximately 40 percent of people who are homeless and that families are the fastest-growing segment of the homeless population. Homeless students are hungry more than twice as often as other students. They lack regular medical care, and 21 percent of homeless students repeat a grade because of frequent absences from school. Compared to students who live in homes, homeless students are more likely to be aggressive and non-compliant, shy and withdrawn, anxious, tired, and restless (Grossman, 1995). They have greater difficulty forming relationships with others. They are also more likely to exhibit symptoms associated with stress and lowered self-esteem.

It is important that students like these be encouraged to attend school each day, because school may be the only place in which they are safe and are fed. Therefore, it is critical that these students be made to feel that they are a valuable part of the classroom community. In order to see that basic needs are met, teachers and administrators must work with other agencies that can provide assistance to these students and their families.

ABUSED AND NEGLECTED CHILDREN

The number of abused and neglected children and youth has risen precipitously in recent years. In 1995, Grossman noted that although about 2 million cases of child abuse and neglect are officially reported annually, conservative estimates suggest that the number of children and adolescents who actually suffer abuse and neglect is two to three times that number. Whatever the numbers, it is clear that far too many students suffer the effects of neglect and psychological, physical, and sexual abuse.

Abused students tend to mistrust others, especially adults, and this mistrust is often played out in their relationships with their teachers. They have low self-esteem and poor self-concepts, and compared to nonabused students, they are more likely to develop conduct and emotional problems, to abuse drugs and alcohol, to lack the motivation and energy necessary to succeed in school, and to misunderstand and be suspicious of the behavior and intentions of others.

Abused students tend to demonstrate serious behavioral problems in school. However, the form their behavioral problems takes depends on how they react to the abuse. Those who are victims of aggression and abusive behavior may act out against others; if they have been sexually abused, they may abuse others sexually or at least act out sexually (Grossman, 1995). Teachers must report suspected abuse. They have a legal and moral responsibility to do so.

CHILDREN WITH VIOLENT TENDENCIES

O'Donnel and White (2001) note that despite the best efforts of teachers and administrators, there will always be a small number of students who are aggressive, defiant, and disruptive in schools. Leff, Power, Manz, Costigan, and Nabors (2001) found that 10–20 percent of kindergarten and elementary age children are repeatedly teased, threatened, or attacked by their peers. Even more frightening is research that indicates that early aggressive behavior is highly correlated with later aggressive acts. Acts of aggression in the early grades often progress to more serious acts of violence when students reach middle and high school.

Hardin and Harris (2000) stress that it is critical that teachers recognize when students are a threat to themselves or to others. Teachers are in a unique position to gather information about students from observations, the students themselves, classmates, or overheard conversations. Too often, however, it is difficult to determine when behavior is a serious problem and when it is harmless play. When teachers do not recognize these differences, they can ignore behaviors that may signal potential aggression or violence (Hazler, 1998).

The American Academy of Child and Adolescent Psychiatry (2001) argues that the presence of one or more of the following behaviors increases the risk of violent or dangerous behavior:

- having a history of past violent or aggressive behavior, including uncontrollable angry outbursts;
- being a victim of abuse or neglect;

Acts of aggression in early grades often progress to more serious acts of violence when students reach middle and high school.

- witnessing abuse or violence in the home;
- bullying or intimidating peers or younger children;
- having a recent experience of humiliation, shame, loss, or rejection;
- bringing a weapon to school;
- coping with a combination of stressful family factors (poverty, severe deprivation, or marital breakup);
- suffering from a mental illness such as depression, mania, psychosis, or bipolar disorder;
- belonging to a cult or gang;
- withdrawing socially because of depression, rejection, persecution, unworthiness, or lack of confidence;
- failing to adjust to a new school after an adequate amount of time.

Teachers viewing this list would note that although almost every child in their class-rooms exhibits one of the characteristics listed, few students become a threat or act in an aggressive manner. This list, therefore, should serve as a guide for teachers to identify signs of potential aggression and self-destructive behavior, and teachers should avoid inappropriately labeling or stigmatizing individual students because they appear to fit a profile or a set of early-warning indicators. If teachers have established a close, caring, and supportive relationship with their students, they will know them well enough to recognize when a student's past history and current behaviors signal the potential for future problems.

When there is the potential for violence, however, teachers must act. Too often, teachers tend to respond to acts of violence by students with violence anger, outrage, indignation, and condemnation. Although these reactions are understandable, they interfere with the development of sound strategies for preventing violent acts (Cangelosi, 2000).

All threats by students to harm themselves or others must be taken seriously. The American Academy of Child and Adolescent Psychiatry (2001) stresses that no threat should be dismissed as just idle talk. However, a single educator cannot handle major crisis situations alone and should seek help from the school counselor, principal, school system mental health professionals, or the student's parents. The immediate evaluation and appropriate ongoing treatment of students who make serious threats can reduce the risk of tragedy. Counseling and psychiatric help is critical for many of these students. In some cases, the juvenile justice system will be involved in interventions for these students.

Doing nothing more than attempting to catch violent offenders, so that they can be punished or removed from the school environment, has not worked (Cangelosi, 2000). The prevention of violent behavior is the goal. Curwin and Mendler (1997) advocate a comprehensive schoolwide approach to violence prevention that includes three basic components and provides specific practical strategies. This approach includes:

- *Teaching students alternatives to violence through conflict resolution, peer mediations, and anger control.*
- *Teaching students how to make more effective choices.* When students break a rule or behave disruptively, they need both firm limits and significant alternate choices. Firm limits indicate what teachers and administrators will and will not accept. Significant choices help students realize that they are capable of selecting nonviolent alternatives.
- *Modeling alternative expressions of anger, frustration, and impatience.* All school personnel must model the same choices and behaviors that they want their students to use. By demonstrating how to resolve conflicts in a nonviolent manner, school personnel can teach students how to deal with difficult situations in a nonaggressive manner.

BULLIES AND THE BULLIED

Bullock (2002) states that between 25 and 50 percent of all students report being bullied. Obviously, bullying is a serious matter, with serious psychological and social consequences for both those who are being bullied and those doing the bullying (Pace, 2001). The victims perceive school as a threatening place and experience adjustment difficulties, feelings of loneliness, and a desire to avoid school. The bully is reinforced for inappropriate behavior, leading to even more violent and aggressive behavior in the future. For both the bully and the victim, bullying can have lifelong effects.

Unlike schools in many European countries, schools in the United States have made little or no attempt to deal with the problem. Ross (1996) suggests that one reason that school administrators have ignored bullying is that the gravity of weapon-related violence in schools makes the problem of bullying seem incidental. However, research shows that bullying can be an antecedent of such violence and that dealing with the problem of bullying in the early grades can reduce acts of violence in middle and high school. Some school personnel are unaware of the extent of bullying, and others believe the myth that children "picking on" or teasing one another is a "normal" part childhood (Bullock, 2002). They also may believe that children should resolve these conflicts themselves. Students who are bullied typically feel that adult intervention is ineffective or fear that telling adults will only bring more harassment (Boatwright, Mathis, & Smith-Rex, 1998). The net result of all these points of view is that schools become environments in which bullies flourish and victims deteriorate.

According to Bullock (2002) bullying refers to repeated, unprovoked, harmful actions by one child or children against another. The acts may be physical or psychological. Physical bullying, or **direct bullying**, involves face-to-face confrontation, open attacks, (including physical aggression), and threatening and intimidating gestures. It includes hitting, kicking, pushing, grabbing toys from other children, and engaging in very rough and intimidating play. Direct bullying tends to increase through the elementary school years, peak in middle school, and decline during the high school years.

Psychological bullying, or **indirect bullying**, includes name-calling, making faces, teasing, taunting, and making threats. Indirect bullying is less obvious and less visible and includes exclusion and rejection of children from a group. Ross (1996) notes that indirect bullying is a more subtle form of bullying, often involving a third party and resulting in social isolation, rumor spreading, and scapegoating.

Students who engage in bullying behaviors seem to have a need to feel powerful and in control. They derive satisfaction from inflicting injury and suffering on others. They have little empathy for their victims, and often defend their actions by saying that their victims provoked them in some way. Many of these students have been taught to strike out physically as a way of handling problems. Students who regularly display bullying behaviors are generally defiant or oppositional toward adults. Boatwright et al. (1998) note that bullies appear to have little anxiety and to possess strong self-esteem. They stress that there is little evidence to support the contention that bullies victimize others because they feel bad about themselves.

Bullock (2002) notes that students who are bullied are often younger, weaker, and more passive than the bully. They appear anxious, insecure, cautious, sensitive, and quiet, and often react by crying and withdrawing. They are often lonely and lack close friendships at school. They may lack social skills and friends, and thus are often socially isolated. Many of these students have physical characteristics that promote teasing. Without adult intervention, these children are likely to be repeatedly bullied, putting them at risk for continued social rejection, depression, and impaired self-esteem.

Ross (1996) suggests that bullying in the school setting does not exist in isolation and is characteristic of a school out of control. Therefore, the solution must involve a strong commitment and concerted action on the part of school personnel, parents, and students. To address the issue of bullying, Bullock (2002) stresses that schools need a comprehensive plan that provides intervention on three levels: schoolwide, in specific classrooms, and with individual students.

A schoolwide plan includes three important components:

1. Awareness on the part of school personnel and parents of bullying problems in their school.
2. A genuine interest by school personnel in addressing the problem of bullying.
3. Schoolwide support for children who are bullied.

A schoolwide plan begins with a clear policy statement against bullying and intervention strategies for addressing it. Another essential element is awareness by parents and students of the sanctions against bullying.

Boatwright et al. (1998) and Ross (1996) suggest that teachers do the following to create a classroom atmosphere that prevents or lessens bullying incidents:

- Provide opportunities for students to talk about bullying and why it is inappropriate and unacceptable behavior. Students must discuss the harm that bullying can cause and the things they can do to reduce the amount of bullying that occurs in a classroom.
- Develop a classroom plan and make sure students know what to do when they see a bullying incident.
- Help students develop a set of rules about bullying, with the goal of reducing bully-victim problems.
- Provide cooperative learning activities in which small groups of students work on a common goal, with the evaluation of the activity focusing on the performance of the group.
- Attend to students' behaviors throughout the day (recess and lunchtime) to prevent bullying incidents.
- Act immediately when bullying is reported. Students must understand that bullying will not be tolerated.

In order to intervene individually, teachers and parents must learn the signs that a student may be a victim of bullying. According to Pace (2001), indicators that a student may be a victim of bullying are:

- avoiding certain situations, people, or places, such as pretending to be sick so that he or she does not have to go to school;
- exhibiting changes in behavior, such as being withdrawn and passive, being overly active and aggressive, or being self-destructive;
- showing signs of fear when asked about certain situations, people, or places;
- receiving lower grades or showing signs of learning problems;
- having unexplained physical symptoms such as stomach pains and fatigue.

CREATING SAFE AND WELCOMING CLASSROOMS FOR ALL STUDENTS

Scenario

When third-grade teacher Haley Whitson was told that a refugee child from Rwanda would be entering her classroom, she was apprehensive. However, her compassion for the nine-year-old, who had witnessed the murder of his parents, quickly overcame her fears and concerns.

Before Didace arrived, Haley tried to learn as much about his country and his circumstances as possible. She knew he would be living with a missionary family who had known Didace's family in Rwanda. She arranged to meet with a professor from the local university who was from an area of Africa close to Didace's village. Part of her concern about having Didace in her class was that he spoke Kinyarwanda, and she could find no one who spoke that language other than his foster parents. Through the professor, Haley learned of another refugee child from Rwanda, Joseph Baldo, who lived an hour's drive away. While visiting with Joseph and his parents, she arranged for Joseph to be in class the first day Didace arrived and to spend one Saturday a month with him.

Haley was concerned about how much her class should know about Didace's circumstances before he left Rwanda. She met with the school counselor and Didace's foster parents, and together they decided that she would tell her class that Didace was orphaned but not about the circumstances surrounding the deaths of his parents.

Before Didace had arrived, Joseph taught Haley a few key words in Kinyarwanda. So, by the time Didace arrived, she could say "Good morning," "Come here," "Goodbye," and "What do you need?" She also learned that Didace could say a few words in French, and she had enlisted the aid of a fellow teacher who spoke French to help her if necessary.

Joseph explained that in Rwanda it was customary for students to stand when a guest entered their classroom and for each student to give the guest a small gift. So, on the day that Didace arrived, the students stood and each student presented Didace with a small gift as they told him their names.

By the end of the school year, everyone in Haley's class agreed that their lives had been enriched by their year with Didace. Didace was well adjusted and could speak enough English to tease his classmates. The students in Haley's class learned a great deal about the world from the experiences, and Haley was certain she had grown as a teacher.

KEY TERMINOLOGY

Definitions for these terms appear in the glossary:

Accommodation	Empowerment approach
Assimilation	Indirect bullying
Bicultural approach	Individual education program (IEP)
Culture shock	Individuals with Disabilities Education Act
Direct bullying	Least-restrictive environment

CHAPTER ACTIVITIES

Reflecting on the Theory

1. When fifth-grader Kalpana Kumar entered Mr. Wilson's classroom during the week before Thanksgiving, she appeared extremely shy. Now, Mr. Wilson is wondering if other factors are at play. Kalpana rarely talks to Mr. Wilson or her classmates. He has never seen her smile. Although she is polite, she refuses to do any work.

   What might be some of the reasons for Kalpana's behavior? How would you help Kalpana become a member of your class?

2. In the first scenario, Rebecca questioned the accommodation provided for Travis. Do you share her concerns? Do you think Travis was fairly treated? Was the way Travis was treated fair to all students? Why or why not?

3. This chapter presents four methods for helping deal with conflicts between the school and students' culture: accommodations, assimilation, the bicultural approach, and empowerment. Which of these methods would you be most comfortable using in your classroom? Explain your reasoning.

Developing Your Portfolio

1. Interview a teacher who has students with disabilities in his or her classroom. What types of instructional accommodations are provided for special-needs students? What types of accommodations are made in classroom management?

Developing Your Personal Philosophy of Classroom Management

1. This text has presented twelve models of classroom management. Does one of the models appear to be more appropriate for working with exceptional students? If so, why?

2. How could an existing model be modified to work more effectively with students from diverse backgrounds?

CHAPTER REFERENCES

American Academy of Child and Adolescent Psychiatry. (2001). Understanding violent behavior in children and adolescents (no. 55). *Facts for Families.* Washington, DC: Author.

Boatwright, B. H., Mathis., T. A., & Smith-Rex, S. J. (1998). *Getting equipped to stop bullying: A kid's survival kit for understanding and coping with violence in the school.* Minneapolis, MN: Educational Media Corporation.

Bullock, J. R. (2002). Bullying among children. *Childhood Education, 78,*130–134.

Burns, J., & Allen, J. D. (1998). Managing the inclusive classroom. *Kappan Delta Phi Record, 35,* 28–30.

Cangelosi, J. S. (2000). *Classroom management strategies: Gaining and maintaining students' cooperation.* New York: John Wiley.

Cartledge, G., & Milburn, J. F. (1996). *Cultural diversity and social skills instruction.* Champaign, IL: Research Press.

Curwin, R. L., & Mendler, A. N. (1997). *As tough as necessary: Countering violence, aggression, and hostility in our schools.* Alexandria, VA: Association for Supervision and Curriculum Development.

Evertson, C., Emmer, E. T., & Worsham, M. E. (2000). *Classroom management for elementary teachers* (5th ed.). Boston: Allyn & Bacon.

Grossman, H. (1995). *Classroom behavior management in a diverse society* (2nd ed.). Mountain View, CA: Mayfield.

Hardin, C. J., & Harris, E. A. (2000). *Managing classroom crisis: Fastback no. 465.* Bloomington, IN: Phi Delta Kappa Educational Foundation.

Hazler, R. J. (1998). Promoting personal investment in systemic approaches to school violence. *Education, 119,* 221–232.

Leff, S. S., Power, T. J., Manz, P. H., Costigan, T. E., & Nabors, L. A. (2001). School-based aggression prevention programs for young children: Current status and implementations for violence prevention. *School Psychology Review, 30,* 344–363.

National Coalition for the Homeless (1999). *Homeless families with children.* NCH Fact Sheet #7. Washington, DC: National Coalition for the Homeless.

O'Donnel, R., & White, G. P. (2001). Teaching realistic consequences to the most angry and aggressive students. *Middle School Journal, 32,* 40–45.

Osborne, A. G., & DiMattia, P. A. (1998). *Classroom management: A case study handbook for teachers of challenging learners.* Durham, NC: Carolina Academic Press.

Pace, B. (2001) Bullying. *The Journal of the American Medical Association, 285,* 2156.

Ross, D. M. (1996). *Childhood bullying and teasing: What school personnel, other professionals, and parents can do.* Alexandria, VA: American Counseling Association.

Schulz, Jane B., Carpenter, C. D., and Turnbull, A. P. (1991) *Mainstreaming exceptional students: A guide for classroom teachers* (3rd ed.). Boston: Allyn & Bacon.

Schwartz, W. (2001). *School practices for equitable discipline of African American students.* ERIC Clearinghouse on Urban Education, Number 166. Columbia, NY: Institute for Urban and Minority Education.

Weinstein, C. S., & Mignano, A. J. (1997). *Elementary classroom management: Lessons from research and practice.* New York: McGraw-Hill.

Chapter *15*

Creating Your Own System

Objectives

Chapter 15 prepares preservice teachers to meet INTASC standards #1 (Content Pedagogy), #3 (Diverse Learners), #4 (Instructional Strategies), #5 (Motivation and Management), #9 (Reflective Practitioner), and #10 (School and Community) by helping them to:

- evaluate the impact of a teacher's philosophy, personality, and teaching style on the selection of a classroom-management plan.
- evaluate the impact of teaching strategies on the selection of a classroom-management plan.
- determine whether they will use a teacher-centered or student-centered approach to classroom management.
- develop a personal classroom-management plan.
- select specific classroom-management strategies they will use in their individual classrooms.
- determine ways to prevent student misbehavior.
- select methods for dealing with inappropriate behavior.
- evaluate how subject-area content impacts classroom-management strategies.
- determine how the school environment impacts individual management plans.

Scenario

As part of the recruitment process for the Denton School District, a team of principals interviews all candidates using a predetermined list of questions. Two of the questions deal with classroom management, and candidates are asked to provide a personal definition of effective classroom management and to describe the classroom-management plan they intend to use in their classrooms. Today, recent graduates Denise Sowell, Martin Segovia, and Brianne Kraeske are being interviewed.

Denise hesitated only a moment before answering the two questions. She had anticipated the questions and said, "I think that effective classroom management is having sufficient control of your classroom so that everyone can learn. To do this, I plan to use Assertive Discipline. I studied Assertive Discipline when I was in college, and my cooperating teacher was using Assertive Discipline as her management plan when I student taught. So, I've had a lot of opportunity to see its application. I think I will feel comfortable using this model."

Martin was visibly nervous when he was interviewed, and his hands shook as he responded to the questions. "I see classroom management as managing all the elements of the classroom so that learning can occur. That means I have to carefully plan how my room is arranged, my class rules, and the procedures for how we will do our activities. I don't have a specific plan in mind. I hope to follow the plan the school has adopted or to use what the majority of the teachers in the school use, because I think there should be consistency within a school."

Brianne was pleased when she was asked the question. She had spent a lot of time thinking about the management plan she would adopt. She had even brought diagrams of how she hoped to arrange her classroom. "I want to use a very student-centered approach with my students. That means I want them to help me create our rules and our consequences. I plan to have a student-centered classroom with lots of activities, so I will need to carefully plan the procedures I will use for group management. I guess I would define effective classroom management as helping students learn to be responsible for their own behavior. That will be my ultimate goal: to help students learn to manage themselves."

INTRODUCTION

The panel of principals may have a difficult time selecting from the three candidates, because none of their answers were incorrect. Their answers represented the philosophy, personality, and teaching style of each candidate. Therefore, any of the three candidates would be an appropriate choice if the teacher's plan fits into the philosophy and management style of the principal.

Ultimately, the most effective classroom-management plan is one that meets the needs of the individual teacher, the teacher's students, and the school environment. In many cases, an existing model will be the best choice. In other cases, the teacher will find it best to merge parts of several models to meet the requirements of the classroom and school environment. Often, the teacher is more comfortable creating a plan that meets the teacher's unique needs. Swick (1985) suggests that the selection of the appropriate classroom-management plan requires teachers to give careful consideration to their own philosophies, personalities, teaching styles, and teaching experiences, and to carefully evaluate the mission and environment of their school and community.

THE PHILOSOPHY OF THE TEACHER

Gathercoal (2001) notes that the basis of a teacher's philosophy is generally formed from fundamental beliefs concerning the basic nature of students, the way students learn, the amount of control or freedom students need, and the way students should respond to the authority of the teacher. This philosophy will provide the foundation for the classroom-management plan selected and used by the teacher.

Martin and Baldwin (1993) suggest that there is an ideological continuum along which a teacher's philosophy will fall. At one end of the continuum is the belief that a student must learn appropriate behaviors and that one of the functions of the teacher is to maintain classroom control while this learning process occurs. At the other end of the continuum is the belief that it is a student's nature to "be good" and that a student will behave appropriately if given the freedom and responsibility to do so.

Gathercoal (2001) also argues that two different educational philosophies exist regarding the nature of students. One philosophy contends that students are evil from birth and that this evil nature can be corrected only by a strong teacher who uses authoritarian methods. The other philosophy views students as innately good and the teacher's role as nurturing the growth of this goodness through positive interactions.

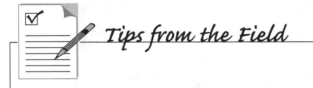

Tips from the Field

I use "magic numbers" as a way to organize my classroom and to manage many of the tasks I'm required to do. On the first day of school, each child is assigned a magic number. I simply start with the first student on my roll, and that student becomes Number 1. To help students remember their numbers, they wear their magic numbers for a few days. When we line up to go out of the room, I use the magic numbers to line up. Sometimes we line up in order, sometimes in reverse order, and sometimes by even or odd numbers. Students write their magic numbers on their papers so that I can put papers in numerical order before placing grades in my roll book. I even use magic numbers to make sure everyone has a chance to answer questions or to do an activity. I have a basket filled with clothes pins on which the magic numbers are written. During question/answer periods, I pull out a magic number from the basket to decide which student will be called. If the student answers correctly, I clip the pen to the side of the basket so I will know not to call on that student again. If they miss the question, the clip goes back in the basket so the student will have a second chance.

Cindy Browning
Grade 1 Teacher
Siegel Elementary School
Murfreesboro, TN

Teachers like Denise, who consider it the responsibility of teachers to maintain control in the classroom, are considered **teacher-centered** in their approach. In the past few years, teacher-centered approaches have been viewed negatively by educators as new research on teaching has focused on the effectiveness of student-centered approaches. However, many teachers think students need guidance by a trained teacher as they move through various stages of cognitive, social, and moral development. Often, it is not their view of students as "evil" that causes teachers to support a teacher-centered approach, but rather their belief that the student's environment influences behavior and that student behavior can be changed by reward, reinforcement, and punishment (Martin & Baldwin, 1993). In the teacher-centered classroom, rules begin with student responsibilities. The breaking of rules requires interventions in the form of punishments or consequences to help students make mental connections between behavior and the consequences of behavior. Privileges in a teacher-centered classroom are earned through appropriate behavior.

At the opposite end of the continuum are teachers like Brianne, who propose a **student-centered approach** to teaching and classroom management. The student-centered teacher

The most effective classroom management plan is one that meets the needs of an individual teacher, the teacher's students, and the school environment.

presupposes that the student has an inner drive to do what is right and learn responsibility through interactions and experiences in a safe, welcoming environment. Gathercoal (2001) notes that student-centered teachers think of students as inherently good and believe they can trust students. Therefore, they are quite comfortable putting into practice methods designed to help students learn and develop attitudes of respect and responsibility. When behavior problems occur, the student-centered teacher is concerned with which strategies will be most effective in bringing about a reasonable resolution to the problem. Every interaction with misbehaving students centers on the resolution of the problem by creating learning experiences that allow them to grow and recover from mistakes. This growth results in students learning responsibility. Choice is important in a student-centered classroom because of the belief that students are active, positive, motivated, and unique problem solvers.

Few teachers act totally according to either of these extreme philosophies or are either totally teacher- or student-centered. Most teachers weigh their basic philosophies about students with educational research and their own experiences to provide a more balanced approach in their teaching practices and management strategies.

THE PERSONALITY OF THE TEACHER

Martin and Baldwin (1993) propose that the personality of the teacher is the most significant variable in classroom success. However, they found no real research that defines the ideal personality for a teacher. Students, too, would have difficulty describing the ideal personality for a teacher. During their twelve years of school, students will encounter teachers with a variety of personalities. Some teachers can tolerate a great deal of noise in their classrooms, whereas others want their classrooms to be a quiet place. Some teachers joke and kid with their students, while others maintain a serious, businesslike demeanor. A look into classrooms will find some that are messy, with materials scattered around the room, and others that are neat, with everything carefully organized and in its place. Some teachers allow students to leave their seats to sharpen their pencils and retrieve materials, while others will allow students to leave their seats only with permission. Teachers vary in a thousand ways, and, amazingly, most students manage to deal relatively effectively with this variety of personalities.

Perhaps, then, it is not a specific teacher personality that creates a successful classroom but the congruence between the teacher's personality and the teacher's actions. Teachers often adopt a particular instructional or discipline technique because research shows it is effective or there is a mandate from the administration. However, if that technique does not fit the teacher's personality, the technique will fail, students will be frustrated, and problems will occur.

Martin found this to be true during his student teaching experience. Both Martin's cooperating teacher and his university supervisor encouraged him to use cooperative learning as a part of his teaching strategies. However, Martin found that he was constantly telling students to lower their voices. Although his cooperating teacher thought the noise level appropriate, Martin felt the class was constantly out of control, and he often resorted to shouting at students to lower their voices. Brianne had the opposite experience. Observing a very traditional classroom, Brianne found the activities boring and wondered what kept the students from falling asleep. She vowed that when she had her own classroom, students would move, talk, and work together.

A second key to finding the balance between teaching personality and classroom management lies with the teacher's expectations. Students can and do deal effectively with a variety of teaching styles, management styles, and teacher personalities as long as they understand what the teacher expects and the teacher is consistent in those expectations. When expectations are not clearly defined, however, students may feel they are treated unfairly and conflicts may develop between students and the teacher. It is important, therefore, that the management plan selected fits the personality of the teacher, and that all components of the plan, including rules, consequences, and procedures, are clearly defined for students from the first day of school.

THE TEACHING STYLE OF THE TEACHER

Brianne's answer about her classroom-management plan showed an unusual understanding of the connections between teaching style and classroom management. Having given careful consideration to how she wanted to provide instruction, she used her approach to teaching as the springboard for selecting the plan she would use. Swick (1985) agrees that room size, seating arrangements, time spent in various activities, available learning resources, subject-area transitions, and group interactions are typical management issues that teachers need to work out in advance of actual teaching and in conjunction with the teaching strategies they plan to use.

Many classroom-management instructional issues are dictated by the subject area taught. Lab classes, vocational classes, and fine arts classes require differing approaches to classroom management because of the physical design of the classroom, the activities involved, group interactions, transitions, procedures, and safety requirements. However, these same issues must be considered with regard to the learning environment in traditional classrooms. Therefore, classroom-management plans must be developed with consideration given to both the subject area taught and the teaching style of the classroom teacher.

Brianne plans to use a student-centered approach to her teaching. As she noted in her response to the panel of principals, this approach requires that she give careful thought to the grouping of students, the management of transitions, and procedures for working in cooperative groups. She may find it helpful to adopt a model such as Glasser's *Reality Therapy and Control Theory*, Curwin and Mendler's *Discipline with Dignity*, Ginott and Kohn's *Building Community*, or Evertson's *Classroom Organization and Management Program (COMP)*, because these models support student-centered teaching strategies. She may find elements from several of these models helpful and create a model that combines many of the ideas and strategies presented in these existing models.

Teachers who plan to use teacher-centered approaches have other issues to consider, and must develop a classroom-management plan that supports the instructional practices they intend to use. Lectures, tutorials, drills, demonstrations, and other forms of teacher-controlled teaching tend to be the focus of instruction in teacher-centered classrooms. Such activities require that the seating arrangement allow all students to see and hear the teacher. In classrooms in which students respond to teacher-directed questions, the teacher must develop clear rules for engaging in the discussion process. Because teacher-centered classrooms tend to use distinct time periods for each subject area, it is important that students progress through the day in an orderly fashion. Teachers using a teacher-centered approach to teaching may want to adopt Skinner's *Behavioral Management*, Canter's *Assertive Discipline*, Jones's *Positive Classroom Discipline*, or Dreikurs's *Logical Consequences*, because all of these models work well in teacher-centered classrooms.

The establishment and maintenance of an effective classroom-management plan is derived not only from knowledge about management theory and strategies but also from the teacher's content and procedural knowledge of the subject matter. Daily planning by the teacher must include thoughtful consideration about both classroom management and instruction.

THE TEACHER'S EVALUATION OF THE SCHOOL ENVIRONMENT

Martin looked to the school and its administration for guidance in developing his classroom-management plan. To create his plan, Martin will assess the school environment, because

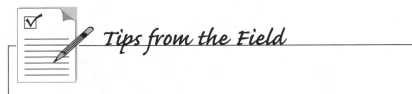

Tips from the Field

I believe a peaceful classroom begins with Good **CONDUCT**. Students are instructed on the meaning of the following character traits:

Cooperate: work together, share, be kind

Organize: be prepared, turn in homework and assignments on time

Negotiate: admit your mistakes, learn to give and take

Discipline Yourself: exhibit self-control, follow directions

Understand Your Feelings: express your feelings, positive attitude

Communicate: listen, observe, speak softly

Tolerate: respect others' differences, abilities, feelings, and needs.

Andrea Galliano
Grades K–3 Gifted Teacher
Mulberry Elementary School
Houma, LA

he understands that a knowledge of the mission of the school; the policies of the school, district, and state; and the management style of the administration will impact his plans for classroom management. Martin must also consider the size of the school and the cultural, gender, and socioeconomic makeup of the student body as he develops his plan.

Swick (1985) recommends that a teacher's classroom-management approach evolve from the total-school setting and reflect the ecology of the school. He advises that classroom management should be proactive and related to all the factors that influence the functioning of teachers, students, parents, and administrators in the classroom and the school. Swick identifies six elements of a school ecology that directly influence classroom management:

1. *Behavior of School Personnel*: A visit to any school immediately gives a view of the interactions between school personnel and the student body. Often overlooked are the interactions of the office staff, custodians, and other support people. If these personnel see their jobs as important to the functioning of the school and understand that their interactions contribute to the overall climate of the school, the atmosphere will be one of mutual respect among staff, faculty, students, and administrators.

2. *The Campus*: The physical layout of the campus contributes to the overall feeling of safety and security felt by students and teachers. Classrooms that are isolated or that are housed in portable facilities present unique management issues. The neighborhood bordering the campus must also be evaluated for additional security issues.

3. *Existing Discipline Practice*: Many schools have a schoolwide discipline plan. As Martin pointed out in his interview, confusion develops when teachers fail to follow the schoolwide plan. It is important that teachers understand the school's plan for discipline before accepting a position. The three candidates should also question the principals about their individual school's discipline policies, so they can determine whether their philosophies will fit into the existing discipline policies.

4. *Parental Involvement*: Parents will not be supportive if they do not think that the school and its personnel have their students' best interest at heart. Parents must feel comfortable coming to teachers and administrators with their concerns. When parents feel part of the school community, they will support teachers and administrators as they make difficult management decisions.

5. *Current Student Behavior Pattern*: A walk down any school hallway reveals much about the existing behavior pattern of a school. The noise level, degree of student engagement, amount of movement within the classrooms, and room arrangements speak volumes about how students behave. Change in existing behavior patterns comes slowly and requires all faculty to make a commitment to new patterns.

6. *School Administrators*: The amount of administrative support provided to teachers will determine how successful they will be in carrying out their discipline plans. Therefore, it is important that teachers share their plans with their administrators before implementing them. Denise wants to use Assertive Discipline as her classroom-management plan. However, if her principal doesn't value or agree with the principles of Assertive Discipline, Denise will find it difficult to carry out her plan.

The Teacher's Experiences in the Classroom

Gathercoal (2001) notes that there is often a difference between what a teacher considers philosophically to be an appropriate action and what the teacher actually does when a problem occurs. This is because actual classroom situations are complicated by the need for quick action, unforeseen situational factors, and emotions that are not present when a teacher abstractly plans for classroom management. As a result, until teachers are put under pressure to act, they are never really sure how they will behave. Such will be the case for Denise, Martin, and Brianne. Although they all think they know the classroom management plan they will use, ultimately what they do will be determined by a multitude of factors, many of which cannot be planned for in advance.

Each year teachers are required to revise their plans as they evaluate their experiences, learn about new research about classroom management, deal with changing school and district policies, and strive to meet the changing needs of students. Therefore, few teachers will use a single classroom-management plan throughout their careers; instead, over the years they will modify their plans and develop new ones as they reflect on their teaching and their students and as they learn from experience.

Key Terminology

Definitions for these terms appear in the glossary:

Student-centered approach   Teacher-centered approach

Chapter Activities

1. Throughout this text, numerous strategies for effective classroom management have been presented. In some cases, theorists suggest the same strategies (for example, rule development) but have different theories about how the strategy should be implemented. Review the theories presented in this text and identify the strategies you will incorporate into your classroom-management plan.

2. Imagine that the same panel of principals that interviewed Denise, Martin, and Brianne is interviewing you. How would you define classroom management?

3. State your philosophy of teaching. In developing your philosophy, consider the following:

   - How do you view students? Must they learn appropriate behaviors because their basic nature is to be "bad," or do you consider that most students are "good" and want to behave appropriately?
   - How much control should the teacher maintain?
   - How much freedom are you prepared to give students?
   - Do you want a teacher-centered or student-centered classroom?

4. How will your personality impact your classroom management? Evaluate your personality by considering the following with regard to your classroom-management plan:

   - What is your tolerance for noise?
   - What will be your tolerance level for student movement within the classroom?
   - What, if any, place is there in your classroom for joking and humor?
   - Do you consider yourself organized and structured?

5. What will be your instructional style? What teaching strategies will you use? How will your teaching style impact your classroom-management plan?

6. What will you do to prevent behavioral problems in your classroom?

7. How will you correct behavioral problems in your classroom? What will be the consequences for inappropriate behavior?

8. There are three options in choosing a classroom plan: (a) adoption of an existing model, (b) adaptation of one or two existing models, or (c) the creation of a model that is unique to you and your students. Which of these options will you use? Describe the classroom-management plan you will use.

CHAPTER REFERENCES

Gathercoal, F. (2001). *Judicious discipline*. San Francisco: Caddo Gap Press.

Martin, N. K., & Baldwin, B. (1993). *Validation of an inventory of classroom management style: Difference between novice and experienced teachers*. Atlanta, GA: American Educational Research Association. (ERIC Document Reproduction Service No. ED359240).

Swick, K. J. (1985). *A proactive approach to discipline: Six professional development modules for educators*. Washington, DC: National Education Association. (ERIC Document Reproduction Service No. ED267027).

Glossary

80-15-5 Principle: concept proposed by Richard Curwin and Allen Mendler that suggests that 80 percent of students rarely break rules or violate principles, 15 percent of students break rules on a somewhat regular basis, and 5 percent of students are chronic rule breakers and out of control most of the time.

Accessibility: a classroom arrangement that allows teachers to maintain on-task behavior by proximity control and to reach every student in the classroom quickly and without disturbing other students.

Accommodation approach: an approach to meeting the needs of culturally diverse students that requires teachers to adapt their management techniques to students' ethnic, socioeconomic, contextual, gender, and other individual characteristics.

Acquisition phase: the time of the school year when students are first learning classroom rules.

Activity reinforcers: participation in a preferred activity that is earned after completion of a required activity.

Applied behavior analysis: a systematic approach to changing undesired behaviors; sometimes used as an alternative term for behavior modification.

Appreciative praise: praise that describes a student's work, action, or accomplishments.

Assertive Discipline: a classroom-management program developed by Lee and Marlene Canter in the early 1970s.

Assertive teachers: teachers who clearly and firmly express their requirements.

Assimilation approach: an approach for meeting the needs of culturally diverse students that requires students to adopt the culture of the school.

Attention seeking: one of the four reasons students misbehave.

Backbone classroom: a term developed by Barbara Coloroso to describe a classroom that is a consistent structure in which students are listened to and learn to respect themselves and others.

Backup system: a systematic, hierarchic organization of negative sanctions for misbehavior.

Behavior modification: a systematic program developed to change the behavior of individual students.

Behavioral techniques: classroom practices that use reinforcement and punishment to modify behaviors.

Bicultural approach: an approach to meeting the needs of culturally diverse students that teaches students to adapt their behaviors to the requirements of the situation, thus allowing them to fit into both the culture of the school and that of their home.

Brick-wall classroom: a term developed by Barbara Coloroso to describe a classroom that is a dictatorship and in which rules are rigid and unbending.

Choice theory: an approach proposed by William Glasser in which he reaffirms that individuals control their own behavior rather than being pawns to external stimuli.

Classroom community: a classroom in which communities are built upon a foundation of cooperation throughout the day, with students continually being allowed to work together.

Classroom Organization and Management Program (COMP): a classroom-management program developed by Carolyn Evertson.

Classroom principles: statements that represent the value system of the classroom that define attitudes and expectations for long-term behavioral growth.

Compelling state interests: four time-tested public-interest arguments crafted in the courts for the precise purpose of limiting constitutionally protected freedoms. The Judicious Discipline model uses four arguments as the basis for rule development.

Conflict resolution: a viable alternative to traditional classroom-management programs, in which students are taught alternatives for resolving personal conflict.

Consensus decision making: a group problem-solving strategy in which all parties affected by the conflict collaborate to resolve the conflict.

Consequences: the results of a student's behavior. When the behavior is inappropriate, the consequences are typically punitive in nature. This can be a synonym for punishment.

Continuous schedule of reinforcement: the reinforcement of behavior every time it occurs.

Control theory: a concept proposed by William Glasser that maintains that the only behavior one can control is one's own.

Corrective consequences: specific strategies for helping students manage their own behavior.

Culture shock: the disorientation and confusion caused when students enter a school in which the culture is different from what they experience at home or elsewhere.

Curriculum approach: an approach to conflict resolution in which students receive instruction in a separate course, distinct curriculum, or daily or weekly lesson plan.

Desists: the actions and words used to stop misbehavior.

Direct bullying: bullying that involves face-to-face confrontation, open attacks (including physical aggression), and threatening and intimidating gestures.

Discipline hierarchy: a listing of consequences for misbehavior that begins with a warning and increases in severity with each infraction of a class or school rule.

Discipline with Dignity: a classroom-management theory developed by Richard Curwin and Allen Mendler that has as a fundamental principle the idea that everyone in the school setting is to be treated with dignity.

Distractions: things or people in the room that compete for the teacher's attention or encourage off-task behavior.

Empowerment approach: an approach for accommodating students from different cultures that encourages students to resolve their cultural conflicts.

Evaluative praise: praise that evaluates personality or judges student character.

Exclusionary time–out: the removal of a disruptive child from the immediate instructional area to another part of the room for a specified amount of time.

Extinction: the weakening or elimination of behavior by withdrawing reinforcement.

Failure-avoiding: one of the four reasons students misbehave.

Feedback: an element of *Skillstreaming* in which students are informed of how they performed during role playing.

Flag rules: rules developed by the teacher that are nonnegotiable.

Grandmama's rule: the concept that students must complete a required task before participating in a preferred activity.

Hard response: a reaction to conflict in which adversaries compete until one is victorious.

Hostile teacher: a teacher who responds to students in a manner that disregards the needs and feelings of students and in many cases violates students' rights.

Indirect bullying: bullying that is psychological in nature and includes name calling, making faces, teasing, taunting, and making threats.

Individual contract: a plan developed with an individual student when the social contract in the classroom fails to work.

Individual education program (IEP): a program designed for students with disabilities outlining specific needs, required accommodations, and expected outcomes.

In loco parentis: a legal stance that grants to educators the same legal authority over students as that of parents.

Inner Discipline: a classroom-management model developed by Barbara Coloroso.

Intermittent schedule of reinforcement: the reinforcing of behavior on some occasions but not each time the behavior occurs.

Interval schedule of reinforcement: the distribution of reinforcements based on the passage of time.

Intervention strategies: strategies used to redirect emerging student misbehavior.

Jellyfish classroom: a term developed by Barbara Coloroso to describe a classroom that has no structure and in which the teacher's expectations are constantly changing.

Judicious Discipline: a classroom-management system developed by Forrest Gathercoal that is based on the synthesis of professional ethics, good educational practice, and students' constitutional rights and responsibilities.

Law of Effect: the concept that if behavior is rewarded it will be repeated, and if behavior is not rewarded it will cease.

Least restrictive environment: the placement situation for students with disabilities which is the closest to that of nondisabled students, based on each student's particular needs and problems.

Limit Setting: a technique from Fredric Jones's *Positive Classroom Discipline* through which teachers systematically teach students to obey the classroom rules.

Logical Consequences: a classroom-management program developed by Rudolf Dreikurs that suggests that the consequences of behavior should be natural, or logically tied to the behavior. Also: teacher arranged consequences that are logically tied to the misbehavior.

Mediation: an approach to conflict resolution that uses trained selected individuals (adults or students) to act as neutral third parties who help conflicting students resolve their differences.

Modeling: a step in the *Skillstreaming* teaching model in which the behavior to be learned is demonstrated.

Natural consequences: the results of ill-advised acts by students that are not imposed by the teacher or administrators but are the natural result of the behavior.

Negative consequences: undesired consequences that follow a behavior that are used to decrease the unwanted behavior.

Negative reinforcement: the removal or avoidance of an aversive stimulus following a desired behavior, which strengthens the likelihood that the desired behavior will be repeated in the future.

Negotiation: a process that allows conflicting students to work together to solve their dispute.

Nonassertive teacher: a teacher that does not make his or her needs or wants known and allows students to take advantage of him or her.

Nonseclusionary time–out: punishment of a student by excluding him or her from participation in classroom activities for a specified amount of time.

Omission Training: the name given to an incentive system that rewards the omission of unwanted behavior. In Omission Training, the teacher rewards the individual student for behaving appropriately for a certain period of time.

Overlapping: the teacher's ability to manage two issues simultaneously.

Peaceable classroom: an approach to conflict resolution in which the classroom becomes a warm and caring community.

Peaceable school: an approach to conflict resolution that applies the peaceable-classroom approach to managing the entire school.

Perspective taking: a strategy that teaches students to look at the world from another person's point of view.

PL 94 142: Education for All Handicapped Children Act. Now known as IDEA–Individuals with Disabilities Education Act.

Positive Classroom Discipline: a classroom-management model developed by Fredric Jones.

Positive consequences: the presentation of extrinsic incentives or rewards following behavior to increase or maintain behavior.

Positive reinforcement: the presentation of a reinforcer desired by the student after he or she has exhibited desired behavior.

Power-seeking: one of the goals of misbehavior, in which the students try to control the teacher.

Premack Principle: a concept developed by David Premack suggesting that participation in a preferred activity can be used to reinforce a less-desired activity.

Presentation punishment: the presentation of an aversive stimulus in order to decrease inappropriate behavior.

Primary reinforcements: reinforcers that satisfy the biological needs or drives of a student.

Principled response: a response to conflict in which students use conflict-resolution skills.

Preferred Activity Time (PAT): activities students enjoy are earned by completing required work.

Procedures: the specific "how to's" that show students step by step how to successfully follow the rules.

Proximity control: the management of classroom behavior by moving throughout the classroom and being physically close to students.

Punishment: the application of an unpleasant stimulus or the withdrawal of a pleasant reward in an attempt to weaken a response.

Punishment lite: a term used by Alfie Kohn to describe consequences.

Quality School: an approach to school developed by William Glasser in which student/student, students/teacher, and students/administrator relationships are based upon trust and respect.

Range of consequences: an element of *Discipline with Dignity* that suggests that a consequence for misbehavior be selected, based on the needs of the individual student, from an established list.

Ratio schedule of reinforcement: the distribution of reinforcements based on the number of responses given.

Real-world consequences: a concept developed by Barbara Coloroso suggesting that consequences for misbehavior should either happen naturally or be reasonable consequences that are intrinsically related to a student's actions.

Reality Therapy: William Glasser's theory hypothesizing that all behavior is internally motivated.

Reconciliation: the process of helping those hurt during conflict or misbehavior to heal.

Reconciliatory Justice: a three-step process through which students are taught to fix problems they create, to prevent similar situations from recurring, and to heal their relationships with people they have harmed.

Reinforcement: the presentation of a desired reward to increase the likelihood that the desired behavior will be repeated under the same or similar circumstances.

Removal punishment: the removal of a pleasant stimulus or the eligibility to receive a positive reinforcement as a consequence for inappropriate behavior.

Resolution: the process of identifying and correcting the deeper issues causing a conflict.

Responsibility Training: a group incentive program in which students are accountable for each other.

Restitution: the process of repairing the damage that has been done to another person's property.

Revenge-seeking behavior: the result of a long series of discouragements in which the student has decided that there is no way to acquire the attention or power desired, and that only revenge will compensate for the lack of belonging.

Ripple effect: the concept that the teacher's method of handling misbehavior by one student influences the behavior of other students in the classroom.

Role playing: a step in *Skillstreaming* that gives students a chance to demonstrate their understanding of the concept presented.

Seclusionary time–out: the removal of a disruptive child for a specified period of time.

Secondary reinforcement: a stimulus that is not reinforcing in itself but that becomes a reinforcer as a result of the connections students make to it.

Severity plan: the immediate removal from the classroom of a student whose severe misbehavior places students or the teacher in danger or prevents instruction from taking place.

Shaping: the process of teaching new behaviors and new skills through the reinforcement of successive approximations of a terminal behavior.

Skillstreaming: a prosocial instructional program developed by Ellen McGinnis and Arnold Goldstein.

Social contract: a system for managing the classroom designed to enhance human interaction in the classroom.

Social reinforcer: a behavior by teachers, parents, peers, or administrators that reinforces students and therefore increases desired behaviors.

Sociometric tests: a way of measuring relationships between students so that the teacher can understand and integrate subgroups in the class, integrate the isolated students, and improve relationships and social interactions within the classroom.

Sociometry: the study of the relationships among people.

Soft responses: a reaction by students to conflict in which they give in as a way to keep peace in the classroom, school, or neighborhood.

Student-centered approach: an approach to classroom management that focuses on helping students learn responsibility through interactions and experiences in a safe, welcoming environment.

Teacher-centered approach: an approach to classroom management that places the total responsibility for maintaining control with the teacher.

Token reinforcer: a reinforcer that has no intrinsic reinforcing properties; it obtains its value because it can be exchanged for something tangible or a desired activity.

Transfer: a step in *Skillstreaming* in which students apply the skills learned to their daily lives.

Transition smoothness: the teacher's management of the transition from one activity to another throughout the day.

Variable schedule of reinforcement: the distribution of reinforcers in such a way that no pattern can be established, and the students cannot predict when they will be reinforced.

Visibility: a classroom arrangement that allows every student to see teacher-led instruction, demonstrations, and presentations.

Withitness: the teacher's ability to know everything that is happening in the classroom and an awareness of the verbal and nonverbal interactions of students with the teacher and classmates.

Author Index

Subject Index

Note: Page entries in *italics* refer to figures.